Hot Stocks

Hot Stocks

Investing for Impact and Profit in a Warming World

James Ellman

ROWMAN & LITTLEFIELD
Lanham • Boulder • New York • London

Published by Rowman & Littlefield
An imprint of The Rowman & Littlefield Publishing Group, Inc.
4501 Forbes Boulevard, Suite 200, Lanham, Maryland 20706
www.rowman.com

6 Tinworth Street, London SE11 5AL, United Kingdom

British Library Cataloguing in Publication Information Available

Library of Congress Control Number: 2020933261
ISBN: 978-1-5381-3746-8 (cloth : alk. paper)
ISBN: 978-1-5381-3747-5 (electronic)

∞™ The paper used in this publication meets the minimum requirements of
American National Standard for Information Sciences—Permanence of Paper
for Printed Library Materials, ANSI/NISO Z39.48-1992.

225-7768

To my lovely and patient Kathryn, coiner of the phrase:
"Behind almost every successful man is a wife rolling her eyes."

Contents

Introduction

Welcome to the Anthropocene!

Most books about global warming are devoted to scaring you into driving a hybrid car, eating only locally raised food, recycling your soda cans, or donating to a nonprofit. While these are positive goals in and of themselves, this book has a different focus.

It is time to position portfolios to maximize returns in a world undergoing climate change. When most investors hear "investing for global warming," they think the subject spans only the narrow field of alternative energy with its makers of solar panels, wind turbines, and electric cars. While this book evaluates these companies, the effects of global warming on many of the largest sectors of our modern economy are also considered: industries as far-flung as agrochemicals, office REITs, engineering services, banking, petrochemicals, and property insurance will rise or fall as the planet warms.

It is the opinion of this author that there is no reason an investment strategy attempting to maximize returns in an era of changing climate cannot be both lucrative and ethical. As investors and customers turn away from companies that harm the environment, the cost of capital for these firms will rise. Many such businesses will be unable to modify their practices sufficiently and will eventually face insolvency. Avoiding or even actively shorting the securities of such companies will improve investment performance. Conversely, a portfolio positioned for an era of climate change will help drive capital to those firms whose efforts maximize the chances that our progeny will not be confined to lives in the polar regions of the planet.

To analyze how a changing climate will impact the capital markets, we first have to understand how we are warming the earth and the resulting changes that are sweeping across the globe. Some readers will already be familiar with much of the following review in this Introduction regarding the causes and impacts of human-driven climate change. Be assured that this is not an "academic" book about the science of global warming but rather a primer on the capital markets and the investment case for individual equities in an era of climate change. If you believe yourself to be well versed in concepts such as ocean acidification and the positive correlation between temperature levels and human violence, please skip ahead to chapter 1. In addition, if you don't need any convincing that companies are changing their practices due to climate change and capital markets are moving to price in its impact, then please dive right into the stock picking and portfolio construction "meat" of this book, which begins in chapter 2. Otherwise, please read on: this section will cover some basic scientific points and build a framework for understanding our hydrocarbon-based civilization's effect on the atmosphere and how equity investing will be impacted by these changes.

Scientists argue that the Holocene geological epoch of the earth's history recently ended and we are now living in the Anthropocene. This is an era dominated by human impact on the earth's atmosphere, geology, and ecosystems. The most obvious effect we are having on the planet is to cause global warming. On November 23, 2018, The US government released the Fourth National Climate Assessment, which states the following:

- "Earth's climate is now changing faster than at any point in the history of modern civilization, primarily as a result of human activities."[1]
- "Without substantial and sustained global mitigation and regional adaptation efforts, climate change is expected to cause growing losses to American infrastructure and property and impede the rate of economic growth over this century."[2]
- "With continued growth in emissions at historic rates, annual losses in some economic sectors are projected to reach hundreds of billions of dollars by the end of the century—more than the current gross domestic product (GDP) of many U.S. states."[3]

The concept behind anthropogenic climate change is quite simple at the core. The sun's light strikes the earth's surface where it is absorbed and converted into heat. Much of this warmth then radiates into the atmosphere. Certain greenhouse gases trap a portion of this heat and keep it from escaping back into space. The prevailing levels of these gases prior to the advent of the Industrial Revolution resulted in the earth's surface being about 35 degrees Celsius warmer than it would have been otherwise. Thus, the greenhouse effect made life possible on the planet.

But now our globalized industrial society releases ever-larger volumes of these gases into the atmosphere each decade. The result is a planet with rising temperatures in its air, on its continents, and in its oceans. Our civilization arose with its centers of commerce, agriculture, industry, and population where they are due to relatively stable levels of climate across different regions. Change those temperatures just a small amount, tweak prevailing rainfall patterns, raise sea levels a meter or so, and humanity will be forced to make significant changes.

The primary greenhouse gases (GHGs) emitted by human activity are carbon dioxide (CO_2), methane (CH_4), and nitrous oxide (N_2O). Annual emissions of these three substances have respectively risen, as measured in billions of tons, from 14.8, 5.3, and 2.2 in 1970 to 36.1, 8.0, and 3.2 by 2014.[4] CO_2 is the least potent but most important greenhouse gas. It is released in massive and rising volume from the burning of fossil fuels (petroleum, natural gas, coal) and land use (deforestation, slash-and-burn agriculture). More potent, but released in overall volume that is less impactful, is CH_4, which is a by-product of livestock digestion, fossil fuel extraction, and the decay of agricultural waste. This is followed by N_2O, which is released by industrial processes and agriculture.

It almost seems as if the human race is engaged in a conscious effort to see just how quickly it can increase levels of CO_2 in the atmosphere. We dig up billions of pounds of hydrocarbons and set them on fire to power our modern lives. We also continue to burn huge expanses of carbon-based forests to make room for our growing cities and food production.

As the initial nations to industrialize, the developed economies of western Europe and North America have emitted the largest cumulative amounts of GHG, with the United States in first place.

However, the rapid industrial development of China has led that nation to catch up rapidly and surpass the United States in annual GHG

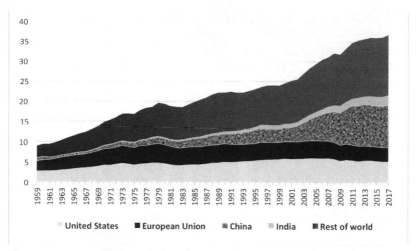

Figure I.1. Annual CO$_2$ Emissions from Fossil Fuels by Region in Gigatons[5]

output. China now pumps more CO$_2$, CH$_4$, and N$_2$O into the atmosphere than the United States, the European Union, and Japan combined.[6] India is also swiftly increasing its GHG output as its economy modernizes.

The result of pumping all this carbon dioxide into the atmosphere is, of course, more carbon dioxide in the atmosphere. Over the last sixty years, the US National Oceanic and Atmospheric Administration has recorded a 30 percent increase in CO$_2$ concentrations at its facility on top of Mauna Loa in Hawaii. In 1960 the reading was less than 320 parts per million (PPM). By 1980 it was over 330, and twenty years later it topped 360. By 2019 the level exceeded 400 PPM and continues to rise.[7]

Scientists have been hauling up huge ice cores from the polar regions that yield a record of the composition of the atmosphere stretching back millennia. Each year a new layer accumulates on the top of these sheets of ice, encasing tiny bubbles of air. When analyzed, the data shows the dramatic increase in CO$_2$ levels with the advent of an industrialized global economy. Even more concerning is that for the last 400,000 years, CO$_2$ levels have fluctuated between 160 and 300 PPM. Thus, our current levels in excess of 400 PPM are unprecedented, and alarmingly, continue to rise.

There is little controversy that concentrations of CO_2, CH_4, and N_2O in the atmosphere have been rising. However, sadly, the theory that this change results in a warming of the planet has become extremely politicized in the United States. The process of curtailing greenhouse gas emissions to a level where we will not cook ourselves in our own waste will likely reduce global GDP growth, impact the profits of the world's largest corporations, threaten the wealth of many plutocrats, push politicians from office, and condemn hundreds of millions to lives of relative if not abject poverty. Thus, we should not be surprised that companies threatened by such curtailment support the work of "climate change denial" scientists who sow doubt and confusion regarding the issue. Many of those attacking the concept of man-made global warming were previously employed to perform a similar role by the tobacco industry.

The tradition in the Western press is to give equal coverage to both sides of the story. Thus, when climate change is discussed, we often read/see/hear from denialists that "most people and many scientists just don't believe that global warming is occurring." Such statements are simply false. For example, when Pew Research conducted a global poll in 2016, more than three-quarters of respondents said that climate change is currently harming or will soon harm the world's population. Agreement with this viewpoint ranges from 95 percent in Latin America to a still large majority of 69 percent in the United States. Two-thirds of global respondents believe that people will have to make major lifestyle changes due to global warming. Even 50 percent of Republicans in the United States support limiting greenhouse gas emissions.[8]

Many who dispute the validity of anthropogenic climate change claim that there is no scientific consensus that human activity is warming the planet. Such an assertion is untrue. Almost all scientists agree that global warming is a man-made phenomenon. Only a tiny percentage of scientists and an even smaller fraction of peer-reviewed published papers dispute such a conclusion.[9]

It is difficult to understand why thousands of scientists would argue that global warming needs to be stopped if they did not believe its future effects on our species to be dire. Denialists claim this is because researchers only receive funding for their work if they conform to the "false conspiracy" of human-caused climate change. Such an argument makes little sense. After all, ExxonMobil, the Southern Company, or Koch Industries will gladly finance climate scientists whose work repudiates the consensus. Yet only a few step forward to accept such funding. Instead, the vast majority of these trained professionals warn that global warming, if not stopped, will lead to economic collapse, mass species extinction, global famines, and inundation of the world's coastal cities. Almost all scientific organizations on a worldwide basis promote the position that climate change is human caused.[10]

Many news outlets are beginning to move away from the traditional system of "giving equal voice to both sides of the story" when covering global warming. For example, the BBC is now demanding that its reporters "challenge" the statements of any interviewed climate deniers just as it would someone claiming that the earth is flat or that long-term cigarette smoking is safe for human health.[11]

While there are climate change skeptics out there on a global basis, polling shows that they are in the minority. This is true even in the United States, where large numbers of intelligent Americans do not believe that the earth is warming or that such a change is the result of human effort. We live in a democracy. You are free to come to and express your own conclusions. However, even if you do not personally believe in the concept of anthropogenic global warming, a growing majority of those active in the capital markets accept the theory as fact.

Whether you are a believer or an open-minded climate change skeptic, please keep reading. It is time to consider how to maximize your portfolio returns and protect your capital in a warming world. After all, not only your family's lives but also your money is at risk.

HOW GREENHOUSE
GASSES ARE CHANGING THE PLANET

So let us return to the "theory" of human-caused climate change. If we accept that GHG emissions lead to a warmer earth, we need to ask:

1. How much extra energy is being trapped?
2. Where is this heat going?
3. How is this warming impacting the planet?

Only after answering these questions can we start to analyze how values in the capital markets will be influenced by climate change.

The sun generates a massive amount of energy, of which only a tiny fraction reaches the earth. This fraction is still huge, as our planet is bombarded by more than 5 quintillion joules of solar energy every minute. To put this in context, every eighty minutes of sunlight striking the earth is roughly equal to all of mankind's energy consumption in 2001.[12] The greenhouse effect caused by our cumulative emissions results in more energy being absorbed than historically would have escaped the earth's atmosphere back into space. How much is this "more"? It currently represents a tiny 0.3 percent of the sun's energy hitting the planet. That sounds like a very small amount, but it represents 250 trillion joules per second, which is equivalent to the earth being warmed by the same amount of energy as the detonation of four Hiroshima atomic bombs . . . per second.[13] By this measure, the earth has absorbed more excess heat than the energy of two billion such atomic detonations in the last twenty years. All this extra energy has resulted in steadily rising surface temperatures versus long-term averages as cumulative GHG emissions have trapped ever more solar energy.

To date, air temperatures have increased only about one degree Celsius due to the impact of GHG. The problem is that it is only one degree, so far. There is a lag in time between the higher CO_2 levels and rising temperatures. Many climate models predict that with significant and continual reduction in GHG emissions we may be able to limit atmospheric temperature rise to only two degrees Celsius. Such an increase

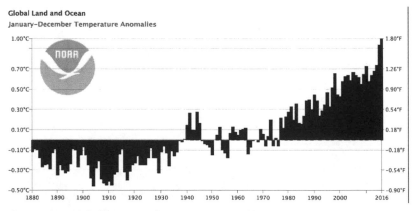

Figure I.2. Global Mean Surface Temperatures[14]

will have significant negative global impacts on our world, but ones we should be able to mitigate at a cost. However, if emissions do not start to decline rapidly in the near future, average warming will likely be three to ten degrees over the next hundred years, with truly devastating consequences.[15]

The atmosphere absorbs only about 3 percent of the heat trapped by the human-caused greenhouse effect. Sea ice, ice sheets, and glaciers absorb a similarly small percentage, but it is enough to accelerate melting over time, resulting in more water in the oceans and higher sea levels.

The remainder of the energy trapped by anthropogenic GHG, more than 90 percent of the total, has been absorbed by the oceans, which act as an enormous heat sink.[16] The oceans are so vast that the rate of warming has been gradual. However, this rate of increase has shown signs of accelerating.[17]

So now that we have looked at where this extra energy is going, let us consider how it is changing the globe. First, as water becomes warmer, it expands. As glaciers and ice sheets experience net melting, there is that much more water in the oceans. A combination of these effects has resulted in rising sea levels around the world.

Sea level rise to date has not been catastrophic, but the populations of the world's coastal cities will be challenged if water levels increase one

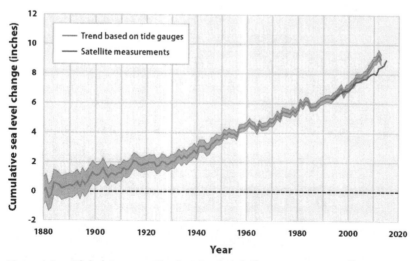

Figure I.3.   Global Average Absolute Sea Level Change, 1880–2015[18]

or two meters by 2100. Such a range is what we should expect unless GHG emissions drop precipitously in the immediate future.[19]

Higher ocean temperatures have been forcing many marine species to migrate toward the poles or deeper to colder depths. A specific example is the American lobster, which used to be caught in great numbers from New Jersey to the Canadian border. As the Atlantic has warmed, the clawed crustaceans have moved north, leading to a collapse of the fisheries in southern New England and a boom for fishermen farther north. Back in the 1980s and 1990s, only 50 percent of the domestic lobster catch was from Maine; now it is 85 percent. This movement toward the poles is widespread: "In the U.S. North Atlantic, fisheries data show that at least 85 percent of the nearly 70 federally tracked species have shifted north or deeper, or both, in recent years when compared to the norm over the past half-century. And the most dramatic of species shifts have occurred in the last 10 or 15 years."[20]

As the oceans warm, many species that cannot migrate, such as corals, die. This is a problem for the billions of humans who live in coastal areas in the lower latitudes and depend upon the ocean for food. Of potentially even greater impact is that as CO_2 accumulates in the atmosphere, much of it is then absorbed into the seas, making them more acidic. In 1985 the CO_2 concentration of ocean water was around 330 atm (standard atmosphere), and its acidity on the pH scale was close to 8.12. As of 2005 these figures had shifted to 360 and 8.09, respectively.[21] "Since the beginning of the Industrial Revolution, the pH of surface ocean waters has fallen by 0.1 pH units. Since the pH scale, like the Richter scale, is logarithmic, this change represents approximately a 30 percent increase in acidity."[22]

"Ocean acidification" makes life more difficult for many aquatic species. Oysters, clams, corals, and many phytoplankton are particularly impacted, as they are unable to build their carbonate-based shells in water with a lower pH. Without shells, they die. As these animals provide the base of much of the oceanic food web, their demise could lead to a collapse of the seas as a source of protein for much of the human race.

As the earth warms, heat waves and droughts are extending in duration and brutality. Many areas are becoming hotter and drier in the American West, the Mediterranean Basin, Southern Africa, and Australia. This is leading to massive tree die-off, more destructive forest fire seasons, and crop failures. Greater levels of famine and poverty are the perfect environment to spark wars, civil unrest, and mass migrations. Even where civilization holds together, rising temperatures are also positively correlated with higher levels of suicide, rape, assault, and murder.[23]

In contrast to dry areas becoming drier, wet areas are generally becoming wetter and experiencing more severe storm events. With rapid reductions in GHG emissions, we may experience relatively small fluctuations in precipitation across much of the more densely inhabited regions of the world. However, if these reductions do not take place, most of the planet will experience either an increase or decrease in precipitation of 20 percent or more on an annual basis.[24]

Man-made climate change will also increase the number of damaging heavy storms: "One consequence of global warming is an increase in both ocean evaporation into the atmosphere, and the amount of water vapor the atmosphere can hold. Higher levels of water vapor in the atmosphere in turn create conditions more favorable for heavier precipitation in the form of intense rain and snow storms."[25] The result is more flooding, more severe hurricanes, and more tornados.

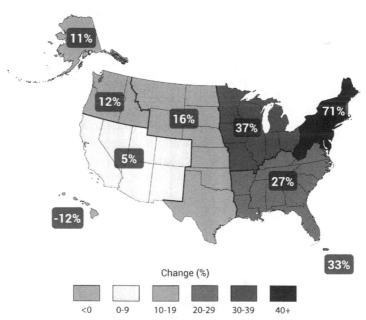

Figure I.4.   US Regional Increase in Very Heavy Precipitation Events 1958–2012[26]

A TALE OF TWO WORLDS: CARBON EMISSIONS TO 2030

A major shift in the geographic sources of GHG emissions has taken place over the last half century. CO_2 output peaked and is now in decline in the more developed economies of the higher latitudes, while a rapid increase has continued in the poorer nations closer to the equator.

Table I.1. CO_2 Emissions as a Percentage of World Totals[27]

	1960	2014
US	31%	15%
OECD total	61%	34%
China	8%	29%
World ex-OECD	39%	66%

Back in 1960, GHG emissions were primarily the fault of the wealthy OECD nations in general, and the United States in particular. Today, global anthropogenic CO_2 emissions are 400 percent greater, but it is now the less wealthy countries in general, and China in particular, that produce the bulk of GHG entering the atmosphere. Over the last five decades, OECD countries doubled their total CO_2 output before they began a recent gradual decline. In contrast, the other nations of the world have experienced a 650 percent increase in their emissions, which are still rising.[28]

A rational person reading most major newspapers would reasonably conclude that the United States is the great culprit causing climate change. A common editorial tone is that the world would be saved if only President Trump chose to commit his nation to the Paris Climate Accord. In truth, the annual carbon footprint of the United States is now relatively small on a global basis and is significantly smaller than its share of GDP. Its percentage of N_2O and CH_4 emissions are even smaller, falling to 10 percent and 6 percent, respectively, in recent years.[29]

Almost all national governments accept that global GHG emissions represent a grave problem and need to be reduced if the warming of the earth is to be limited to only 1.5 to 2 degrees Celsius. The primary argument at international conclaves is over who will make these painful reductions. This is a major point of controversy as switching to cleaner-burning fuels and renewable energy sources will not be cheap.

Poorer nations demand that they be allowed to continue to industrialize and grow wealthy while rich nations, guilty of emitting the bulk of cumulative CO_2 that has been added to the atmosphere, dramatically reduce their releases. In the 2015 Paris Climate Accord, nations such as India, China, Indonesia, and South Africa pledged only to reduce their *rates of growth* of GHG emissions through 2030. This is in contrast to wealthier entities such as the EU, Australia, and Japan that promised to implement significant immediate *output reductions*. Similarly, even with the United States out of the Paris Accord, its annual emissions have generally been declining in recent years as renewables and relatively cleaner natural gas replace coal as an energy source. Wealthier nations declare that they will do their part but insist that developing nations closer to the equator must also make painful sacrifices.

The argument made by the less wealthy nations certainly has some merit. After all, if you reside in an OECD nation and have enough liquid assets to consider how to invest to profit from climate change, you are rich enough to tighten your belt a bit and lower your GHG emissions. If you live in China or India or Indonesia, and cook indoors over charcoal and ride on the back of a motorbike to get to work, reducing your carbon footprint will have a truly painful impact.

The point here is not who is right, but what is likely to happen over the next ten, twenty, and thirty years: We should expect that the world's wealthy nations to increasingly adapt their economies to reduce GHG emissions, and poorer ones to adjust so that at least their increases will slow. However, with current policies and Paris Accord pledges (which may not be met), the earth is expected to warm by 3 to 5 degrees Celsius by 2100.[30] The result will be an investment environment characterized by business practice changes driven by both carbon footprint mitigation efforts as well as the increasingly apparent impacts of a warming climate.

Let us end this introduction with a few points before moving on to the capital markets and investment strategies for the new world we have fashioned for ourselves:

• As we have pumped gigatons of CO_2 into the atmosphere, we have altered the climate of our planet. The oceans are expanding as they warm and take in enormous amounts of ice melt. Thus, the great coastal cities of our civilization are increasingly at risk of inundation. In addition to warmer water driving species toward the poles, the oceans are becoming more acidic, which dooms many aquatic organisms. Declines in sea life threaten more than a billion people who depend on the ocean for food.

- The changing climate also threatens terrestrial food production as wet areas of the continents are getting wetter and are experiencing more extreme storms and floods while dry areas are increasingly wracked by heat waves and drought. Such changes in sea levels, air temperatures, precipitation, and food production for the poorer populations in the lower latitudes of the earth will likely trigger armed conflict and massive migrations toward the wealthier temperate regions of the world. While anthropogenic global warming will make some areas a true hell on earth, other regions that are currently impoverished may become vibrant and wealthy.

- This brings us back not only to why you should care about climate change as a member of the human race but also why you need to pay attention as an investor. The expected chain of events due to GHG emissions are sure to have a significant impact on the capital markets. Fortunes will be made and others lost as the switch takes place from fossil fuels to those produced from renewable sources. Governments will increasingly tax consumers for the economic externalities (true costs) of fuel, food, and travel. Much of the world's most valuable real estate will either be swallowed up by the oceans or precariously protected by infrastructure projects built at monumental expense. Some of the world's great cities will become uninhabitable, while many at higher latitudes will experience an acceleration of growth.

Chapter One

The Increasing Impact of Climate Change on Markets

Many investors have heard about global warming for years, and learned to shrug. Sure, it might happen in the future, but far in the future. For many, investing for climate change has meant putting money into renewable energy stocks in areas such as wind or solar . . . which have been terribly poor investments. The ten-year underperformance of three major Exchange-Traded Funds (ETFs) in the alternative energy space against that of the broader market is remarkable: from August 3, 2009, to August 1, 2019, the Invesco Solar, Invesco WilderHill Clean Energy, and iShares Global Clean Energy ETFs (TAN, PBW, ICLN) declined 62, 36, and 46 percent, respectively, while the broader S&P 500 Index nearly doubled.[1] Many investors have come to believe that green investing is simply a way to lose money in a noble cause.

I believe that such a mindset will soon be obsolete. While the last chapter focused on laying out the case for how the world will be affected by global warming, this one is dedicated to showing how these impacts are beginning to rapidly affect the capital markets. The costs of climate change are increasingly reflected in business decisions and asset prices. The next ten and twenty years are likely to see significantly better returns for climate change–focused investors. Consider three recent examples from such geographically dispersed locations as London, Sacramento, and Miami:

1) In late 2019, the *Guardian* reported that the number of insurers ceasing to write polices to coal mining projects and power plants doubled in 2019. Seventeen major firms including Chubb, Generali,

Swiss Re, Axis Capital, QBE, and Allianz have now made such announcements since 2017.[2] Insurance giant AXA has gone a step further and chosen to cease providing coverage to any new oil pipelines, coal plants, and tar sands projects. As the company's CEO, Thomas Buberl, put it: "A +4°C world is not insurable."[3]

Such changes are rippling across the financial services industry. The global megabank, HSBC, recently announced a significant shift in its policies regarding lending to the energy sector. No longer will it finance the construction of offshore petroleum projects in the Arctic, tar sands developments in Canada, or most coal-fired power plants. Perhaps of even more import is the declaration that "HSBC has been a long-standing supporter of its customers that operate in the energy sector. It will continue to support those that are making acceptable progress towards international good practice, while ending relationships with those that do not meet minimum standards."[4] Other large banking institutions such as ING, BNP Paribas, Wells Fargo, Morgan Stanley, Legal & General, JPMorgan, Deutsche Bank, and the World Bank have announced similar policies regarding their relationships with fossil fuel companies.

Is this change across the financial industry driven by the managements of these financial behemoths suddenly realizing that they care deeply about the environment? Is it a cynical decision that these energy extraction businesses are going to be unprofitable and may become legal liabilities for the financial firms that service them? Perhaps the answer is both. What matters is that major fossil fuel energy projects require massive upfront capital outlays, and as capital becomes more expensive (or even unobtainable), fewer of their ventures will be started.

These new policies mean that the near-term earnings power of many large financial services companies has declined as they turn away what is currently good business. The same is true for the profit profiles of the fossil fuel companies that will now have to pay more for capital from a smaller set of financing options or forgo previously profitable projects. Conversely, this adjustment means that more capital will become available at lower prices to alternative energy companies. Such a change will make otherwise uneconomical wind and solar projects profitable and facilitate their construction.

2) On the same day as the HSBC announcement, the *Wall Street Journal* ran a story highlighting that home buyers are now paying a premium in coastal communities to live at higher elevations above sea

level.[5] This is particularly true in Miami where frequent flooding in areas of low elevation is leading to slower price appreciation than in other areas of the city. Researchers sifting through home price sales data in Dade County dubbed this "climate gentrification" where those with greater wealth can afford to move to higher ground, while the less fortunate suffer increasing inundations as sea levels rise.[6] Whether or not individuals across the coastal regions of the United States believe in global warming, their collective actions show the impact of an efficient market as more flood-prone housing near sea level now sells at an average 7 percent discount to properties less at risk.

This adjustment will have significant impacts across the capital markets. Lower housing prices in some communities will result in falling property tax receipts, putting pressure on the repayment ability of municipal bonds issued by these cities. A greater number of flood events will further stress these entities as cleanup costs and insurance premiums rise. These inundations from storms and king tides combined with falling prevailing home prices in such areas will lead to a higher level of mortgage defaults and banks taking more severe losses when they have to seize collateral.[7] Shopping centers, coffee shop chains, restaurants, hotels, and a myriad of other businesses built to service these areas with falling values and rising flood incidence will struggle to earn back their cost of capital. In contrast, other areas that are more protected from rising seas will thrive as they experience an influx of wealthy residents.

3) On May 9, 2018, the California Energy Commission unanimously voted to mandate that all new homes built in the state after January 1, 2020, will have to be constructed with solar panel energy systems in place.[8] Stocks of solar installation companies jumped. This new rule will increase the construction costs of a new home in the state by around $10,000. However, assuming stable electricity prices, the cumulative utility bill cost savings to the homeowner of the solar panel system should significantly exceed its upfront costs. California is a clear leader in the United States in both residential as well as utility-grade solar power systems, and often acts as an early adopter of ideas and technologies that sweep east across the nation.

If these systems prove to be successful and economically advantageous, we should expect similar mandates to spread to states such as Arizona, Nevada, and Florida. Hawaii and California have both enacted laws that all electricity generated in these two states will have to be from renewable sources by 2045. Such legislation will likely spread east across the United States as well. If nothing else, these regulatory rules will have significant effects: utilities will sell that much less power in coming years to customers whose homes produce their own electricity, gas pipeline companies will transport that much less revenue-generating fuel, and demand for hydrocarbons in the state will be lower.

As we step back and consider these events, we can see that,

- at the global level, major financial institutions are turning their backs on lending to the fossil fuel industry,
- at the national level, US homebuyers are selling their coastal properties and heading to higher ground, and
- at the state level, the demand for solar power components and installers in the California home construction market will rise significantly.

These changes are being driven by choices made in blue-chip company boardrooms, individual consumer pricing decisions, and government regulatory regimes. The values of trillions of dollars' worth of assets were altered by just these three recent decisions.

This is only the beginning.

Despite the headlines generated by the policies of the Trump administration and its positions on global warming, environmental regulation, and fossil fuel production, a major shift has been taking place in our nation and across the globe. "Every year the World Economic Forum asks 1,000 business, policy and thought leaders to rank about 30 risks facing the world by both impact and likelihood. In this year's report, released Wednesday, climate-related risks top the list."[9]

We will likely never know the exact tipping-point moment when individual investors, professional capital allocators, and major companies collectively started to react to climate change in ways that impact the markets. What is important to understand is that this inflection has taken place and the change is accelerating.

The views of US individual investors regarding these issues have evolved rapidly. In excess of 60 percent of Americans rate climate change to be a "crisis" or a "serious problem."[10] More than 90 percent of voters who are registered Democrats or lean Democratic believe that global warming is affecting the United States, and three-quarters agree that human activity is responsible. In contrast, most supporters of the GOP disagree with these points. However, the younger the registered Republican/lean Republican voter, the more likely he or she is to agree with prevailing Democratic opinions on this subject.[11] A similar dynamic holds true geographically: the closer GOP voters live to the coasts the more likely they are to agree that climate change is impacting their local community.[12]

Global warming is likely to increase energy usage by upward of 20 percent for consumers in southern red states that have traditionally voted for Republican political candidates.[13] The Brookings Institution advanced this thinking further with a recently published study showing that changes in the environment may push many more Republican voters toward an acceptance of the validity of global warming and the need to do something about it. The data is stark when researchers estimated county-level income changes from climate-related impacts due to coastal flooding, falling agricultural yields, rising levels of violence, more heat-related deaths, and a reduction of labor output. A map of these findings shows that many GOP-leaning red states across the Southeast and Gulf Coast and stretching up into the central plains will experience the worst declines in income by the end of the century. Counties along the northern tier of the nation are actually expected to

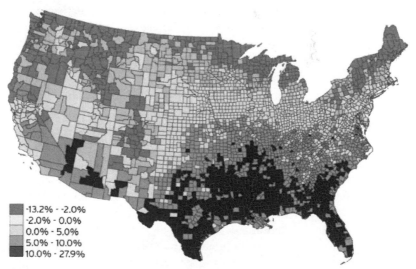

-13.2% - -2.0%
-2.0% - 0.0%
0.0% - 5.0%
5.0% - 10.0%
10.0% - 27.9%

Figure 1.1.   Climate-Related Costs by 2080–2099 as a Share of 2012 County Income[14]

see economic output improve from the same trends. Witnessing the fall-out of global warming with their own eyes may finally convince many voters in the southern United States that the climate is indeed changing. Those who fund climate-denial efforts must worry when even young Republicans are increasingly coming to believe in global warming. The outlook for legacy energy companies is bleak: the majority of Americans favor developing alternative fuel sources at the expense of oil, gas, and coal while imposing stricter emission limits on power plants. Over-whelming numbers of Americans want to see expanded use of wind turbine and solar panel farms while wishing to see a curtailment of hydraulic fracturing, coal mining, and offshore drilling.[15] If these desires are enacted into government policy, they spell trouble for the fossil fuel industry, and a windfall for companies in the renewable power space.

We have likely reached an inflection point in terms of the perceptions of US voters and that of the representatives they elect regarding global warming. Legislative and regulatory action at the state and local level is leading the way. The United States generates the vast bulk of its GDP in coastal areas that increasingly have large majorities that believe in climate change and are likely to elect officials with similar views. This leads to mandates such as the solar power rules recently enacted in California. Even in coastal states usually considered Republican strong-holds, such as Texas, the overall population is younger than the national average, which may lead to "greener" policies over time. Perhaps Donald Trump will have the Twenty-Second Amendment repealed and be elected to a third or fourth term, but he is likely to be our last "denier-in-chief" president. As most US electoral votes come from coastal states, and as current younger "green" Republican Party members naturally age, we will likely have a federal government in the future more interested in decarbonization policies than the one we have today.

Moving on from the broader public, institutional investors are adjusting their attitudes and their allocation policies regarding companies that emit large amounts of GHG. Many have simply chosen to wash their hands of these companies altogether, as with tobacco, alcohol, casino, and other "sin" stocks. In 2014, institutions with $52 billion in assets under management committed to divest their holdings of fossil fuel stocks. By late 2019, that figure had grown dramatically to more than 1,100 institutions controlling in excess of $11.5 trillion.[16]

Other large investors have chosen to retain their holdings but work to actively promote change. The Climate Action 100+ was launched at the end of 2017 and has rapidly attracted 370 signatory investors managing assets in excess of $35 trillion. These institutions are pressuring public company managements and boards of directors in several target industries (fossil fuels, mining, etc.) to enact greener policies, increase environment disclosures, and systematically cut their GHG emissions. To date, the Climate Action 100+ claims that more than one in five of its "focus companies" in the fossil fuel, mining, and automotive industries have committed to science-based emission reduction targets.[17]

Historically, institutional investors have been held to a fiduciary duty to maximize short-term returns. Now, a growing body of work indicates that in more recent years the stocks of companies that are reducing GHG emissions and preparing for a low-carbon future generate higher overall returns. In contrast, those that are "carbon-inefficient" are market laggards.[18] Larry Fink, the head of BlackRock, with more than $6 trillion in assets under management, recently released an open letter to global CEOs that proclaims, "As a fiduciary, BlackRock engages with companies to drive the sustainable, long-term growth that our clients need to meet their goals." This document continues, "The time has come for a new model of shareholder engagement."[19] Fink demands that companies account, measure, and report their effects on society with a specific emphasis on environmental impacts. Mr. Fink points out that his firm's $1.7 trillion of active funds can easily dump stocks and bonds in companies that do not meet BlackRock's standards. However, the manager's much larger passive index-tracking portfolios are unable to sell off assets in companies that do not conform with his company's goals. Thus, Fink concludes, "Our responsibility to engage and vote is more important than ever. In this sense, index investors are the ultimate long-term investors—providing patient capital for companies to grow and prosper."[20]

Either as a reflection of this evolution in attitude among the general population and institutional investors or due to gentle nudges of the market's invisible hand, large corporations are increasingly directing their capital to reduce GHG emissions. While this may lower profits in the short term, it is good business if it builds loyalty among customers and investors. More than a thousand major companies such as AB

InBev, Apple, DuPont, Unilever, and PG&E are currently members of the "We Mean Business" initiative. These firms, with more than $20 trill on in market capitalization, have pledged to enter into programs such as rolling out corporate fleets of electric vehicles, moving to 100 percent renewable power usage, adopting emissions reduction targets, removing deforestation products from supply chains, imposing internal carbon prices to decision making, and switching to alternative fuels.[21]

Some of these pledges will end up being just that. However, many individual companies and their managers are making decisions based on climate change that cumulatively will have large impacts on the capital markets. Consider the following three examples:

1) Royal Dutch Shell Plc is the second largest of the six giant companies that make up "Big Oil." The company's CEO and CFO (Ben van Beurden and Jessica Uhl, respectively) have turned in their traditional internal combustion engine cars and the company is replacing its entire fleet of gasoline vehicles with plug-in hybrids.[22] In recent years, Shell has spent many billions buying natural gas assets in expectation that this fuel will continue to be used for longer than petroleum due to its lower GHG emissions profile. The company has also begun investing significant sums in electric car infrastructure with the acquisition in 2017 of NewMotion, which operates tens of thousands of charging stations across Europe.

2) Ikea, the world's largest furniture retailer, received significant criticism for the short life span of many of its products, which promote a culture of wasteful consumerism. In response, the company has altered its practices in several ways. It has meaningfully reduced its virgin wood consumption by switching to recyclable loading pallets, is moving to sell only energy-efficient LED lightbulbs, and has pledged that by 2020 its company-owned renewable power production will match its total energy consumption. Ikea now owns more than three hundred wind turbines and has installed seven hundred thousand solar panels on its buildings.[23]

3) Kimberly-Clark is one of the world's largest personal care companies with brand leadership in many product areas including Cottonelle toilet paper, Kleenex facial tissue, Kotex tampons, and Huggies disposable diapers. For years, it suffered from negative publicity from environmental groups such as Greenpeace, which linked the company's products to the clear-cutting of virgin boreal forests that fostered rising

CO_2 levels in the atmosphere. In the face of this pressure, Kimberly-Clarke has chosen to embark on a number of environmental initiatives in recent years. These include reducing its water use by more than two million cubic meters, diverting 95 percent of its manufacturing waste from landfills by utilizing recycling technologies, reducing its GHG emissions by 18 percent, and sourcing all of its virgin wood fiber from certified sustainable forest providers.[24]

To summarize this chapter:

- Institutional investors and the general public increasingly believe that global warming is a problem that demands action. As they ramp up efforts to force companies to change, it is increasingly clear that we have entered an era of capitalism and commerce where climate change will influence returns across many aspects of the capital markets.
- Rising numbers of multinational companies with poor environmental records in industries as diverse as oil exploration, couch sales, and disposable swim diapers are modifying their operations to reduce GHG emissions.

These strategy shifts may impact short-term profits, but they are likely to lead to higher returns over time versus continuing current practices and risking the wrath of investor divestment and consumer boycotts. Prudent investors would be wise to take notice. Let us now survey the major economic sectors that will win or lose as this shift gathers pace.

Chapter Two

Renewable Energy

Operators and Installers

If climate change and efforts to mitigate it are to create a winner in the capital markets, it will be the renewable power industry. A portfolio of stocks of companies that manufacture, install, and operate wind and solar power systems will likely outperform the market by a considerable margin over the next twenty years. These renewable systems offer massive advantages for our modern society as they generate almost no GHG emissions, little toxic pollution compared to the use of hydrocarbons, and eliminate the need to transport huge volumes of physical fuels over great distances. While this book on climate change and the capital markets is not just about green energy, it does make sense to start our review in the renewable power area due to the impact of rising levels of GHGs in the atmosphere.

While these technologies are exciting, most of the stocks of companies in the alternative energy space have been terrible performers over the last two decades for a number of reasons:

- The costs of harvesting power from sun and wind had been significantly greater than the direct expenses of producing an equivalent amount of energy from fossil fuels. Thus, renewable power projects were historically only economically feasible with major government subsidies or tax incentive programs.
- The externality costs of the extraction, transport, and burning of fossil fuels have not been levied on the firms that bring the coal, petroleum,

and natural gas to market, nor on those industries and consumers who utilize the fuels. These "ignored externalities" include groundwater contamination, release of toxic substances into the environment, airborne particulate irritants, and of course, GHG emissions.

- Government incentive programs to promote wind and solar have waxed and waned. This has created a boom and bust cycle in the renewable power industry, raised the cost of capital for investment in the field, and resulted in poor financial performance for many companies in this space.

These trends are changing. We are now entering an era of rapid conversion away from fossil fuels to the use of renewable power sources. The primary drivers of this change are "significant historical cost declines for utility-scale Alternative Energy generation technologies driven by, among other factors, decreasing supply chain costs, improving technologies and increased competition."[1]

Such rapidly falling costs have resulted in a significant shift in the allocation of capital for electric power plant construction. Annual US investment in wind and solar plants now significantly outstrips that for hydrocarbon projects.[2] The same is true on a global basis where capital allocated to building renewable power generation is now 300 percent of

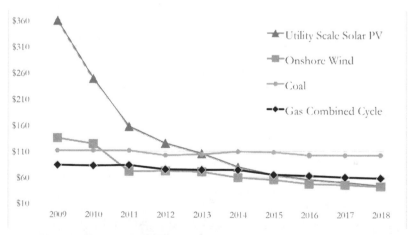

Figure 2.1.   Average Unsubsidized Levelized Cost of Energy Generation in US$/ Megawatt[3]

that being spent on new hydrocarbon facilities. Solar is now the leading energy technology being installed across the world, with China deploying 53,000 megawatts (MW) of the 98,000 added in 2017.

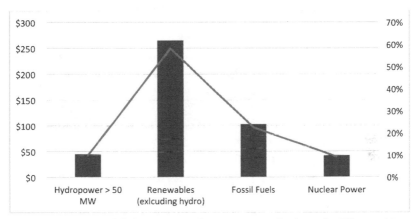

Figure 2.2.   2017 Global Investment in Power Capacity in US$ Billion and Percentage of Total[4]

The current rapid growth rate is set to accelerate. Unsubsidized solar and wind power technology is already comparable in price or cheaper than that for new fossil fuel projects, and these renewable technologies are forecast to drop significantly in cost in coming years. At the same time, governments are imposing or increasing GHG emission taxes that make fossil fuel power more expensive. Depending on the acceleration of the rate of these changes, it may become economically necessary to retire many gas and coal powered electricity plants early and replace them with cheaper wind and solar projects.

Over the five years leading up to 2018, Bloomberg New Energy Finance reports $1.5 trillion was invested in renewable power systems that added more than 1,000,000 MW to global electricity grids. Bloomberg also forecasts that an additional $11.5 trillion will be invested in this space from 2018 to 2050, by which time wind and solar will generate almost half of global electricity production. Over this same period, the cost of the average solar PV plant is expected to fall by 71 percent, wind power by 58 percent, and battery storage systems by an even greater amount.[5]

GOVERNMENT INTERFERENCE

Government rules and taxes that encumber operations of hydrocarbon companies and harm their profits while supporting renewable power are increasing rapidly. The number of laws enacted and executive orders announced related to climate change on a global basis have grown exponentially over the last two decades. From only a handful in the mid-1990s, the quantity on a global basis has exploded to well over a thousand today.[6] As the use of hydrocarbons represents the world's largest contributor to GHG emissions, such increases in regulation symbolize an existential threat to the legacy energy industry's profitability. At the same time, such a change in government policy is spurring the growth of investment in solar and wind power.

Multiple factors are driving the shift in government oversight of the oil, gas, and coal industries. As renewable power generation becomes ever cheaper, nations with little in the way of hydrocarbon reserves have an opportunity to significantly:

- reduce the volatility in the cost of energy supplies,
- gain a measure of domestic energy independence, and
- cease transferring massive flows of wealth to repressive regimes that voters in pluralistic nations find reprehensible.

In addition, a shift in public concern regarding the risks to the planet from climate change is driving governmental policy. All regimes survive over time only at the sufferance of their citizens. Even the Chinese imperial dynasties of old understood the need to retain "the mandate of heaven." Thus, as citizens react to the impact of global warming, climate change laws are not only becoming prevalent in democracies such as Canada, India, and Germany but also in authoritarian states such as Russia, China, and Turkey.

The ways government actions can incent a switch to renewables are many and varied. Most obvious is the potential imposition of carbon taxes on GHG emitters. Certainly, taxing every ton of CO_2 output is a simple and direct method of reducing the demand for burning hydrocarbons. While the United States has resisted this global trend to date, there are now almost fifty national and regional carbon tax or emission cap-and-trade programs around the world. Significantly, China's system goes into effect in 2020.[7] While most of these laws currently levy a relatively small amount for emitting a ton of CO_2, costs are set to rise over time, which will make sourcing power from renewables ever more economically profitable.[8]

Clearly, government actions are driving consumers and industry toward investments in green energy sources. The question is how fast that transition will take place. Falling production costs, technological advancement, and customer choice are driving the shift to renewable power at an accelerating pace in our nation. This despite the United States having massive reserves of oil, gas, and coal sited close to its major population and industrial centers.[9] From close to zero in 2008, solar power has soared to 67 billion kWh (kilowatt hours) in 2018. Electricity generated by wind, starting at a larger base of 50 billion kWh a decade ago, increased to 275 billion kWh in 2018.[10]

These trends in the United States have resulted in investment in wind and solar power generation growing faster than many market watchers expected. In 2013, the US Energy Information Administration (EIA) forecast that installed American solar power capacity would grow 1,000 percent from its 2011 level by 2040. However, it reached that milestone in 2017.[11] While not seeing quite the same exponential growth rates as solar, wind-generated energy has also experienced a rapid increase.[12] Current robust rates of growth of energy captured by wind and solar energy in the United States are set to rise dramatically as a result of political change and consumer choice.

Many members of the Democratic Party have been agitating for a "Green New Deal," which would impose taxes on fossil fuel use and incentives to invest in more renewable power systems. A focus would be on systems that would generate the largest number of low- and middle-skilled jobs as well as improve the financial health of the middle class. Virtually all the major Democratic Party candidates for the presidency in 2020 were proponents of a version of a Green New Deal. This list includes Joe Biden, Cory Booker, Pete Buttigieg, Amy Klobuchar, Kamala Harris, Bernie Sanders, Mike Bloomberg, and Elizabeth Warren.[13] Polls show that the Green New Deal has a more than 50 percent approval rating among all voters and is of course particularly popular among registered Democrats. The point here is that Democratic candidates conclude that they need to support green economic policies to win the support of their party's voters. While nothing in politics is assured, assuming that the United States continues to have elections that lead to regular peaceful changes of the party in control of government, greater public incentives for the renewable power industry along with rising costs on the burning of hydrocarbons are coming in the near future.

Finally, not only is wind and solar growing as a percentage of electricity generated but also the demand for electricity is likely to rise quickly as the auto, truck, and even much of the airplane fleet comes to rely on battery power rather than burning fossil fuels. Space heating is increasingly being provided by electricity as well in many temperate parts of the world. Electrification of transportation and space heating will likely overwhelm any reduction in power use due to potential improvements in efficiency and replacement of older systems (incandescent bulbs to LEDs, better insulation, upgraded HVAC systems, etc.). Bloomberg New Energy Finance forecasts that electric vehicles will demand 2 billion MW of power by 2040 and will account for around 10 percent of all electricity consumed by midcentury.[14]

WHAT TO BUY?

Investing in the renewable power space remains risky but is less so than in the past. There are still many small firms in the space with new technologies, and only a few will prove to be commercially successful. However, investors can now choose among the stocks of several large entities with lengthy track records, a history of profit generation, and robust business models. Equities of companies in the renewable energy space currently represent only a tiny corner of the overall market. This area is poised to become one of the fastest growing sectors in the US economy over the next twenty years.

We will now review a number of these established companies in the renewable energy space with equities that trade on the US markets. While each of these stocks is unlikely to be a winner, as a group these names are well positioned to outperform the overall market due to rapid top-line growth rates driven by technological change, government policy, and consumer choice. As part of a broader equity portfolio, these investments are likely to outpace returns for traditional energy stocks that investors should consider divesting over time. (The fossil fuel industry will be covered in chapter 4.)

No prudent investor puts all of his or her eggs in one basket, and I would not recommend allocating too large a percentage of a portfolio into renewable power stocks. However, the companies highlighted in this chapter and the next:

- Command a combined market capitalization of well over $100 billion and represent real businesses with strong future prospects.
- Are the largest renewable power stocks available for general investment in the United States and may come to command premium valuations as the impact of climate change intensifies.
- Provide for significant diversification due to multiple business lines, technologies, market cap sizes, and geographic domiciles.
- Offer a mix of fast-growing technologically advanced component manufacturers as well as several stocks that generate strong dividend yields to provide for current income.

UTILITY-SCALE RENEWABLE POWER OPERATORS

The majority of renewable power capacity installed across the United States are in large "utility-scale" projects. We will cover regulated utilities stocks themselves in chapter 8, and in this section we will consider the investment merits of several companies that own renewable power facilities and sell their output to grid providers. These firms are usually referred to as Independent Power Providers (IPPs) that operate under the following basic strategy:

- They raise capital to purchase or build power projects.
- The electricity generated is sold at wholesale prices according to negotiated rates in long-term contracts with large utility companies.
- Cash flow generated is used to maintain the equipment, service debt, pay dividends, and finance the next project.

IPPs have been able to carve out this niche as regulated utilities have not been able to build and operate renewable power station projects at sustainable returns on investment due to complicated laws and regulations regarding the setting of consumer pricing charges, use of tax incentives, and depreciation rates. Falling prices for renewable power construction costs along with expiring tax rules may allow utilities to build more of their own renewable projects. However, these same changes may also lead to the IPPs being bought out at premiums by the big utility companies.

Some of these IPPs are sophisticated engineering and construction management firms, while others are externally managed financial shells that do little more than own energy facilities and process revenues and payments. A few retain significant fossil fuel electricity generation plants while moving toward a mix richer in renewables. All have a development pipeline of new projects that should lead to rising levels of revenue, profits, and/or dividends to provide investors with current yield as well as potential stock appreciation. In addition, these companies are well positioned for the imposition or expansion of carbon emission taxes and renewable power mandates in the nations where they operate. Such changes in government policy would raise the price of electricity in the wholesale market and force the early retirement of many older generation plants that burn fossil fuels. In such a scenario, renewable power generators would see significant increases in profit margins as well as demand for increased production.

Ørsted (formerly DONG Energy—it's a long story) is arguably the most sophisticated designer, builder, and manager of offshore wind farms in the world. Based in Denmark, the company has installed capacity of 12,000 MW and has close to another 5,000 under construction. Its stated goals are to add 15,000 MW in capacity by 2025 and have 30,000 MW in operation by 2030. Offshore wind is a small industry poised for rapid growth, which has received little attention in the press or from investors. The positives of offshore wind are significant versus those of onshore projects:

- It is often more feasible to build wind turbine towers to significantly greater heights (100 meters or more) in offshore settings. Average wind speeds increase with height, and taller towers allow for the installation of longer blades that capture more energy. Individual wind turbines that produce 8.8 MW of power have been deployed, 10 MW units are now being built, and 13 to 15 MW models are expected by 2025.
- Open stretches of ocean allow for precise placement of towers to maximize the efficiency of a given wind farm compared to onshore

Table 2.1. Selected Renewable Power Operators Ranked by Market Capitalization[15]

Ticker	Name	Mcap in $B	Dividend Yield	Power Mix
DNNGY	Ørsted	39.0	1.6%	100% wind
BEP	Brookfield Renewable	12.1	5.2%	76% hydro, 20% wind
NPIFF	Northland Power	3.7	4.7%	45% wind, 40% nat gas, 5% solar
CWEN	Clearway Energy	3.5	4.5%	38% wind, 31% solar, 30% nat gas
NEP	NextEra Energy Partners	2.9	3.9%	75% wind & solar, 25% nat gas pipeline
TERP*	TerraForm Power	3.7	4.5%	63% wind, 37% solar
TRSWF	TransAlta Renewables	2.7	7.0%	46% wind, 47% nat Gas
PEGI**	Pattern Energy	2.7	6.2%	100% solar & wind
AY	Atlantica Yield	2.4	6.6%	90% solar, 10% wind
INGXF	Innergex Renewables	1.6	4.6%	55% wind, 38% hydro
AZRE	Azure Global	0.5	0.0%	100% solar

* BEP announced a bid to buy the rest of TERP it did not already own in January 2020.
** Pattern Energy agreed to be acquired by the Canada Pension Plan Investment Board in November 2019.

projects where designers have to account for the location of roads, buildings, and other existing infrastructure. Offshore locations are usually out of sight of onshore property owners and away from low-level aviation routes.

- Giant wind components (towers, turbines, blades, etc.) can be delivered to offshore sites by ship, which is significantly cheaper than land transport. Arrival by sea also avoids the logistical challenges of negotiating narrow tunnels, roads, and more. Note that each blade in many of these modern wind turbines is longer than the wingspan of a Boeing 747.
- Offshore wind projects transmit their power relatively short distances to population centers via undersea cable compared to the transport of power or fuel required for most other electricity generation (coal, gas, hydro, etc.).
- Offshore wind tends to generate the greatest output in the middle of the day, which conforms to peak energy demand. This is in contrast to onshore wind that usually is most productive in the evening and early morning.

Ørsted's established wind farms are based in the seas off Denmark, Germany, the UK, and now the United States. A new project along the west cost of Taiwan is in development. Japan, India, South Korea, and Poland represent potential additional markets where Ørsted expects to bid on projects in the near future.

The US Northeast offers a particularly attractive geography for Ørsted due to the region's high population density, traditional dependence on coal, relatively low solar yield, and significant offshore wind resources. Stanford University researchers estimate that there is enough offshore wind energy along the coast from Maine to Virginia to fulfill one-third of US energy demand.[16] An Ørsted subsidiary built and operated the first active US offshore wind farm near Block Island, Rhode Island, and is negotiating to build an additional 6,000 MW of capacity in the region. Seven states along the Eastern Seaboard have set targets to auction offshore projects in the next few years.[17]

Other nations opening up their offshore regions to wind farm development offer additional growth opportunities. Germany plans to install up to 1,000 MW per year through 2030, while the UK's goal is 1,000 to 2,000 MW of new annual capacity. Japan wants to have 10,000 MW

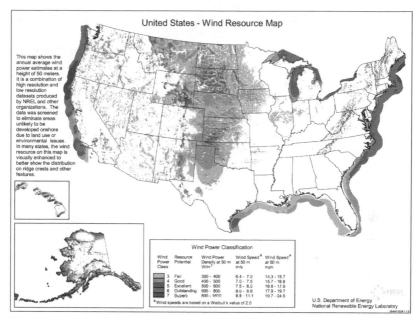

Figure 2.3. US Wind Resource Map—Average Annual Windspeed at 50 Meters[18]

built by 2030, South Korea is targeting 13,000 MW, and India may aim for 30,000 MW by that date.[19] Such initial buildouts may be just the start of a long phase of exponential growth, as it is estimated that the United States has in excess of 2,000,000 MW of feasibly harvestable annual offshore wind capacity while Japan has more than 1,500,000.[20]

With a reasonable and stable dividend, excellent growth prospects, and industry-leading technology and expertise, Ørsted stock is certainly one that investors should consider for their portfolios. Returns could rise significantly if carbon emission taxation becomes more onerous for fossil fuel–generated power in nations such as the UK, Germany, and the United States. While it is significantly more liquid on the Copenhagen stock exchange, Ørsted ADRs trade sufficiently for most US individuals to purchase a desired position.[21]

Brookfield Renewable Partners is a large owner/operator of power assets including more than two hundred hydroelectric facilities and one hundred wind farms. While this is primarily a hydro company, it has been increasing its solar and onshore wind assets rapidly. Total growth in capacity has increased from less than 6,000 MW in 2013 to more than 17,000 MW today, while the company has expanded its operational footprint from three to ten nations.[22] The profitability of established hydro projects may rise as they are used increasingly as enormous commercial "batteries" to store power generated by solar and wind projects at times of the day when it is not needed. This "excess" electricity can be used to run pumps that move water up from the river below to the reservoir behind large dams. Then, when power demand spikes, this water is allowed to flow once again through the hydroelectric generation turbines.[23]

One word of caution regarding climate change to investors considering holdings of such businesses in their portfolios: While we usually consider hydroelectricity production to be "green," there is increasing evidence that it can be as polluting in terms of carbon intensity as coal-fired power plants.[24] In hotter climates where a large volume of nitrate fertilizer enters the water flow upstream of dams, wide and shallow man-made reservoirs may spur massive aquatic vegetation blooms and die-offs, which turn these lakes into giant methane factories.[25] This means that GHG emission taxation schemes could hit certain hydroelectric businesses as hard as those generating power from fossil fuels. There may be a bit of a mitigating factor here as scientists have proposed harvesting this "biogenic" natural gas using systems that collect the CH_4 as it is released in dam spillways.[26]

As BEP has several hydro facilities in tropical areas of Brazil and Colombia, this methane issue is worth considering as a potential investment risk. More study needs to be done, but certainly building dams to replace fossil fuels may not be as green an option as usually thought. On a more positive note, many of BEP's acquisitions have been made at attractive prices in distressed situations that have paid off. In other words, management has a track record of doing deals at the right time and the right price.

Note that BEP is not a "normal" corporation but rather a Master Limited Partnership (MLP). BEP investors purchase and own "units" instead of shares. This legal structure has the advantage that the annual distribution yield is tax advantaged, but with the "negative" that owners receive a K-1 each year, which requires a bit more work when it comes time to prepare personal tax returns. Some 30 percent of BEP units are owned by its General Partner, Brookfield Asset Management, a conglomerate that has a solid, long-term record of delivering value to its shareholders. For owners of BEP this has resulted in the quarterly distribution rising from $.36 per unit in 2013 to $.52 in early 2019.[27] For those climate change–focused investors willing to own an MLP, Brookfield Renewable is an attractive liquid holding combining current yield and potential for growth.

We now move on to a group of yieldcos that are not MLPs and have a more traditional corporate charter, pay regular dividends to shareholders, and are externally managed by a financial sponsor.[28] The first is Northland Power, a Toronto-based power generation company with 2,000 MW of current generation capacity. It is rapidly moving away from natural gas in its energy mix to one more focused on wind and solar. Wind power is 45 percent of its portfolio, with solar another 5 percent and almost all its assets in Canada. Its construction/development pipeline is significant, and the company has the near term goal of wind becoming 60 percent and solar 10 percent of its production mix.[29] If successful, the company will also evolve to having a much more geographically diverse base of earning assets. The Deutsche Bucht 269 MW wind farm off the coast of Germany is on track to be completed by the end of 2019, which should lead to increases in cash flow and stock dividends in 2020. Still in the planning stages, the Hai Long 1,000 MW wind farm off the west coast of Taiwan is slated for a 2026 completion date.

Northland's management team has produced a strong investment return over the last decade, and has a clear path for earnings and dividend growth as it becomes a more geographically diverse company with a greater focus on renewable energy. However, it is worth noting that the stock's current dividend yield of around 4.5 percent is significantly lower than several other yieldcos reviewed in this section.

Next is Clearway Energy, which was previously named NRG Yield. The entity was originally set up by NRG, a large utility, to hold a portfolio of mostly renewable power generation assets that grew rapidly under its former CEO, David Crane. After a run of poor stock performance, the utility's Board of Directors fired Crane, and the company then sold its interest in NRG Yield in 2018. The entity was renamed Clearway and is now sponsored and managed by Global Infrastructure Partners (GIP), which oversees more than $50 billion of hard assets around the world.

CWEN's facilities are all in the United States, with about 70 percent of its 7,000 MW of production assets being solar or wind. This percentage should rise over time as the company's development pipeline consists solely of renewable power plants, with 1,000 MW expected to come online in the near future and another 8,000 MW under development. These new projects not currently owned will be offered for sale to Clearway under what are known as ROFO (right of first offer) agreements after GIP completes the construction phase of the specific wind or solar plant.

Clearway currently yields a dividend north of 3.5 percent with a target to grow its payout by 5 to 8 percent per year. Such a platform is likely to generate steady if unspectacular returns as long as the company is able to renew its power sales contracts at acceptable rates, and can access the market to raise capital for its planned acquisitions. Clearway is an excellent play on a future where the cost of utility-scale wind and solar project construction costs fall while some sort of carbon emission taxation comes into effect in the United States. With a strong sponsor, quality assets, and a competitive current yield, Clearway is an attractive investment.

NextEra Energy Partners is a yieldco sponsored by the giant utility NextEra Energy (NEE), which has north of $100 billion in market capitalization. The strange thing about NEE is that while its regulated utility markets are in sunny Florida, in that state it is happy to make its money burning natural gas (NEE is covered in more detail in chapter 8). Almost all the company's wind and solar projects are elsewhere—in Texas, California, Oklahoma, Ontario, North Dakota, and elsewhere—where it acts as an IPP and sells power on to local utilities.

If there is a problem with NEP it is that the market views it as being one of the best investments in the space, and so it often trades on one of the lowest yields. Its dividend has marched relentlessly higher since it went public in 2014, with its quarterly payout rising from $0.19 to $0.50 by the middle of 2019. For investors willing to accept a lower yield now and hope for a larger payout in the future, NEP is a good choice.

TerraForm Power, another yieldco, is a way to buy Brookfield's wind and solar assets unbundled from the hydropower assets in BEP. Brookfield entities own 65 percent of TERP shares, which leaves a "free float" of more than $800 million of stock for individual investors to buy. Two-thirds of the company's 3,600 MW generating capacity is based in the United States, with most of the remainder in Europe. As with several similar investments in this section, TERP is an attractive takeout target and BEP announced a bid to purchase the rest of the company's shares in January 2020.

TransAlta Renewables, a yieldco managed by Calgary's TransAlta Corporation, owns a 2,400 MW collection of power assets across Canada, the United States, and Australia. The company has a bit more than half of its generation capacity coming from renewables, and will likely purchase a few additional wind projects under ROFO contracts when they are completed. However, as management continues to consider additional natural gas plant acquisitions, it is not entirely clear that TransAlta Renewables will continue to have a majority of its revenue coming from renewable sources in the future. The stock has an attractive yield of close to 5.5 percent with a dividend payout that has grown steadily since its 2013 IPO. While not a top choice, there is no reason a yield-oriented investor concerned about climate change and carbon taxation wouldn't want to add this name to a portfolio.

Pattern Energy is yet another yieldco. Riverstone Holdings acts as the sponsor and controls Pattern's board of directors. The company is solely focused on solar and wind energy, and its path to higher revenues and dividends is clear with a ROFO pipeline from Pattern Development Companies that exceeds 10,000 MW. Execution of this plan would increase Pattern Energy's output by more than 300 percent. Projects under construction include what will be the Western Hemisphere's largest wind farm near Corona, New Mexico. The eastern part of that state is a particularly windy area of the United States, and several wind farms are being built there.[30] New Mexico's legislature is considering increasing its 2040 renewable power mandate from 20 percent to 80 percent, and the electricity output of these wind farms can be exported to nearby population centers such as Dallas/Fort Worth. Sadly, public investors are likely to have lost their chance to invest in PEGI by the time this book is published as it has agreed to be taken private by rapacious Canadian pensioners at a price that I believe to be significantly too low.

Atlantica Yield PLC, a British-based yieldco, is similar to Clearway in that it was renamed with a change in financial sponsor. Originally launched as Albengoa Yield, the company is now controlled by its 25 percent owner, Algonquin Power (AQN). Atlantica primarily owns solar farms in Spain and the United States, which generate 1,400 MW.

The company also owns a collection of other revenue-producing assets such as a natural gas power plant in Mexico, wind farms in Uruguay, two desalination plants in Algeria, and 1,100 miles of electric transmission lines in Chile and Peru.

While the dividend is higher now than immediately after the 2014 IPO, it is lower than where it peaked in late 2015. The company is looking to buy additional electric transmission assets and desalination plants under ROFO agreements, which may be financially sound but are not necessarily attractive for the investor looking at the stock as a way to play the renewable energy space. However, the current dividend yield is attractive at more than 5 percent, and the company's stated goal is to increase the payout by 8 to 10 percent per year through 2022.

Innergex Renewable is another smaller renewable power producer. It has a bit more than 2,000 MW in operation, and projects under construction and development will increase output by more than 50 percent. The company's HQ and roots are in Canada, where it produces most of its output from hydro projects. However, Innergex has been expanding both by technology (into wind, solar, and geothermal) and geographically (to the United States, Iceland, France, and Chile). While attractive as a "green" energy investment, the stock has a smaller market cap and lower dividend yield (around 3.5 percent) than some of the other names considered in this section.

Finally, in this review of renewable power producers, we come to Azure Power Global Ltd., which is in the business of building and operating utility-scale solar projects in India. The company differs from others discussed in this chapter as it is a small, new, fast-growing firm that is currently not paying dividends. As such, both the upside and downside are greater for this stock, as is its likely future volatility. The company currently has production facilities generating 3,000 MW, is rapidly expanding with another 2,000 MW of capacity in its pipeline, and owns India's largest organic solar power portfolio. Cash flows are being recycled into growth with expectations that India will auction off an additional 30,000 MW of solar power project contracts per year for the next decade. If the management team can execute on its plan, Azure could become one of the world's largest solar power companies by 2030.

While the potential for growth in solar in India is dramatic, the risks of investing in this emerging market are significant as well. As an example, Azure stock fell from $16 to $8.50 in the fourth quarter of 2018.

This was partly in reaction to the imposition of a new 25 percent tariff regime on imported solar panel equipment. The Indian government is attempting to jump-start domestic production, but in the near term its efforts will lead to higher equipment prices for solar installers. Nevertheless, even with these new costs, solar power is still significantly cheaper than fossil fuel alternatives in India, whose growing economy and middle class consumers are hungry for additional flows of electricity.[31] While speculative, Azure is an interesting investment in an otherwise more stable, yield-focused renewable power generation space.

SOLAR INSTALLERS

Solar power now is capturing more than half of all investment in new renewable power systems across the United States. While utility-scale projects represent the bulk of this spending, PV panels mounted on the roofs of homes are the most visible sign of this growth to individual investors. Known as "distributed power," consumers have been rapidly adopting the technology and saving rising amounts of money due to:

- the rapid decline in costs and efficiency improvements of solar power systems.[32]
- increasing retail rates of electricity purchased by consumers from grid utilities. The national average price per kilowatt (kW) paid by consumers rose more than 50 percent from 2000 to 2017, and is expected to climb further over the foreseeable future.[33]
- a widening array of financing options for homeowners, including lease of the equipment, power purchase agreements (PPAs) from installers, as well as the more traditional outright purchase of the systems.

The United States is lucky enough to have a large percentage of its residential homes located in regions where photovoltaic solar resources are significant. This makes installing a rooftop solar PV system an attractive investment for many consumers.

States in the southwestern quadrant of the United States (California, Nevada, Arizona, New Mexico, Texas) receive the largest amount of solar energy per day. Thus, it should be no surprise that this region

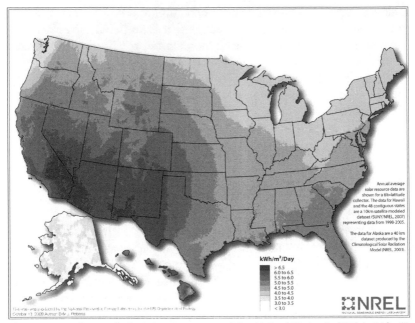

Figure 2.4.   Photovoltaic Solar Resources of the United States in kWh/m²/day[34]

also has the most installed residential systems as a percentage of total homes. However, the average penetration rate of residential solar power systems in these states remains under 10 percent. On a national basis the figure is significantly lower, and many market forecasters expect overall US levels to soar more than fivefold to 12 percent over the next decade.[35]

The cost of installing an owner-purchased residential system in the United States, including all taxes, installer profit, equipment, permitting, and more, has fallen from $7,240 per kilowatt in 2010 to $2,800 in 2017.[36] With the system average size at 5.7 kW, the cost to a residential consumer is now running around $16,000 before any tax credits or local incentives are taken into account.

At current retail electricity costs, the average solar PV system will save a California resident more than $29,000 in utility bill costs over a twenty-year period. This represents approximately a 3.5 percent after-tax annualized return, which compares favorably to current interest rates paid on bank accounts and high-grade bonds. This investment profile improves when one takes into account that today's solar PV panels are expected to still produce 80 to 90 percent of their original power after twenty years.[37] The rate of return on a home solar PV system improves if grid-purchased electricity costs rise over time (and they are expected to do so). High local retail electricity rates make solar investments economic in less sunny locations as well with a twenty-year utility bill savings of $31,000 in Massachusetts, $26,000 in New York, and $20,000 in New Jersey.[38] While savings are a bit lower in the Southeast due to low current electricity prices, PV system installations are still ramping up in places such as Florida and North Carolina.[39] In addition, by absorbing the sun's energy, rooftop solar panels lead to buildings on which they are mounted being a few degrees cooler on hot days. This reduces air conditioning use and represents an additional approximate 5 percent savings in electric utility costs.[40]

Solar installers are also now offering home battery backup systems manufactured by companies such as Tesla, Sonnen, and LG. As battery prices have fallen, the net installed cost of such a system has dropped to around $8,000. When paired with a solar PV system, these batteries can generate significant electricity bill cost savings. Most residential PV owners elect to be billed on a time-of-use plan with their utility. This allows them to utilize solar energy generated from their panels in the middle of the day when prices are highest, and they buy cheaper power from the grid at night after the sun has gone down. With a residential battery system in place, excess solar power generated in the morning can be stored at the house rather than sold into the grid at low rates. Then, when retail electricity prices spike in the middle of the day, the battery kicks in and powers the home, allowing solar-generated output to be sold into the grid at a higher level of profit.

The rollout of home battery systems has another benefit as they lead to a lower peak demand on the grid, fewer brownouts, and reduce the need to turn on peaker power plants, which run on fossil fuels that are both expensive and polluting. Finally, in addition to the profitable investment characteristics of a residential battery system, homeowners gain peace of mind that their houses will not go dark when there is a grid power outage. The rollout of these products offers solar installers another profitable item to sell, which should lead to an increase in revenues and net income per customer over time and offset the falling price of PV systems.

Three of the "national" installation companies are publicly traded—Sunrun, Tesla (formerly "Solar City"), and Vivint Solar (RUN, TSLA, VSLR). Tesla, dominated by its automotive business, will be covered in the chapter on transportation stocks.

So, on to RUN and VSLR: they are both "small-cap" stocks today, but with a combined market capitalization of over $3 billion they are certainly liquid enough for a position in individual investors' portfolios. These two companies operate in a rapidly growing business, and have been gaining market share from their competitors.[41] In 2014 the two companies had combined revenues of $224 million. By 2018 this figure had soared 460 percent to more than $1 billion.[42]

The largest irritant for shareholders of these two companies to date is that the rapid growth of revenues has not consistently resulted in bottom-line profits. A primary reason for this is because the solar installers offer residential customers three options to pay for a new system to be placed on the homeowner's roof:

1. Purchase the power system outright for full cost.
2. Lease the power equipment and pay the installer back over fifteen to twenty years.
3. Enter into a PPA with the installer, and the consumer pays a contracted low rate for power to the installer for twenty years.

Option 1 provides the installer with an immediate profit. However, installers claim that the latter two options provide for a higher total profit over time, even though it creates a loss in the year the equipment is placed into service. PPAs and solar leases also require installers to obtain ongoing lines of credit and add significant debt to their balance sheets. Finally, these residential financing options create credit risk for Sunrun and Vivint as consumers may default on their payments. The debt is secured by the equity in the house and appears to be safe. However, as we saw in the 2008 financial crisis, when home values decline, homeowners will walk away from "underwater" properties.

In recent years, installers have changed their pricing to steer more homeowners toward purchases of PV systems. This has led to the desired change in behavior, and customers have increasingly been buying their systems outright, but at the cost of slowing installation growth for the industry. In 2014 fewer than 30 percent of installations were customer owned. By 2017 more than 50 percent were.[43] This resulted in improved earnings for the installers in that year. However, the subsequent negative impact of tariffs imposed on Chinese-made solar panels by the Trump administration as well as the recent expiry of some state tax incentives on residential renewable power projects reduced installer profit levels in 2018 and 2019.

The short-term outlook for the installers is mixed as federal tax incentives for residential solar power installations are set to phase out starting in 2020, and it is not clear if they will be renewed, expanded, or eliminated. Uncertainty regarding tariff duties on imported solar panel equipment also presents a current overhang for the stocks. In addition, the industry needs to do a better job policing its salesforce as some homeowners have been talked into entering into inappropriate contracts that cost them more than buying electricity at retail rates from the grid. Such actions have allegedly taken place often enough that Vivint has been sued by the attorney general of New Mexico for "unfair and unconscionable business practices" and has received several hundred complaints on the Better Business Bureau website.[44]

Despite these difficulties, longer term, the outlook for Sunrun and Vivint is positive for the following reasons:

- Prices of solar power equipment are forecast to continue their rapid decline, as are continued improvements in the efficiency of PV panels to convert sunlight into electric power. Consumers are increasingly able to invest in rooftop systems that produce 100 percent of their annual power needs at progressively lower prices.
- Retail electricity rates are rising as utilities recoup the costs of ongoing infrastructure investments. This trend increases the economic value of residential PV systems and may be most pronounced in California, where the bankruptcy of PG&E is expected to lead to significant grid rate hikes for consumers in the near future.
- Pressure appears to be building across the political spectrum for additional incentives for investments in renewable power. As already discussed, a Green New Deal plan may become a major plank of the Democratic Party platform, and one that results in competing initiatives from the GOP. State governments in other sunny parts of the United States may impose rules similar to those of California's, which mandate that all new homes include a solar PV system. Such political changes would be positives for Sunrun and Vivint.

- The tariffs on Chinese-made PV equipment, the high cost of capital to finance solar leases, and a decline in total installations led a few significant competitors to exit the market, including NRG Home Solar, Sungevity, and Direct Energy. Tesla (Solar City) has also been losing share as the company focuses on its auto business. This decline in competition may act as a significant boost for sales and profits for Sunrun and Vivint in the next few years.
- Increasing acceptance and falling prices of home batteries is driving demand for both these storage devices *and* residential solar power systems. This trend will likely accelerate with climate change, leading to increased incidence of heavy storm events and extended grid outages.
- Sunrun recently released a report showing how large its business of solar PV systems married to battery systems could become. Los Angeles currently has three natural gas-fired plants approaching retirement age. "Repowering" (rebuilding/upgrading the current generators) these plants with newer natural gas technology would cost more than $2 billion. Sunrun's proposal is to move away from gas and instead spend slightly less money on forty thousand rooftop PV systems with battery storage in LA.[45] Allowing the local utility to tap these battery reserves on demand would satisfy a similar amount of power as the old natural gas plants while also providing a significant level of energy self-sufficiency across the city in the event of an earthquake or other disaster that disrupts the traditional electrical grid. LA recently announced it would not repower the gas plants and would look to alternative "green energy" instead. It is certainly possible that a large American city will choose to replace fossil fuel power with a large network of PV and battery systems in the near future.

Let us conclude this chapter with some summary points:

- US-based investors convinced that climate change is going to increasingly impact the capital markets should consider renewable power producer stocks for a portion of their portfolios. Most have attractive current dividend yields with moderate expected growth and an embedded option on imposition of carbon taxation on the burning of fossil fuels.
- Residential solar installers are also likely to become attractive investments as strong revenue growth will eventually translate into higher and more stable earnings. Falling solar PV system prices and home battery systems should accelerate client growth over time.

Chapter Three

Renewable Energy
Equipment Manufacturers

We will now consider manufacturers of the equipment used to generate renewable power.

WIND POWER MANUFACTURERS

As discussed in the previous chapter, wind power is an industry experiencing rapid growth. Greater government regulation and taxation of carbon emissions will accelerate adoption of wind energy as with other green sources of power. Wind is plentiful, the price of capturing it for electricity generation has been dropping rapidly, and unlike solar farms, wind turbines allow farmers and ranchers to generate extra revenue while still utilizing most of their acreage for agriculture or grazing. While onshore wind power is primarily harvested in the evenings, it can be married with solar to generate a more level load. Or, increasingly, this electricity can be stored utilizing many green methods until it is needed. As most people live near coastlines, offshore wind production, positioned just over the horizon, can be an even more profitable endeavor and is growing at an even faster pace.

Concerns about wind turbines killing birds are more than a bit overblown. According to a recent peer-reviewed study, these machines kill more than 350,000 birds in the United States per year. That is certainly a lot of birds, but it is a fraction of the 1.4 to 3.7 *billion* birds killed annually by cats in our nation![1] President Trump's comments that the noise from wind turbines causes cancer in humans have been roundly dismissed as being "ridiculous" and not grounded in fact.[2] Worries about views of wind turbines reducing property values have also been shown to be dramatically exaggerated.[3] Note that back in the 1930s, many wealthy homeowners in San Francisco's Pacific Heights neighborhood complained that their property values would plummet as soon as their views were marred by the newly built Golden Gate Bridge.

The wind turbine manufacturing industry is attractive for equity investors. A small number of profitable companies dominate the space (outside of China) and are rapidly improving their products with larger, more efficient, and technologically advanced offerings. These bigger companies can afford the R&D necessary to continue pushing down the price of wind-generated energy as well as tap the capital markets to invest in the giant manufacturing facilities required to build ever-larger blades, towers, and nacelles. Established companies with long track records such as Vestas, Siemens Gamesa, and GE Wind Energy have acted as rational competitors balancing the need to expand and increase revenues while still driving profits to the bottom line.

Certainly, the industry faces challenges. Rapidly falling costs of wind power represent a challenge to manufacturers as unit prices decline. However, this trend has been offset through total growth in market demand as well as the launch of successively larger and more expensive towers and turbine blades that produce more energy with greater efficiency. China has repeatedly proclaimed its goal to dominate the global manufacturing markets of both solar and wind power equipment. It reiterated this objective with the release of the thirteenth five-year plan in early 2017 with a budget to spend $360 billion on renewable power projects by 2021.[4] Such objectives leave little room in the world for wind turbine makers *not* owned by Chinese interests, and this represents a risk to several stocks we will now consider.

Vestas Wind, based in Denmark (VWDRY—ADR), has for some time been the world's largest manufacturer of wind turbines, towers, and affiliated equipment. The company has in excess of twenty-four thousand employees, its equipment is technologically advanced, and it commands a capitalization in excess of $20 billion as of this writing. Vestas is a premier holding for investors looking for long-term returns in the green energy space.

Despite significant competition, Vestas actually increased its sales dominance in 2018 as it commissioned turbines with a capacity of more

Table 3.1. Global Onshore Installed Wind Turbine Market
Share 2016–2018[5]

	2018	2017	2016
Vestas	22.0%	16.4%	16.5%
Goldwind	14.5%	11.6%	12.1%
GE Wind	10.8%	10.3%	12.3%
Siemens Gamesa	9.0%	14.6%	10.9%
Envision	7.0%	6.1%	3.7%
Evercon	6.0%	6.6%	6.6%
Ming Yang	5.0%	4.7%	3.7%
Nordex	5.0%	6.6%	5.0%
Other	20.7%	23.1%	29.2%

than 10 GW resulting in a global market share of 22 percent. This was almost as much as the next two competitors combined.[6] Analysts expect wind power installations will continue to grow steadily, with market research company Technavio expecting a compound annual growth rate of 6 percent through 2023.[7]

Vestas and Mitsubishi Heavy Industries each own half of MHI Vestas Offshore Wind. This joint venture is currently producing the world's largest offshore wind turbines, which are each rated up to 8.8 MW of output. These mammoth structures can individually power more than seven thousand homes, and 9.5 MW turbines are now being tested. As discussed in the previous chapter, growth in this area is rapid, and Fortune Business Insights expects a CAGR of generation capacity in excess of 19 percent for the offshore wind power market through 2026.[8] MHI Vestas Offshore Wind continues to dominate the space, and in 2017 it was awarded more than 700 MW of turbine orders just for two projects off the coast of Germany. The JV's manufacturing facilities across northern Europe are hitting economies of scale, and the unit is expected to break into the black in 2019 to 2020.[9]

Coming in at number two in the 2018 world market share rankings is China's largest wind company. Xinjiang Goldwind has an illiquid ADR (XJNGF), a liquid listing in Hong Kong for investors who are able to trade there (2208.HK), and an overall equity capitalization in excess of $5.5 billion. Based in Beijing, it has the positive feature of primarily selling its products in the world's largest wind power market. The Chinese government subsidizes domestic wind power firms in myriad ways while blocking sales by foreign players such as Vestas and Siemens Gamesa using methods that are blatant violations of WTO rules.[10] Such government influence has led to Goldwind's local market share expanding past foreign competitors to a remarkable 30 percent while that of Vestas's and Siemens Gamesa's has shrunk to low single digits. Goldwind's order backlog has grown robustly, and the company is starting to win its first contracts outside of China.[11] So for an investor, what's not to like?

For better or worse, there are problems with the story. First of all, margins in China are lower than elsewhere. As several other domestic players are willing to cut prices in order to grow, Goldwind's market share dominance has only come at the cost of flat annual revenues and profits since 2015. Also, the company's great success at home has led to a significant reliance on that one market with more than 95 percent of its order backlog located in China. In other words, it is extremely exposed to the continued health of wind power growth in one nation and the ability of the government in Beijing to keep the market largely closed to foreign competitors. It is not clear that this situation will continue.

The United States has been actively working on "opening" the Chinese market to a more level playing field for foreign firms while cracking down on nontariff barriers, forced technology transfer, and intellectual property theft. More quietly, European governments have been doing the same.[12] Efforts to limit international sales of telecom equipment by China's Huawei and ZTE are only the most public battles being waged on this front. It seems clear that not only has China been in breach of WTO rules on a daily basis since the day it joined in 2001, but also that its largest trade partners may have finally decided to do something about it.

This backlash has begun to impact the wind turbine industry. Until recently, Western companies often chose not to sue Chinese competitors for unfair practices due to fear that doing so would shut them out of the lucrative Chinese market. This has been changing. An example is the successful legal battle waged by US firm AMSC against Chinese wind turbine maker Sinovel Wind. The latter was convicted in US federal civil court in 2018 of conspiracy, technology theft, and wire fraud charges. Sinovel stole and utilized AMSC's software for regulating electricity flow from wind turbines rather than continuing to purchase it as per an executed contract, leading to a drop in AMSC's market value in excess of $1 billion and the loss of more than seven hundred jobs in the United States. That Sinovel was only ordered to pay $60 million in restitution shows that the system is still working for Chinese firms, but perhaps, not for much longer.[13]

Next, we move on to another wind turbine manufacturer in Siemens Gamesa Renewable Energy, SA. (GCTAF—ADR). Based in Spain, this is a recent merger of the local Gamesa and the wind power operations of German conglomerate Siemens. While smaller than Vestas, Siemens Gamesa still commands an $11 billion market capitalization, and it is a large player in both the onshore and offshore wind power market. It is very much a global company with manufacturing centers not just in Europe, but also in Egypt, Morocco, Canada, China, the United States, and India.

The company has also been rolling out its Electric Thermal Energy Storage (ETES) technology, which uses excess electricity from wind (or other renewable power sources), when cheap, to heat rocks up to 600 degrees Celsius. This heat can then be converted back to electricity using a conventional steam generator when demand for power is higher. ETES is designed for retrofitting older coal-fired power plants and similar operations, which allows owners of these facilities to decarbonize and extend the life of their plant and equipment as intermittent renewable energy systems are ramped up in size.

The last company to be considered in this section is TPI Composites (TPIC), which produces wind turbine blades for large customers such as Vestas, GE, and Siemens Gamesa. A small cap stock valued by the market at around $900 million, TPI is well positioned for continued growth in the wind power market. Large turbine manufacturers have been increasingly outsourcing the production of their wind blades, and TPI has seen its global market share of onshore blades rise from 3 percent in 2013 to 14 percent in 2018.[14] That it has accomplished this rising market penetration rate to date with virtually no sales to Chinese domestic players is impressive.

While TPIC certainly has risks, the company operates with economies of scale and has low cost, technologically adept operations. This should allow an investor to participate in accelerating growth in wind power migration without having to worry about which turbine manufacturer wins in the marketplace. The largest issue in the medium term is if the company can follow through on its goal of doubling its wind blade sales from 2018 to 2021. Large investments in new manufacturing plants and equipment have kept revenue increases in recent years from making it to the bottom line. We will soon learn if TPIC's manufacturing expansion into places such as Yangzhou, China, and Chennai, India, are to pay off for investors.

SOLAR POWER MANUFACTURERS

There are several manufacturers of solar power equipment for investors to consider. We will start with public solar panel manufacturers: First, Solar, Jinko Solar, Canadian Solar, and SunPower (FSLR, JKS, CSIQ, SPWR) command more than $10 billion in combined market capitalization as of late 2019. Then we will move on to inverter manufacturer SolarEdge (SEDG).

The biggest problem for an investor looking to buy stocks of solar equipment makers is that many of the large global players are in East Asia and have shown themselves to be less than focused on short- or medium-term profit maximization. I vividly recall my first international investment trip, which took me to South Korea in 1996. My initial meeting was with a manufacturing company. After the requisite formal, two-handed exchange of business cards, I started off by asking, "How is business?" The answer I received was, "Business is excellent so we are expanding production as fast as possible." The next company I visited was in the same industry. When I again asked, "How is business?," the answer I received was "Business is terrible so we are expanding production as fast as possible." Over the next two decades I heard that answer over and over again from companies across East Asia. This mindset continues to dominate among executives in many industries in the region, especially those "targeted" for growth by the Chinese government. This results in a tougher operating environment for all competitors in the space regardless of an individual company wanting to act as a rational market player.

While rapid increases in output are often positive for market share and revenue growth, it is not necessarily a recipe for rising profits and share prices. In particular, many economists have singled out China in the last decade as massively overinvesting in capital goods and equipment due to overly easy credit and political encouragement to maximize employment.[15] For players in many fragmented industries where Chinese competitors are large participants, it is difficult to generate significant profits. This has been particularly true in the solar power space that Beijing has targeted for growth and global dominance. The result is a glut of solar panel manufacturing capacity, and a history of sales into the global market at prices so low they appear to be aimed at driving non-Chinese competitors out of business.

In addition to volume-focused versus profit-focused competitors, solar power equipment manufacturers have been cut by the doubled-edged sword of technological advancement that has rapidly driven down manufacturing costs and unit sale prices. In an extremely cutthroat market, this has led to average prices of equipment falling more than 70 percent from 2010 to 2018, outpacing significant increases in unit sales.[16] Solar PV sales are often limited by the amount of real estate available to be covered by panels (roof size, acreage for a solar farm, etc.). Thus, it has often been more difficult for solar panel manufacturers to make up for falling unit prices in volume. For the immediate future, investors need to tread with caution in this space.

First Solar (FSLR) has some unique characteristics that have allowed it to partially avoid some of the worst negative trends in the space. This $6 billion market cap company based in Arizona makes proprietary solar panels with differentiated cadmium telluride (CdTe) thin-film technology that can be manufactured more cheaply than offerings from competitors selling more traditional silicon-based PV systems. These CdTe panels also have a superior energy yield in hot and/or humid conditions and shed snow and dust more easily. While CdTe is toxic if ingested and must be disposed of properly, First Solar has turned this into an advantage. It has set up recycling centers for its products when they reach the end of their twenty-five-year lives, which allow for 90 percent of both the glass and the semiconductors in the panels to be reused. This has strengthened the company's green bona fides.

In addition to technology advantages, most of First Solar's manufacturing facilities are outside of China (in Malaysia, Vietnam, and Ohio), which has allowed First Solar products to mostly avoid the ongoing tariff battles between the world's two largest economies. Deliveries of the company's Series 6 product line are ramping up, should double from 2019 to 2021, and its expected output is already mostly presold over this time period. The company also has a robust balance sheet with little debt and large amounts of liquid assets.

Nevertheless, First Solar has not been able to avoid the financial pain prevalent throughout the industry over the last several years. The company has been surprisingly honest in its willingness to call out Chinese manufacturers for receiving government subsidies, overproducing to grab market share, and dumping product at or below manufacturing cost, which would represent clear violations of WTO rules. Note this passage from FSLR's 2018 annual report:

> Certain of our existing or future competitors may have direct or indirect access to sovereign capital, which could enable such competitors to operate at minimal or negative operating margins for sustained periods of time. . . . If competitors reduce module pricing to levels near or below their manufacturing costs, or are able to operate at minimal or negative operating margins for sustained periods of time, our results of operations could be adversely affected. We believe the solar industry may from time to time experience periods of structural imbalance between supply and demand (i.e., where production capacity exceeds global demand), and that such periods will put pressure on pricing, which could adversely affect our results of operations. We believe the solar industry is currently in such a period, due in part to recent developments in China. . . . An increased global supply of PV modules has caused and may continue to cause structural imbalances in which global PV module supply exceeds demand, which could have a material adverse effect on our business, financial condition, and results of operations.[17]

Despite these headwinds, FSLR has continued to generate profits and has reported strong sales growth in markets such as Japan, India, and Australia, even as falling unit prices led to a significant reduction in revenues in the United States. If an investor wishes to invest in a solar panel manufacturing company with a diversified geographic footprint and a level of technological advantages, FSLR is probably the best bet.

Next, we consider Jinko Solar Holding (JKS), the world's largest manufacturer of solar PV panels. Based in China, the company has a full listing on the New York Stock Exchange and recorded in excess of $3.5 billion in sales in 2018. However, low profit margins of 1 to 2 percent result in a current market capitalization of "only" a bit more than $1 billion. The company has shown a strong ability to execute on its expansion plans. Total panel (module) manufacturing capacity increased from 2 GW in 2013 to almost 11 GW in 2018, with a goal to increase this to 15 GW by the end of 2019.

Current tariffs imposed by the United States on Chinese solar panel products have reduced the share of Jinko's revenues from our nation from 36 percent to 11 percent over 2016 to 2018. The company has been reasonably successful in its attempts to diversify its geographic base of sales with modest gains in European sales and significant increases in shipments over recent years to Mexico, Australia, Japan, and the United Arab Emirates.[18]

JKS represents an inexpensive way to bet on rapid growth of solar PV sales around the world. However, risks are significant that local Chinese margins will remain depressed, and WTO decisions could be detrimental to Jinko shareholders.

On to Canadian Solar (CSIQ) based in Guelph, Ontario, with a market cap in excess of $1.2 billion. While the company is technically Canadian in its domicile, it is as much a Chinese firm as a Canadian one. Its CEO, Shawn Qu, emigrated from China to Canada before founding the company and still owns more than 20 percent of the shares. All other C-Suite executives are either Chinese nationals or of Chinese extraction. Most of the company's manufacturing operations are in China, which also represents the company's largest market as measured by MW of installed base.[19]

As with other "commodity" manufacturers of solar panels, Canadian Solar has had difficulty generating profits as the industry's manufacturing capacity continues to expand faster than rapidly growing global demand. However, the company has demonstrated an ability to stay in the black, been able to push out the maturity of its borrowings, and has a relatively liquid balance sheet. Fitting in somewhere between the more advantageous position of FSLR and the commodity production of JKS, CSIQ is another stock for investors to consider as they look toward a global economy shifting away from carbon-based energy sources.

Finally, in the PV manufacturer space we get to SunPower (SPWR), a $1.4 billion market cap company based in San Jose. The company has experienced significant growing pains over recent years as plunging unit prices and sticky operating expense levels offset improvements in sales volumes resulting in years of financial losses.

To stabilize the situation, the company has embarked on a strategy, mostly complete, to shed assets and units and simplify its business. It is no longer putting residential PV system loans and leases on its books, outsourced a portion of its manufacturing, deleveraged its balance sheet, pushed out debt maturities, and cut costs. Currently it is focused on advancing its solar power technology, simplifying manufacturing processes, and retaining its significant market share in the United States for both commercial and residential sales. With manufacturing operations in Malaysia allowing the company to avoid some of the impact of US tariffs on Chinese solar power equipment, strong sales growth outside the United States, and continued overall solar power demand expansion, SPWR has a shot at returning to profitability in 2020.

We finish this chapter with SolarEdge (SEDG), an Israeli firm with a full NASDAQ listing, primarily engaged in the production of solar inverters. Solar panels generate direct current (DC) electricity, which needs to be converted ("inverted") to alternating current (AC) so that it can be fed into a commercial utility grid or used by a residential home. Solar panel systems have generally been moving away from conventional "string," systems, which utilize one inverter that is connected to multiple panels, toward the use of microinverters that are built into each panel and often lead to higher output, lower costs, and reduced maintenance for a system over its useful life. Inverter systems have been getting smaller, cheaper, smarter, and network enabled. These are trends that potentially will allow for a level of technological advantages and premium unit sales prices for leading companies in the space.

SolarEdge is the world's largest inverter manufacturer. It certainly has competition, but it currently boasts a market share among residential solar panel systems greater than 55 percent and a top share in the commercial space (though much lower at 14 percent).[20] Its largest competitor is Huawei, which obviously has significant security issues with Western governments. It is a small step from worry that Huawei's telecom systems could be commandeered by the Chinese government to fears that the same company's web-linked solar panel "brains" could be "turned off" by Beijing at a time of its choosing.

As solar panel system costs continue to fall, governments mandate greater use of such equipment, and total unit sales increase, the demand for inverters should remain strong. SEDG is well positioned for these trends, and it trades on a reasonable forward P/E ratio. Investors interested in this space can also consider Enphase Energy (ENPH). While its revenues are lower and it has struggled to report profits, ENPH and SEDG have similar market caps.

We can wrap up this chapter on alternative energy stock investing with a few summary points:

- There are now several stocks of significant size and levels of stability in which an investor can direct a portion of his portfolio. I would certainly not suggest putting all of one's eggs in this basket, but there are a range of manufacturers and service companies, both yield generating and speculative, in which to choose.
- More conservative investors should consider a larger weighting in yield-oriented service providers such as Brookfield Renewable, Ørsted, and Atlantica Yield (BEP, DNNGY, and AY). Those more willing to take risk and looking for higher returns over time can invest in more speculative names such as Azure Power, Vestas, First Solar, and SolarEdge (AZRE, VWDRY, FSLR, and SEDG).
- To make room for such stocks in a portfolio, we now turn to an area that should be underweighted by investors in an era when climate change increasingly impacts the capital markets—fossil fuel.

Chapter Four

Hydrocarbons

The Biggest Loser

If a major sector of the equity market is to suffer severely due to climate change, it will be the legacy energy space. We have already considered how a combination of government policy, technological advancement, and public pressure has led to an exponential acceleration in investment in renewable power generation. Now it is time to evaluate how this trend will shift world energy demand away from oil, gas, and coal faster than many expect. The following pages will review:

1. the relative GHG emissions released by the burning of various fossil fuels;
2. the size of the oil, gas, and coal sector in the market;
3. the challenges faced by companies in the space; and
4. how to manage portfolio risks for investors who choose to underweight or completely divest from this sector.

NOT ALL FOSSIL FUELS ARE CREATED EQUAL

As we move forward in time, the world is likely to experience both disruption to the global economy due to climate change as well as increasing government actions to mitigate it. The risks are such that investors should increasingly avoid committing capital to stocks in the fossil fuel sector. To make a recommendation to *not* invest in these stocks, the risks must be significant, numerous, and potentially insurmountable.

This chapter will attempt to make the case that this is the coming reality for the fossil fuel industry. The effects of government interference, changing consumer attitudes, more rapid switching to renewables, litigation, stranded assets, and obsolete infrastructure are likely to overwhelm many hydrocarbon companies in the years ahead.

It is important to understand that all fossil fuels are not equally polluting when it comes to causing global warming. In addition to taking a high toll on human health and the environment, coal is by far the dirtiest of the major fuels in terms of GHG emissions. Natural gas is about 50 percent cleaner, and different compounds of petroleum (oil) fall in the middle:

Table 4.1.　Pounds of CO_2 Emitted by Fuel per Million BTUs of Energy Produced[1]

Coal (anthracite)	229
Coal (lignite)	215
Coal (subbituminous)	214
Coal (bituminous)	206
Diesel fuel	161
Heating Oil	161
Gasoline	157
Propane	139
Natural Gas	117

This measurement of CO_2 released per unit of energy produced is referred to as "carbon intensity." Unfortunately, carbon-intense coal still accounted for 28 percent of the world's energy consumption in 2017, and the somewhat less polluting petroleum accounted for another one-third. While gaining share, natural gas and nonhydro renewables were still only 23 percent and 4 percent, respectively.

For civilization's sake, the faster the world can phase out the burning of coal the better. The most likely path forward is to switch from coal and petroleum to the much lower carbon footprint of natural gas as a bridge fuel, which is itself then phased out by wind, solar, and other renewable energy generation. The United States is further along this route than much of the rest of the world. The nation's annual electrical generation since 2000 has been relatively stable at around four million gigawatt hours, and over that time the use of coal has been reduced by more than 40 percent.[2] Government regulation has had little to do with this significant decline of US coal consumption. Instead, the use of hydraulic fracturing and horizontal drilling technology has led to a surge in domestic production of inexpensive natural gas. In addition, the rapid growth in the use of wind and solar power has also been starting to crowd out the use of coal. In the year 2001 the United States generated 51 percent of its electricity from coal, 21 percent from nuclear, 17 percent from natural gas, and 11 percent from renewables. By 2017, natural gas had surged ahead to 32 percent, coal had declined to 30 percent, nuclear was stable at 20 percent, and renewables had increased to 18 percent.[3]

After natural gas and coal, the other major fossil fuel consumed in the United States is crude oil, of which we burn more than seven billion barrels per year. More than 70 percent of this oil is turned into gasoline, diesel fuel, etc., and used for transportation needs. The type of hydrocarbon produced by individual companies becomes important when we shift our attention to a review of the capitalization of the fossil fuel sector in the US stock market. Certainly, this is an extremely large and valuable industry. Energy stocks made up 5.7 percent of the S&P 500 Index in 2019, with more than $1.3 trillion in market capitalization. Outside the United States, the numbers are even larger, with energy companies representing 6.3 percent of the MSCI All Country World Index and more than $2.7 trillion in market capitalization.

There are thirty stocks classified as energy companies in the S&P 500 Index. All are engaged in at least one aspect of the extraction, transportation, processing, or sale of petroleum and natural gas. Many of these companies are household names, such as the giant integrated conglomerates ExxonMobil, Chevron, and ConocoPhillips (XOM, CVX, COP). Several somewhat smaller, generally more US-focused "independent" producers include EOG Resources, Devon Energy, and Pioneer (EOG, DVN, PXD). Others, such as Schlumberger, Baker Hughes, and Halliburton (SLB, BHGE, HAL), do not lease or own drilling sites but act as oil field services companies that make their livings getting the fossil fuels out of the ground for others. Finally, there are the companies such as pipeline operators Kinder Morgan and ONEOK, and refiners Valero and Marathon Petroleum (KMI, OKE, VLO, MPC), that process hydrocarbons and transport them to market.

Note that none of these companies are in the business of mining, processing, or burning coal. The last coal company in the S&P 500,

Peabody Energy (BTU), was booted out in 2014 less than two years before it was forced into bankruptcy reorganization. There are still a few US-domiciled stocks that are focused on coal mining, but they make up a small corner of the market and have struggled to report profits in recent years. In addition to BTU, these include CONSOL, Cloud Peak, Arch Coal, and Foresight Energy (CEIX, CLD, ARLP, FELP). All have market capitalizations smaller than the energy company with the lowest valuation in the S&P 500.

Table 4.2.   Energy Sector Components of the S&P 500[4]

Ticker and Name	MKT Cap in $B
XOM EXXON MOBIL CORPORATION	342
CVX CHEVRON CORPORATION	228
COP CONOCOPHILLIPS	77
SLB SCHLUMBERGER N.V.	70
EOG EOG RESOURCES, INC.	61
OXY OCCIDENTAL PETROLEUM CORPORATION	55
MPC MARATHON PETROLEUM CORPORATION	46
PSX PHILLIPS 66	46
KMI KINDER MORGAN, INC.	39
VLO VALERO ENERGY CORPORATION	37
WMB WILLIAMS COMPANIES, INC. (THE)	31
HAL HALLIBURTON COMPANY	31
APC ANADARKO PETROLEUM CORPORATION	29
BHGE BAKER HUGHES, A GE COMPANY CLASS A	28
CXO CONCHO RESOURCES, INC.	27
PXD PIONEER NATURAL RESOURCES COMPANY	27
OKE ONEOK, INC.	26
HES HESS CORPORATION	18
DVN DEVON ENERGY CORPORATION	16
MRO MARATHON OIL CORPORATION	15
APA APACHE CORPORATION	14
NOV NATIONAL OILWELL VARCO, INC.	14
NBL NOBLE ENERGY, INC.	13
FTI TECHNIPFMC PLC ORDINARY SHARE	12
HFC HOLLYFRONTIER CORPORATION	11
COG CABOT OIL & GAS CORPORATION	11
EQT EQT CORPORATION	9
XEC CIMAREX ENERGY CO.	9
HP HELMERICH & PAYNE, INC.	7
NFX NEWFIELD EXPLORATION COMPANY	4

The energy companies in the S&P 500 generate large current profits, are technologically adept, and control massive amounts of infrastructure critical to the functioning of the global economy. The stocks in the sector have acted "normally" over the last several years—they rise and fall with the price of oil, the level of quarterly earnings per share, and the outlook for supply and demand of petrochemicals in the future. The sector has continued to exhibit its historically higher volatility than the overall market, with periods of outperformance followed by sharp corrections.

Looking at the recent "normal" action in the market, one would be hard-pressed to argue that the average investor believes the age of oil to be at an end. Such a doomsday scenario also seems unlikely when considering the corporate communication of BP PLC. Note that this mega-cap company, formerly British Petroleum, changed its logo to an environmentally friendly-looking green/yellow starburst, and in advertising equates the letters of its name as being the initials standing for "Beyond Petroleum." While BP has made investments in renewable energy, its largest capital outlays have been to buy reserves of natural gas while it continues to explore and drill for new reserves of petroleum. Thus, it is

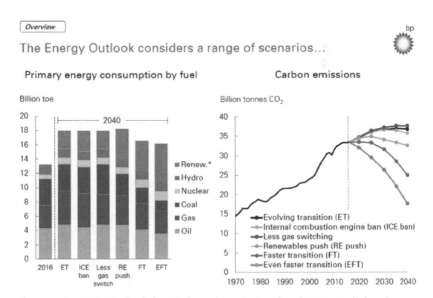

Figure 4.1. BP's Outlook for Hydrocarbon Demand and GHG Emissions[5]

no surprise that the company's 2018 global energy outlook presentation lays out a base case titled "Evolving Transition" that predicts overall demand for oil and gas will continue to rise for many years to come.

As you can see from Figure 4.1, BP accepts that the global economy is adopting alternative sources of energy. However, in the Evolving Transition scenario, that change will not end the growth in global demand for oil and gas. More rapid switching to renewables in BP's "Even Faster Transition" model would still see only a small decline in the total annual use of oil and gas by 2040.

BP is not alone in its optimism for future oil demand. "Most oil companies see a peak around 2040. Others say their industry will enjoy decades of growth as it feeds the energy needs of the world's expanding middle class. Many oil and gas companies expect similar trends to BP, while Saudi Arabia and Russia do not foresee a peak until at least 2050."[6] Of course, one should expect oil and gas companies (and their largest shareholders) to be upbeat about the outlook for their primary product. But what if these detailed forecasts are delusional?

DNV-GL, a major energy and maritime services company based in Norway, has a more pessimistic outlook for the legacy energy sector. It forecasts that demand for oil will peak in 2024 and natural gas usage will top out ten years later. It incorporates into its model that the price of generating power from renewables will continue to fall quickly due to technological advancement. It also forecasts rapid efficiency gains will lead to a steady reduction in absolute world energy demand after 2035 despite global GDP more than doubling by 2050.[7] Even so, DNV-GL's scenario does not bring GHG emissions down to a level that will limit global warming to the Paris Agreement target of no more than two degrees Celsius.

The London-based think tank Carbon Tracker Initiative expects an even more rapid destruction of demand for oil and gas as investment grows in wind and solar power generation coupled with improved battery storage technology. The organization notes that annual consumption of fossil fuels in OECD electricity production began to decline in 2007, and argues that total demand for hydrocarbons will peak in the 2020s with the exact year driven by the rate of global growth and the speed of investment in wind and solar projects.[8] In such a scenario, the rates of decline in annual consumption of fossil fuels will become severe.[9]

The International Energy Agency has consistently underestimated the growth of alternative energy generation and called for ever more development of fossil fuels to supply its industrialized member nations. However, even the IEA now accepts that there is a real possibility of a "Sustainable Development Scenario" in which demand for petroleum peaks in the next few years. In such a development, the IEA believes petroleum consumption would decline by one million barrels per day between now and 2025.[10] While less pessimistic for the fossil fuel industry compared to the outlooks of Climate Tracker and DNV-GL, this is yet another industry observer calling the beginning of the end of the age of oil.

If these more negative forecasts for hydrocarbon demand play out, stocks of legacy energy companies are in for a rough ride in coming years. Problems will play out on both the income statements and balance sheets for these firms:

• Revenues will decline if demand falls.
• Owned reserves of oil and gas underground may become stranded and economically unexploitable.
• The value of hydrocarbon infrastructure assets will decline and potentially face write-downs before expected retirement dates.
• Governments and litigation may exact payments from the industry to finance climate change mitigation efforts.

EVALUATING THE THREATS

As previously noted, the number of laws and executive policies enacted on a global basis to restrict GHG emissions had grown to more than 1,400 by 2017 compared to fewer than one hundred a decade earlier. As the use of hydrocarbons is the world's largest contributor to these emissions, such increases in regulation represent an existential threat to the legacy energy industry's future profits.

The ways government actions can harm the bottom line of companies like ExxonMobil and Chevron are many and varied. They include the potential imposition of carbon taxes on GHG emitters, tighter monitoring and penalties for leaks and spills from wellheads and pipelines, the banning of the sale of internal combustion engine (ICE) vehicles, and mandating increased use of alternative energy sources. To date, most carbon tax regimes around the world that have gone into effect have set the cost of emitting CO_2 low enough to have little impact on the use of petroleum and natural gas. Currently they only threaten the use of more highly polluting coal. However, as prices are ratcheted higher and more nations implement taxes on the release of CO_2, demand for oil and gas will naturally decline and the shift to other, less polluting sources of energy will accelerate.

International bodies are coming to prohibit the use of certain hydrocarbons. The International Maritime Organization (an agency of the UN) is set to implement a ban starting in 2020 on the use of bunker fuel with a sulphur content above 0.5 percent (from 3.5 percent currently). This fuel, currently used by the engines of most oceangoing ships, is effectively the sludge left over when heavy sour crude is refined and more valuable distillates are removed. For decades, ships have often utilized cleaner fuels near port and then switched over to burning bunker fuel when out of sight of land. This practice made the shipping industry one of the "dirtiest" on the planet.

While undoubtedly there will be some initial cheating of the new rules, ships that continue to use high-sulphur content fuel will be liable to lose their insurance, be subject to impoundment in port, and their owners will be the targets of expensive lawsuits. To avoid switching to cleaner but more expensive petroleum fuel, vessels can have expensive scrubbers installed that clean out impurities in exhaust gas. Another option is to have ship engines converted to burn liquefied natural gas. However, capacity constraints on production and installation of this equipment mean that retrofitting to either option would take decades to complete across the global fleet.[11]

Market observers forecast that the International Maritime Organization's new rule will increase demand for low-sulphur fuels, add $4 or more to the global price of a barrel of petroleum, and increase seaborne shipping rates by 25 percent or more. Such impacts would likely make it uneconomic to produce crude from many "sour crude" wells in such places as Venezuela, Alberta, and the Gulf of Mexico.

Government actions are also beginning to restrict individual consumers' use of hydrocarbons. The iconic image of petroleum in the modern world is to fill up an automobile's tank with gasoline. For better or worse, buying a vehicle powered by an ICE around the world is going to get more difficult in coming years. The potential electrification of the bulk of the terrestrial transportation fleet is a massive threat to legacy energy companies. After all, more than half of all petroleum demand in 2016 was for road transportation.[12]

Several nations have announced policies to ban the sale of ICE-powered vehicles in the near future. Other countries are currently debating the imposition of similar prohibitions. The details of each regulatory regime are different, but in general the goal is a gradual replacement of the current ICE fleet with one powered by natural gas, electric-hybrid engines, and/or fully electric vehicles (EVs).

Table 4.3. Nations Enacting Policies Banning the Sale of ICE Vehicles[13]

Country	Ban Announced	Ban to Commence
Norway	2016	2025
Denmark	2018	2030
Germany	2016	2030
India	2017	2030
Ireland	2018	2030
Israel	2018	2030
Netherlands	2017	2030
Scotland	2017	2032
UK (ex-Scotland)	2017	2035
China	2017	2040
France	2017	2040
Taiwan	2018	2040

While these total bans have not yet gone into effect, in some nations such as China, getting permission to buy an ICE car has become extremely difficult. The quota system there now makes it much easier to buy a hybrid or EV, and there are two thousand applicants for each ICE vehicle permit on offer.[14] In addition to these national bans, individual cities including Rome, London, Athens, Paris, Guangzhou, Oslo, Mexico City, Madrid, and Copenhagen have announced upcoming bans on nonresident ICE cars and/or operating diesel-powered vehicles in municipal limits.

Many of these prohibitions at both the national and city level have not yet been legislated into law. At this point most only exist as guidelines, goals, or executive orders likely to be decided in litigation. Certainly, there is sure to be some "slippage" in enacting these new rules.

However, it is clear that in many parts of the world it will become increasingly difficult to buy or drive ICE vehicles.

EVs will grow in share not only through government policy "push" but also through consumer choice "pull." A recent Ipsos Mori poll found that 40 percent of European respondents believe that their next car will be an EV. This is a dramatic difference compared to the current 2 percent penetration rate across the continent. The higher cost of an EV remains the biggest concern among European consumers, but battery prices have been falling quickly and Volkswagen announced that from 2019 its Golf sedan will be the same price in either a battery or ICE configuration.[15]

In the United States, where driving distances tend to be greater, only 20 percent of Americans said they planned to replace their current car with an EV, according to a 2018 survey by AAA. However, that is up from 15 percent just the year before. With lower battery costs and improved technology, "range anxiety" is beginning to ease and adoption rates will likely rise quickly from the current 1 percent in the United States.[16] EVs are not only growing quickly in popularity in developed markets but also in nations such as China, whose consumers bought more electric cars in 2017 than the rest of the world combined.

EVs will increasingly come to be priced at parity (or below) ICE cars. That change will incent consumers to test drive these cars and appreciate their superior acceleration and silent operation. Public knowledge of EV's lower maintenance and operating costs will increase. The popularity, acceptance, and penetration rate of the new technology is likely to soar.

In addition to ICE bans, which may push many consumers to buy EVs in the future, governments have also implemented policies to force utilities to begin switching from hydrocarbons to alternative power sources. Scores of nations have mandated minimum amounts of electric power generation to come from renewables by certain future target dates. As it takes years to permit, build, and bring large power plants online, utilities are redirecting their current investment decisions toward solar, wind, and hydro projects. Some of these national targets are absurdly low, such as Russia's 2.5 percent by 2025, and will be of little consequence for hydrocarbon demand. In contrast, many are ambitious, such as New Zealand's goal of 90 percent by 2025 (renewables were 82 percent in 2017), Austria's goal of 100 percent by 2030 (73 percent in 2018), and Spain's similar 100 percent goal by 2050 (43 percent in 2014). In many countries where national legislation has not yet been enacted, regional governments are leading the way. For example, twenty-nine US states and nine Canadian provinces have announced their own mandates for minimum alternative power in the overall mix of electricity generation.[17]

Carbon emission taxes, ICE sales bans, alternative electrical power mandates, and stricter regulations on methane leakage are only some of the ongoing government actions that reduce demand and drive up the costs of hydrocarbons. The real question at this point is how quickly will these policies reduce sales, profits, and share prices of companies in the legacy energy sector.

The trend of rapid investment increases in renewable power generation crowding out hydrocarbons is taking place across much of the globe. As noted in a previous chapter, a growing majority of net new electricity generation investment is for wind and solar facilities. As an ever-larger percentage of new electric generation investment shifts to renewables and older plants are retired, demand for oil and gas will decline. In addition, other threats to hydrocarbon demand come from a variety of surprising sources, which include:

- Plastic bottles made at least partially from plant material are rapidly gaining share.[18]
- Biofuel made from agricultural waste is now powering commercial United Airlines flights.[19]
- Stores in an increasing number of nations no longer offer plastic shopping bags to customers.
- Efficiency programs such as "Energy Star" in the United States save consumers many billions of dollars in power costs per year.[20]

Initially, the trends discussed would primarily impact the revenue and profit lines of the legacy energy companies' income statements. Then there are the dangers to the balance sheets themselves.

The most immediate threat is from the tort bar. Lawyers learned that suing the tobacco, asbestos, and medical implant industries could generate billions in legal fees. Many of these seasoned litigators are now teaming up with states and cities to sue large oil and gas companies. These regional governments hope to win payments to mitigate the costs associated with global warming, such as increased flooding and windstorm damage. The most notable of these cases include Oakland, San Francisco, and New York City suing energy companies such as ExxonMobil.

To date, judges have decided in favor of fossil fuel company defendants. It is worth noting that the tobacco industry also prevailed for a time in the courts when confronted with the harm their products had caused to human health. As more data emerges concerning what Big Oil knew about the threat of global warming and when it knew it, the potential will only rise that multi-billion-dollar judgments will rip holes in these companies' balance sheets.

This litigation risk does not only exist in the United States. Legal actions against Big Oil and other CO_2 polluters are sprouting up around the world. For example, the Philippines set up a tribunal to consider claims that typhoon damage to the island nation is rising due to GHG emissions caused by companies such as Chevron and BP.[21] Similar claims are starting to work their way into the courts in locations as diverse as Germany, Vanuatu, and Marin County, California. Courts in desperate countries located closer to the equator may be less impartial when deciding such cases as the costs of climate change rise.

While no court has yet handed down a judgment that orders Big Oil to pay $1 trillion, $2 trillion, or $10 trillion in damages to climate change victims, the day that occurs may be rapidly approaching. Legacy energy companies will certainly appeal any such award, but litigation costs will mount. Lawyers for the plaintiffs would likely attempt to block any further payment of dividends by oil companies to their shareholders under the argument that such disbursements represent fraudulent conveyance.

Next to be discussed is the emerging issue of stranded assets. This concept can be explained in a reasonably simple two-part process:

1. If the world chooses to limit GHG emissions so that prevailing temperatures rise no more than two degrees Celsius, then most of the hydrocarbons in the ground will have to remain there and cannot be extracted, processed, and burned. These limits could be imposed through carbon emission taxes, renewable energy mandates, or simple government fiat.
2. Legacy energy companies record their oil and gas reserves as assets on their balance sheets. If it turns out that those hydrocarbons have

to remain in the ground, their value will need to be written down with a resulting negative impact on the total equity of the energy companies in question.

In 2012 the IEA calculated that only one-third of global fossil fuel reserves could be burned if the world were to achieve a warming goal of no more than two degrees Celsius.[22] Proven reserves have continued to grow since then, driven primarily by US expansion in horizontal drilling and hydraulic fracturing. Thus, ever larger percentages of legacy energy companies' assets in the ground are potentially subject to value impairment and stranding.

To take one significant example, ExxonMobil's 2017 annual report lists massive hydrocarbon reserves valued at $90.2 billion.[23] This asset value represents almost half of the company's total equity of $194.5 billion. Obviously, if a large percentage of those hydrocarbon reserves were to become worthless, the impact on the price of XOM stock would be significant. Of course, writing down reserve values would trigger other balance sheet actions. In such a scenario, the company would also have to adjust downward the value of much of its plant and equipment as it would be idled long before its expected retirement date. ExxonMobil reported $252.6 billion of property, plant, and equipment assets in 2017, and further impairments to this total in addition to reserve value write-downs could potentially wipe out 100 percent of the company's book equity. Such asset stranding would impact the balance sheet values of equipment including offshore oil drillers, pipeline operators, and refineries.

Of course, most large oil and gas companies argue that the threat of stranded hydrocarbon assets is spurious and that they will profitably exploit their booked reserves. They expect that governments will not have the will to limit fossil fuel combustion. The political winds are blowing against them, but it is possible that the fossil fuel industry will be able to fight a successful rearguard action against carbon emission taxation and regulation. However, even if governments do not act, it is also conceivable that another factor will lead to fossil fuel reserves becoming stranded assets.

As detailed in previous chapters, technological improvements have been rapidly driving down the cost of generating renewable power. Over the next decade this trend may lead to such a drop in new production costs of solar and wind projects that many proven reserves of hydrocarbons will cease to be economical to exploit. The Bronze Age did not end for lack of bronze; it ended due to technological advancement leading to the production of iron. We are living through the final days of the Oil Age.

Certainly, the actions of some energy majors belie such confidence in the business-as-usual model. Royal Dutch Shell (RDS.A) has been allowing its proven reserves to shrink. At the end of 2017 the company had reserves of 12.2 billion barrels of oil equivalent compared to 13.3 in 2016 and 14.3 in 2010.[24] At these levels, Shell can only sustain its current annual production of 1.4 billion barrels for nine years. The company recently published a lengthy report on the ongoing transition in the energy industry that contained the following:

> We conclude there is a low risk of Shell having stranded assets, or reserves that we cannot produce economically in the medium term. . . . At December 31, 2017, we estimate that around 80% of our current proved oil and gas reserves, will be produced by 2030 and only around 20% after that time. Production that is already on stream will continue as long as we cover our marginal costs. . . . For Shell, this means that we will still produce and sell the oil and gas that society needs, while preparing our portfolio to move into lower-carbon energy, where this makes commercial sense.[25]

Shell has expanded its investments in natural gas and more recently began to diversify into offshore wind farms and electric vehicle charging stations. The company is clearly attempting to surf the disruptive waves of technological and political change and maintain its current level of profitability. It may pull off this trick, but the record of buggy-whip companies that successfully moved into auto parts, or mainframe computer makers that became leaders in laptops, or camera makers able to leap into producing smartphones is woefully small.

An additional problem is that Shell, and the stocks of the other large, integrated "oil majors," trade in the capital markets at significant premiums to the value of their book equity. Investors assume that the parts are worth more than the whole, or that future fossil fuel finds will increase out-year profitability levels. These price-to-book premiums may experience significant compression as shareholders increasingly take note that the companies that produce fossil fuels are themselves investing elsewhere.

If hydrocarbon asset stranding does take place, its pace and cause (government action or technological change) will be important to the future path of equity values of US companies such as ExxonMobil, Chevron, BP, and Shell. The Western oil companies primarily pump out their product in locations where production costs are relatively high and the incentive is to maximize short-term positive cash flows. In contrast, the state companies of most OPEC nations (and Russia) have much lower average pumping cash costs to supply the global market, and their incentive is to manage production levels downward to limit supply and maximize long-term profitability.

If fossil fuel reserves are stranded due to governmental measures, it is possible that the Western companies with their higher production cost locations may suffer the most pain. In contrast, if hydrocarbon asset stranding takes place due to technological change and cost reductions in the price of renewable power systems, then volume-oriented US companies may have time to deplete most of their reserves while national oil companies in such places as Saudi Arabia and Iran will wish they had pumped more and faster.

Of course, the most likely scenario is a synergistic one: government action to limit GHG emissions will spur investment in wind and solar power, and improvements in these technologies will allow governments to impose ever more severe taxes and restrictions on CO_2 pollution.

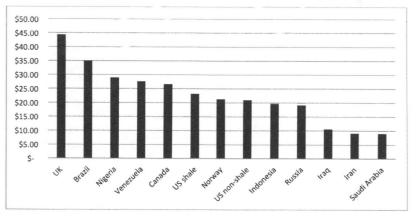

Figure 4.2.   Average Cost to Produce a Barrel of Oil or Gas Equivalent (2016 Data)[26]

Such a future would represent an existential crisis for both the owners of ExxonMobil and the House of Saud.

Before moving on to specific stock recommendations, we can conclude the following regarding investment in the fossil fuel industry from this review:

1. Stock prices and earnings streams of fossil fuel–producing companies are likely to become increasingly volatile due to government regulation, litigation expense, and competing technological disruption. The most impactful of these changes in the short term are likely to be government suppression of global demand for fossil fuel through carbon taxes, pollution reduction mandates, and support for renewable power. Such policies would likely be popular in nations such as the United States, where consumers distrust the oil and gas industry more than any other.[27]
2. To the extent that one does invest in energy stocks, it is important to be mindful of the carbon intensity of the fuel produced by each company. All things being equal, coal businesses are more at risk than petroleum ones, which are in turn riskier than ones that specialize in bringing natural gas to market.
3. Investors also need to be cognizant of the potential for assets such as reserves, pipelines, and drilling rigs having their values impaired. Such an eventuality could wipe out many billions of dollars of balance sheet capital.
4. Rising numbers of investors are divesting their holdings of fossil fuel energy companies for reasons of environmental conscience and expected future financial returns. This is driving up the industry's cost of capital. The remaining shareholder base is increasingly demanding operating changes that are good for the planet but likely to reduce profitability, at least in the short term. Major financial institutions are refusing to offer lending, insurance, or investment banking services to fossil fuel companies. These energy firms may increasingly find that other services and physical inputs become increasingly difficult to obtain.

WHAT SHOULD A RATIONAL INVESTOR DO?

Taken together, these changes should result in the companies of the fossil fuel sector experiencing lower revenues, higher costs, reduced profits, and compressed stock valuations. Certainly, one can make an argument that it would be best to avoid this sector completely, not just for ethical reasons but also to maximize portfolio returns. That is my position: the best and easiest course is simply to not own any fossil fuel energy stocks in a portfolio.

Avoiding fossil fuel stocks entirely will likely lead to portfolio outperformance over time. However, this strategy has its own risk for investors, which is marked underperformance in those periods when energy sector stocks rise quickly. These market moves are usually the result of spiking oil prices due to geopolitical instability and/or potential negative supply shocks. To protect against such "tracking error" compared to index returns, investors can engage in one of the following strategies:

- Own stocks of companies that operate renewable power–producing properties and are in the business of selling electricity to the market. Most of these companies (such as CWEN, AY, BEP, etc.) sell the power they generate through long-term contracts. Thus, their profits will not immediately benefit from higher prevailing prices for fossil fuel. However, over time, if oil and gas prices remain elevated, expiring electricity sales contracts will reset at higher prices, leading to higher profits and share prices for these green power producers.
- Own stocks of companies that produce and/or install renewable energy systems such as Ørsted, Sunrun, Sunpower, and First Solar: high oil prices will trigger more demand for renewable power and more incentives for governments to offer tax subsidies for installation of such systems. Of course, there will be a lag between rising energy prices triggering higher sales of wind and solar power equipment. Thus, there may be significant tracking error with this option as well.
- Own stocks of a few fossil fuel companies that produce low carbon-intense fuels (natural gas, propane, etc.), and have an asset base relatively less exposed to being stranded or suffering impairment charges.

For those investors who wish to choose the last option, let us compare the positioning of Cabot Oil & Gas (COG) versus that of Occidental Petroleum (OXY). Investors concerned about the impact of climate change but hesitant to completely divest from the hydrocarbon sector in their portfolios can sleep better holding COG while avoiding OXY.

Cabot is a "pure-play" on the natural gas output of the Marcellus Shale geological formation that stretches from Kentucky to New York state.[28] Most of Cabot's operations are in Pennsylvania, where its active gas wells and pipelines are located. The gas output of the Marcellus Shale is favorably positioned for a world economy hungry for energy but also increasingly attempting to reduce GHG emissions. These wellheads are geographically close to the heavily urbanized agglomeration of the Boston-Washington corridor, with more than fifty million residents responsible for 20 percent of America's GDP.[29] The Marcellus is arguably the only major oil or gas field situated geographically adjacent to one of the world's major concentrations of political power and economic output.

The carbon intensity of burning gas to provide the electricity and heat demanded by the US Northeast is dramatically less than the region's historic employment of Appalachian coal for that purpose. Of course, Cabot can also ship its output west to the industrial plants and cities of Ohio, such as Cleveland, Dayton, Toledo, and Columbus.

The employment of fracking and horizontal drilling has resulted in a rising supply of gas that is lower in cost than using the region's coal. The market has responded by shifting its fuel demand, and coal has been losing share even in the absence of carbon taxes or mandates designed to reduce national GHG emissions. Such government policies could certainly accelerate the ongoing trend and increase demand for locally sourced natural gas.

Cabot's reserves are almost solely one product: more than nine and a half trillion cubic feet of natural gas with a balance sheet value of around $3 billion. Exploration has been ramping up, and production has increased quickly. It now has more than 550 producing wells, and expects to add 15 percent more per year at some of the three thousand additional undrilled locations it owns or has leased.[30] Fracking shale rock formations produces flows of fossil fuel that deplete in a much shorter time than a traditional well. Historically this was viewed as a negative. However, this becomes an advantage for an investor concerned about the impact of climate change. Gas from a well in a shale formation flows to market quickly and then begins to decline in just a few years. This forces an energy company to limit exploration costs and recoup its capital outlays quickly. Thus, hydrocarbon asset stranding due to GHG emissions regulation or new alternative energy sources is less likely to take place compared to companies extracting fuel from more traditional reservoirs.

In an investment environment increasingly altered by global warming, Cabot's single product sourced from a single region adjacent to its primary market moves from being a concentration risk to a potential positive. Yes, there are threats to Cabot's sales of natural gas—competing product can be shipped in as liquified natural gas (LNG) from Africa, Maritime Canada, or the Gulf of Mexico—but these sources would incur higher processing and shipping costs to get to the US Northeast. In addition, LNG is more carbon intensive than natural gas delivered by pipeline as significant energy is expended cooling the gas and some CO_2 and CH_4 is vented into the atmosphere in the liquification process.

Another risk is from green activists. Cabot's product is certainly not beneficial for the environment: fracking has been accused of contaminating groundwater, causing earthquakes, and releasing CO_2 and methane into the atmosphere.[31] However, the immediate alternative is coal with its high GHG emissions, direct negative health impacts, and environmental degradation of "mountaintop removal" mining in Appalachia. In such a context, it is easy to argue that natural gas from shale formations is the lesser of two evils while we wait for a handoff to renewable power. As noted in a previous chapter, the US Northeast is also relatively poorly situated to make large-scale use of either onshore wind or solar power. There are many billions of dollars' worth of gas to sell in the eastern United States as coal is replaced as a means of producing electricity in the region. Imposition of taxes and additional regulation on GHG emissions will only accelerate this trend.

Now let us compare the single-region natural gas play of Cabot to fossil fuel companies whose products are much more polluting in terms of CO_2 released per unit of energy released.

According to the Climate Accountability Institute, seven out of the fifteen most carbon-intense companies in the world are based in the United States, of which Occidental Petroleum is one of the most polluting. While Occidental does produce natural gas, most of its reserves

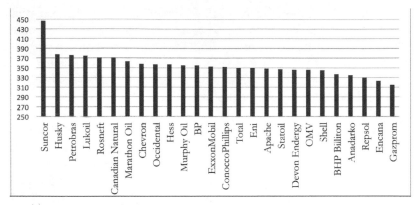

Figure 4.3.　Global Energy Majors Ranked by GHG Emissions Intensity (kgCO$_2$e/boe)[32]

and output are of crude oil. The company pumps out its hydrocarbons in the United States (mostly in Texas), as well as other nations such as Colombia and Oman. The South American production is mostly of sour crude, which may become increasingly uneconomical to bring to market due to its high sulphur content.

Occidental's output from the Persian Gulf is high-quality petroleum and natural gas. Of course, these fossil fuels have to be shipped long distances (adding to their carbon intensity) through politically unsettled sea lanes to get to their end markets. In addition, Occidental's Persian Gulf gas must be turned into LNG before being loaded into specialized tanker ships. The company also has a significant chemicals business in the United States, with much of its input being various hydrocarbons. This diversification of product and geography was historically a positive for legacy energy stocks. However, in a world focusing on reductions of GHG emissions, carbon taxation, vehicle electrification, and renewable power, these strengths may become weaknesses susceptible to carbon taxation, litigation, and technological change.

In the evolving investment landscape impacted by climate change, a strong argument can be made that less carbon-intense natural gas plays in the US Northeast offer the best risk/reward for those who feel the need to own some fossil fuel stocks. Cabot fits this description, as do other Marcellus Shale plays such as EQT Corporation, Antero Resources, Range Resources, and CNX Resources (EQT, AR, RRC,

CNX). The new drilling technology being employed in the Marcellus Shale continues to improve, and there is a massive amount of acreage yet to be explored. The United States would significantly reduce its overall GHG emissions if it simply replaced coal with natural gas for electrical generation east of the Mississippi. Thus, these gas producers of the Northeast currently sit at a favorable junction of profit growth, consumer choice, and likely ongoing government policy.

The Marcellus Shale plays are better positioned than other US natural gas producers such as Chesapeake Energy and Comstock Resources (CHK, CRK). These latter companies also primarily produce natural gas but from a portfolio of properties in less attractive locations such as Oklahoma, Texas, Colorado, North Dakota, and Louisiana, where regional population densities are lower and smaller volumes of coal are utilized as an energy source.

Also, a concern for these companies is that many energy drillers west of the Mississippi are bringing significant supplies of natural gas to the surface as a by-product of their prospecting for petroleum. This drives down local natural gas prices—sometimes to such an extent that they actually go negative. Due to these depressed prices, many energy exploration firms in Texas currently engage in the unconscionable practice of "flaring" their natural gas. This means they burn it at the wellhead, lighting up the night sky to such an extent that the activity can be seen from space. Useless flaring in just this one state was recently releasing greater equivalent daily GHG emissions pollution than that of 2.5 million cars.[33]

To reiterate, at greatest risk and to be avoided are the stocks of carbon-intense companies with large percentages of their reserves in petroleum, such as ExxonMobil, Murphy Oil, Occidental, Marathon Oil, Hess, and Chevron (XOM, MUR, OXY, MRO, HES, CVX).

Such a strategy of overweighting natural gas versus petroleum puts an investor at risk of a gas glut and/or a spike in the price of oil. However, the two commodities have generally moved in tandem over the years.[34] Thus, only owning stocks of companies in the natural gas space will allow a portfolio to participate in a rally in energy prices without being exposed to the most onerous impacts of government-imposed carbon emission taxation and regulation.

WHAT TO OWN OUTSIDE THE US?

Moving on to a global view, only seven of the fifty largest oil and gas companies in the world ranked by revenues are based in the United States.[35] There are more than seventy publicly traded energy names in the Morgan Stanley All Country World Index. The risks to these companies are rising due to global warming just as for fossil fuel energy firms in the United States. While the perils of litigation, carbon emission taxes, bans on ICE vehicle sales, and asset stranding vary by nation, the market for fossil fuels is global in nature, and a drop in demand will impact energy companies wherever they operate.

As with a domestic equity portfolio, the safest bet is to divest from these stocks entirely and partially hedge against spikes in oil and gas prices with holdings of alternative energy suppliers and equipment producers such as Denmark's Vestas, Spain's Siemens Gamesa Renewable Energy, Bermuda's Brookfield Renewable Partners, and China's Jinko Solar (VWDRY, GCTAF, BEP, JKS).

Some investors with global portfolios will shy away from complete divestment of fossil fuel investments. As with US stocks, an intermediate step is to only own those companies with lower carbon intensities. This leads to a focus on stocks of natural gas producers located close to large population and manufacturing centers that still utilize coal to fuel local electricity production. The best names fitting this description include Russia's Gazprom, Canada's Encana, and Spain's Repsol (GZPFY, ECA, REPPY).

Finally, the most dangerous energy stocks to own are those that primarily produce petroleum and rank high on the list of the worlds' most carbon-intense companies. These include Canada's Suncor Energy, Husky Energy, Canadian National Resources, Brazil's Petrobras, and Russia's Lukoil and Rosneft (SU, HUSKF, CNQ, PBR, LUKOY, OJSCY).

The Canadian stocks are particularly risky as they have been increasing their refining of Alberta's tar sands into petroleum. These operations pollute local water supplies, and are about 15 percent more carbon intensive than conventional oil extraction.[36] In addition, it also takes a significant amount of energy to get this oil to far-away markets via lengthy pipeline systems.

The center of tar sand production is the Canadian city of Fort Mc-Murray, which is more than eight hundred miles by road north of the US border and an additional one thousand miles from the main North American petroleum transshipment point in Cushing, Oklahoma. Once there, this Canadian product has to compete with cheaper US production whose volumes have soared due to the fracking revolution. China is a potential market for tar sand oil, but both geography and politics are problems. To sell directly to Asia, the oil would need to be pumped over the Canadian Rockies first before it could be loaded into waiting supertankers. To get there, transmountain pipelines will have to fight gravity, as well as fierce political opposition from the province of British Columbia.

Let us conclude this chapter with a few summary points:

- The fossil fuel sector is becoming arguably the most dangerous industry in which to invest. More than a hundred billion dollars of market value is likely to be wiped out in the next two decades from a range of negative impacts such as faster renewable power system installation, electrification of the terrestrial vehicle fleet, and more government intervention via carbon emission taxes and litigation.
- The speed of this change is the big question mark and will drive the rate at which investors should divest from the sector.
- To reduce index underperformance in periods when oil prices spike, investors can consider owning shares of established and profitable renewable power companies. Or, if less tracking error is desired, stocks can be owned in the hydrocarbon space that have lower carbon intensities than average.

Chapter Five

Financial Services

Underwater ATMs?

The business of the major industries of the financial services sector is, at the end of the day, about managing risk. After assessing potential borrowers, banks make loans and bet they will usually get paid back. Property & Casualty insurance companies issue policies and estimate that only a small percentage of them will have to be paid off. If these firms manage risk well enough, they make money. If they don't, they go under and fail—sometimes spectacularly.

The problem with global warming for the financial services sector is that it is changing the level of risk in many aspects of our economy. Sea levels are rising, severe storms are increasing in frequency, migration patterns may shift, and certain industries such as fossil fuel extraction and chemical production are likely to suffer under increased taxation, regulation, and capital shortages.

COMMERCIAL BANKING

At their core, regional banks concentrate local pools of capital in deposits, pay interest on it, and then lend out a portion of those funds as loans to finance the local economy. A moderate, upward-sloping interest rate curve and an economy growing at a steady pace is a perfect scenario for maximizing bank profitability. Such an environment led to the coining of the "3-6-3" rule, which translates to: pay your depositors 3 percent, lend money out at 6 percent, and be on the golf course at 3 pm.

An occasional flood or severe storm event is a challenge, but the sun comes back out, insurance policies pay off, and FEMA shows up and hands out wads of cash. Lenders suffer some losses but are soon flush with deposits, and loans are made to finance reconstruction. Economic growth rises, infrastructure is rebuilt better than before, and banking profits return. However, this model only works if the big storms and/ or floods are occasional. What happens if they become annual occurrences? What happens if the most valuable real estate in a region slowly sinks beneath the waves?

Let us consider again the chart previously shown in chapter 1 that forecasts the cost by county as a result of global warming:

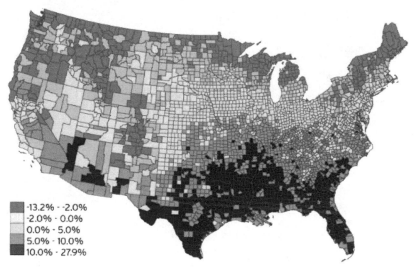

Figure 5.1. Climate-Related Costs by 2080–2099 as a Share of 2012 County Income[1]

A myriad of negatives (flooding, violence, lower outdoor productivity, etc.) means that counties in a huge arc from the western reaches of Texas to southern Florida are expected to experience a 10 to 28 percent decline in annual income from a warmer climate while those stretching along the Canadian border may see up to 13 percent growth in GDP as a result of the same trends. What seems clear is that banks operating in low-lying areas in the Southeast of the nation are at greater risk of business model disruption compared to those in the northern tier of the country. For local banks in places like Miami, Tampa, Mobile, and Houston, the trends are certainly negative. The estimates of these effects are not only due to storms and rising sea levels but also to increased prevalence of violent crime, reduced labor productivity, and higher mortality rates. In contrast, a warmer climate is likely to increase economic growth in the northern tier of the nation. One should not expect an immediate surge in economic activity in Spokane, Grand Rapids, and Buffalo, but the trends are in place and will likely accelerate over time.

Utilizing this data allows us to relatively easily determine a set of Pair Trades: which regional banks should be owned for long-term investment and which should be avoided (or shorted). Consider the list of banks in table 5.1: These twenty-eight companies with a combined market capitalization in excess of $220 billion are primarily engaged in the traditional "bread and butter" of regional banking without particularly outsized asset management, investment banking, or national credit card businesses. Their fortunes are inherently tied to the economic health of the states where they operate. The list of banks on the left (Snow) column primarily do business in the northern tier of US states that will either be marginally impacted or even see positive economic effects from climate change. Due to slower growth over recent decades, it is not surprising that the Snow banks are about 10 percent cheaper by P/E ratio on average than those in the right (Sun) column.

Part of this valuation differential is explained due to the Sun banks being significantly more exposed to the oil and gas industry in Texas, Oklahoma, and Louisiana, which has boomed in the last two decades. Banks in the Southeast have also benefited from a multidecade trend of population migrating south to coastal areas with milder winters and hot summers, where most severe temperature periods are mitigated with prodigious doses of air conditioning. However, these trends are set to stall or even reverse as the banks in the Sun category have their branches located in southern states that border the Gulf of Mexico and the Atlantic where carbon taxation, sea level rise, more intense storm surges, and increases in killing heat are likely to negatively impact local economies.

Florida presents a good case study regarding what those impacts could look like in coming years. In Miami, sea levels have risen ten inches since 1900. This has led to the city experiencing a 400 percent increase in the number of "sunny day" flooding events where simple

Table 5.1. Selected Regional Banks Ranked by Market Capitalization[2]

	Snow					Sun			
Name	Ticker	Market Cap ($B)	P/E	Major States	Name	Ticker	Market Cap ($B)	P/E	Major States
M&T Bank	MTB	23.1	12.3	NY, MD, NJ, PA	BB&T Corp.	BBT	36.9	11.7	NC, VA, FL, GA
Fifth Third Bancorp	FITB	20.4	10.7	OH, MI, IL, FL	Regions Financial	RF	14.8	10.3	AL, FL, TN, LA
KeyCorp	KEY	17.5	9.4	OH, NY, WA, OR	Cullen/Frost Bankers	CFR	5.9	13.1	TX
Citizens Financial	CFG	15.9	9.4	MA, PA, RI, NY	Synovus Financial	SNV	5.4	9.3	GA, AL, SC, FL
Huntington Bancshares	HBAN	14.3	11.0	OH, MI	Popular, Inc.	BPOP	5.2	9.2	PR, NY, FL
Comerica	CMA	11.0	9.3	IL, WI	BOK Financial	BOKF	5.4	11.2	OK, TX
Wintrust Financial	WTFC	4.1	10.0	PA, MD, OH	Prosperity Bancshares	PB	4.6	13.9	TX, OK
F.N.B. Corp	FNB	3.7	10.6	OR, WA, CA	Iberiabank	IBKC	4.1	11.7	LA, FL
Umpqua Holdings	UMPQ	3.6	10.2	WI, IL	BankUnited	BKU	3.2	11.6	FL, NY
Associated Bank	ASB	3.4	11.2	MN, IL, MI	Bank of Hawaii	BOH	3.4	15.2	HI
TCF Financial	TCF	3.4	11.2	MT	Texas Capital Bancshares	TCBI	3.1	10.2	TX, OK
Glacier Bancorp	GBCI	3.4	12.7	ID, MI	BancorpSouth	BXS	2.9	12.6	MI, TX, AK, LA
Chemical Financial	CHFC	2.9	10.7	MI	International Bancshares	IBOC	2.5	11.6	TX, OK
Old National Bancorp	ONB	2.9	12.7	WA, OR, AZ	Trustmark Corp.	TRMK	2.1	15.0	MI, AL, FL
Average		9.3	10.8				7.1	11.9	

high tides cause sea water inundation to close roads, damage homes, and impact business activity.[3] Local government is now spending accelerating amounts of money to upgrade pumps, install one-way water valves, raise roads, and increase the height of seawalls. Salt water is also starting to invade freshwater aquifers, and more intense storms are causing a trend of greater levels of damage over time. These impacts are occurring across most coastal low-lying areas, which for Florida means almost the entire state. These costs are reducing real estate values, will result in more business bankruptcies, and make many think twice before moving to the Sunshine State. Such trends will result in higher loan charge-off costs, less fee revenue, and slower business growth for banks operating in the area.

Since 1970, the United States has experienced an average daily warming of 2.5 degrees Fahrenheit. This trend has been uneven by city, but the data points cluster around the average. Residents of Green Bay, Wisconsin, have likely welcomed the 2.9-degree temperature increase experienced. However, Tampa, Florida, has warmed by the same amount, but such additional heat and humidity is probably not enjoyed by most who live there.[4] While that Florida city used to see the thermometer top out many years at 93 or 94 degrees, summer highs that register 97 or 98 have become common. Tampa increasingly experiences summers where the high of the day is over 90 degrees for weeks at a time.

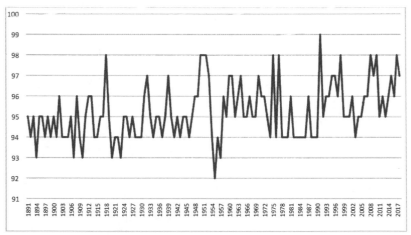

Figure 5.2.   Hottest Day of the Year for Tampa, Florida, in Degrees Fahrenheit[5]

For decades, the US population has been shifting out of the Rust Belt in the Northeast and Midwest to the Sunbelt. The greatest losses were in New York, Pennsylvania, Ohio, and Michigan, with Florida, California, Arizona, and Texas experiencing the biggest corresponding population gains.[6] The 2017 tax bill with its incentives to move to states with low property and income taxes was expected to accelerate this trend. However, worries about greater impacts of climate change on places such as Houston and Miami may be starting to have an effect. Census Bureau estimates released in April 2019 show a sharp slowdown in migration to the Sunbelt.[7] Time will tell if this becomes a trend.

I have been analyzing banks since being employed as a bank examiner at the Federal Reserve starting in 1990. An impression gained over many years is that executives at banks in the Snow Belt are simply tougher than those from companies farther south. Managements at banks in the Sun Belt have learned to expect an ever-continuing influx of new residents to support home prices, retail sales, and overall business activity. Those in the Snow Belt have generally adapted to thrive even in an economy with a declining number of residents. Imagine how much harder life would be for banks in Florida and Texas if residents start to migrate farther north, and how much easier it would become for those in Pennsylvania and Michigan if local populations began to rise faster than the national average.

To our earlier list of regional banks, we can add a couple more pair-trade names consisting of larger, "super-regional" banks.

US Bancorp and PNC Financial both do most of their banking in areas outside the Old Confederacy, which is where climate change is likely to hit hardest. In contrast, much of BAC is the former Nations-Bank franchise that was cobbled together across the Southeast over a quarter century by its former CEO, Hugh McColl. With similar P/E ratios, long positions in Minneapolis-based USB and Pittsburg-based PNC are likely a good bet against Charlotte-based BAC for patient investors. While Bank of America does operate large investment bank and money management operations, core commercial banking still dominates its revenue stream.

Wells Fargo also mostly fits into the "Sun" category after it absorbed the large Southeast franchises of First Union and Wachovia. However, the company has been in turmoil in recent years due to its account-opening fraud scandal. While the stock valuation is currently depressed, it will likely move back up to industry averages over time. Until then,

Table 5.2. Selected Super-Regional Banks Ranked by Market Capitalization[8]

		Snow				Sun		
Name	Ticker	Market Cap ($B)	Major States		Name	Ticker	Market Cap ($B)	Major States
US Bancorp	USB	83.7	MN, OH, CA, WI		Bank of America	BAC	292.6	CA, NC, TX, FL
PNC Financial	PNC	61.5	PA, OH, NJ, MI		Wells Fargo	WFC	217.8	CA, FL, TX, NC

the pair trade of USB and PNC long versus a short on BAC represents a large and liquid opportunity to bet on the evolution of the American economy in an era of increasing impacts of global warming.

INVESTMENT BANKING

Next, we move on to review the investment banking industry as dominated by Goldman Sachs (GS), Morgan Stanley (MS), and the specialized arms of JPMorgan Chase (JPM) and Citigroup (C). Will climate change impact these companies? Of course, it will. The best-selling novel *New York 2140* highlights a future where one of its main characters drives a fancy speedboat to work through the streets of a permanently flooded Manhattan. His job is at an investment bank where he spends his day amorally trading sea-level-rise futures contracts.[9]

Science fiction books aside, it is likely safe to say that the capitalists at Goldman and Morgan et al. will find ways to manage risk, underwrite deals, and make money regardless of the underlying climate. Some investment banks will do better and some a bit worse, but I will leave it to others to determine which stocks in the space are best to own.

INSURANCE

Many assume that insurance will be one of the most negatively impacted industries due to climate change. I am not so sure. Yes, while flooding, hurricanes, wildfires, and crop failures will cause losses at insurance companies, a warming world may be positive over the next two decades for many US- and Bermuda-based companies in the industry that trade on the NYSE and the NASDAQ. Consider the way property and casualty (P&C) insurance companies work:

- The company sells a large number of policies and invests the premium payments in relatively safe and liquid assets. Its balance sheet and equity slowly build over time.
- A major catastrophic ("cat") event takes place such as a hurricane, earthquake, or other.

- The insurance company liquidates investment assets as needed and pays out funds to policyholders who have valid claims.
- The company raises additional capital from the markets if needed to rebuild its balance sheet.
- New policies are sold at now higher prices to customers who have become that much more worried about another cat event, and the process repeats.

Of course, if too severe a disaster takes place and the insurer was taking too much risk in one area, the company may be unable to raise new debt and equity and is then seized by state insurance regulators and placed into runoff. Certainly, climate change increases the possibility of a particularly large storm hitting a region of the United States. However, a couple of factors regarding the structure of the industry protect many of the publicly traded companies. First of all, most flood damage is not covered by private insurance but rather by a money-losing federal program. Similarly, crop failure insurance is also underwritten by Washington, DC. In addition, private companies have shied away from taking on too much risk from specific potentially devastating disasters such as an earthquake in California (most insurance for such an event is issued by a state authority) or a large hurricane in Florida (many homeowners are only able to obtain coverage from the state-owned nonprofit Citizens Property Insurance Corporation).

As the impact of climate change becomes more noticeable, there will likely be more major cat events as severe weather intensifies and storm surges cause greater flooding damage. However, as losses mount, insurers will refuse to cover riskier clients and will raise prices on those still-offered policies. At the same time, demand will likely rise as awareness of risk increases and many businesses and homeowners choose not to self-insure. Primary insurance companies will increase their purchase of reinsurance (insurance companies that sell insurance to insurance companies) so as to manage their exposure to any one negative event.[10] As long as insurers are paying attention to rising threats caused by climate change (they are), price their policies accordingly, and purchase enough reinsurance, they are likely to manage the next two decades of more severe weather events with not much more difficulty than the last two.

However, global warming is going to accelerate a trend in the insurance industry which will provide some opportunity for investors.

Insurers have increasingly been tapping the capital markets to sell "cat bonds," which are synthetic reinsurance securities tied to the risk of a certain catastrophic event taking place. For example, an insurer with a large exposure to policies written in Texas sets up a special-purpose entity that holds the cash raised from the sale of specific bonds. The fine print of the security offering contract promises to pay investors back their capital plus a set interest rate if no hurricane hits Texas for a predetermined number of years.

In contrast, if a storm does hit the state and costs the insurer more than a certain amount of dollars in claims expense, the bond capital is handed over to the insurer.

These cat bonds obviously carry risks, but they are ones not correlated with those of the economic cycle consistent across most other fixed income investments. This has led to growing acceptance of this asset class among institutional investors who are always on the hunt for uncorrelated risk assets in which to invest capital. The positive for the insurer or reinsurer sponsoring the bond is significant, as these instruments allow them to hold less capital on their balance sheet, efficiently reduce risk to any one catastrophic event, and increase ROE in what has historically been a relatively low return industry.

This corner of the capital markets has been growing at a rapid pace. As the severity and frequency of major storms increase, premium rates for some events will rise, as will insurers' desire to sell off (cede) a portion of the risk of a specific cat taking place. This will lead to larger-dollar volumes of these bonds being issued than would likely take place in an environment with fewer damaging weather events. As the cat bond market grows, the number of buildings and businesses that are offered insurance at a given price point can grow quickly, and the dollar amount of coverage will no longer be limited by the size of insurance/reinsurance company balance sheets. While the cat bond market has grown from almost nothing to close to $40 billion in the last two decades, potential future growth is huge. The high-yield bond market has more than $3 trillion in outstandings and exhibits a similar return profile to insurance-linked securities. However, these "junk" bonds have a greater correlation to the performance of equities, real estate, and private equity, which make them less attractive to institutional investors looking for diversification.

The two largest issuers of cat bonds are Arch Capital (ACGL) and Everest RE (RE), with more than $5.5 billion in outstandings repre-

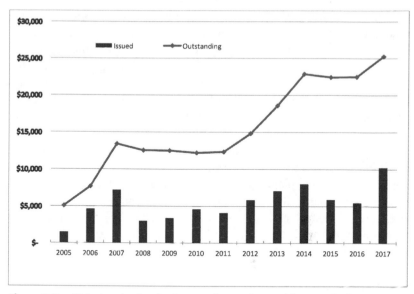

Figure 5.3.   Catastrophe Bonds Outstanding and Issued by Year in $M[11]

senting greater than 20 percent of the total market. These companies, which are both based in Bermuda for tax and regulatory reasons, list the United States as their largest geography where risk is insured. As the cat bond market continues to grow, these two companies are well positioned to expand rapidly, as well as rebuild their capital more readily after major disasters strike. While traditional investment banks such as Goldman Sachs and Deutsche Bank Securities are trying to muscle into the market, the dominant two underwriting/bookrunners in the cat bond space are the securities arms of insurance brokers AON Plc and Marsh & McLennan. The growth of these securities, coupled with a rising demand for insurance coverage driven by increased frequency and severity of storm events, bode well for the business of all four of these large, liquid, globally diversified companies (ACGL, RE, AON, and MMC) as long-term investments.

In contrast, the impact of climate change is likely to be quite painful to the handful of insurance companies that specialize in writing homeowner and commercial insurance policies in Florida. Most of the major national insurance companies (Allstate, Travelers, Hartford, State Farm, etc.) exited the state's market years ago due to the perceived risks of insuring against wind events there. This led to the growth of the state's insurer of last resort (Citizens Property), as well as several other newer companies. Three of the top five insurers of Florida homeowners' policies are publicly traded: United Insurance Holdings, FedNat Holding, and Heritage Property & Casualty (UIHC, FNHC, HRTG), which represent, respectively, the first, fourth, and fifth largest players in the state as of 2016.[12] These are risky investments over time in the face of an increasing impact from climate change.

As we have already discussed, Florida is in a particularly difficult position in relation to global warming. This could spell doom for these three insurance companies. Certainly, bad luck could lead to a progression of three, four, or five large and severe hurricanes hitting the state in consecutive years that will push these geographically focused insurers into runoff and wipe out their equity values. Sea level rise is an even greater, though longer-term, threat. Many climate simulations predict that much of Florida south of Lake Okeechobee will be permanently inundated by rising ocean levels as a result of a 2- or 4-degree Celsius increase in average global temperatures.[13] However, long before southern Florida sinks beneath the waves, many of the homes there will see their value decline or the structures will simply become economically uninhabitable. As ever higher monthly spring tides correspond with even moderate storm surges, flooding will become a regular occurrence in many urban areas.

Municipal taxes and utility rates in the state will need to rise to maintain critical infrastructure that goes far beyond property damaged by flooding. The reason so much of the state is barely above sea level is that it is the construct of an ancient and enormous coral reef made up of porous limestone that grew old when the earth was warmer, the ice caps at the poles had melted away, and sea levels were significantly higher. Today this porous rock allows salt water from rising seas to percolate up through the water table. This salt will contaminate drinking water sources and damage business in several industries. In addition, Florida still burns coal to generate electricity, has almost no wind farms, and only a 0.2 percent residential solar power penetration rate, which is one of the lowest of any state. If some form of carbon taxation comes into effect, storms become more severe, and Florida begins to implement renewable power mandates, utility rates will rise in response to the need to harden infrastructure and finance new generation facilities. Even more than with banking across the Southeast coastal region, the ability to generate profits from the business of property insurance in Florida will be under pressure in coming years.

REITS

This analysis of banks and insurance companies can also be applied to REITs (Real Estate Investment Trusts), which are often grouped in with the rest of the financial services sector due to their reliance on leveraged balance sheets. The S&P 500 contains thirty-one REITs, making up about 3 percent of the index and having a combined market cap in excess of $650 billion.[14] While this is a small percentage, there are several investment opportunities in the real estate space for those considering the impact of climate change.

Some of these stocks are national companies with a large number of individually lower-value properties that are likely to be no more impacted by a warming world than the average company in the S&P 500. Examples include firms running rental locker businesses such as Extra Space Storage and Public Storage (EXR, PSA), document management company Iron Mountain (IRM), data center hosts such as Digital Realty, Equinix, and CoreSite (DLR, EQIX, COR), or communication tower owners American Tower and Crown Castle (AMT, CCI). However, other REITs have significant geographic concentrations that expose them to financial losses and declining property values due to climate change.

Consider one of the largest REITs in the world: Boston Properties (BXP). This $20 billion market cap company owns almost two hundred buildings, with the greatest value comprising landmark downtown office towers with more than 60 percent of NOI (Net Operating Income) derived from locations in Boston and New York City. Another large portfolio of owned buildings is built in downtown San Francisco on landfill adjacent to the bay. Economic power has been increasingly concentrated in a small number of coastal cities at the expense of the rest of the nation over recent decades. This trend has been one of the factors driving BXP's significant long-term outperformance of the S&P 500. However, rising sea levels and more severe hurricanes barreling into the Atlantic coastline threaten to reverse this trend.

Other large REITs with large office concentrations in New York include Vornado and SL Green (VNO, SLG). As sea levels rise, these companies can certainly begin to buy properties located in inland locations, sell some along the coast, and shift their centers of gravity. The problem is that as public companies, such moves will be clear to all to see and signal that remaining owned buildings on the oceanfront may be less than great investments.

Then there are some REITs (not in the S&P 500, but still of significant size) that own properties in the coastal areas of the Southeast already highlighted as being in the path of the storm of impacts of climate change. For example, Invitation Homes (INVH) is one of the nation's largest owners of single-family houses. Camden Properties (CPT) has one of the largest portfolios of residential apartment buildings. Leasing out these properties currently results in a regional breakout as follows:

Table 5.3. Geographic Breakdown of Selected Measures for INVH and CPT[15]

Invitation Homes (INVH) Core Revenue		Camden Property (CPT) Net Operating Income	
17%	Tampa-Orlando	11%	Tampa-Orlando
13%	South Florida	9%	South Florida
13%	Atlanta	9%	Atlanta
7%	Other Southeast	19%	Other Southeast
6%	Houston-Dallas	18%	Houston-Dallas
13%	Southern California	9%	Southern California
10%	Phoenix-Las Vegas	13%	Phoenix-Las Vegas
56%	Subtotal	66%	Subtotal

As you can see, the financial health of these two stocks is tied to areas expected to see the most negative GDP impacts over time from climate change. Outsized exposure to the southern half of Florida should be of particular concern. With such large portfolios, it would be difficult for INVH and CPT to sell down much of their portfolios without roiling the values of their underlying properties.

Another REIT with a Florida focus is Regency Centers (REG), which owns and operates shopping centers anchored by large grocery stores. Some 29 percent of the company's net operating income is generated in Florida, another 7 percent in eastern Texas, and Regency has a collection of additional properties in markets along the coasts of Georgia and South Carolina.[16]

Next, let us consider the climate change risks facing Alexander and Baldwin (ALEX), an owner of commercial properties across Hawaii. Certainly, the Aloha State is a lovely place, and lots of baby boomers have wanted to move there with their wealth as they retire. As with everything else, the boomers get what they want, and the question is if they will still want to move to Hawaii in the future if carbon taxation is imposed on air travel and as the state experiences higher temperatures, increasing incidence of tropical diseases, rising sea levels, bleached coral, and more intense hurricanes. A quick glance at ALEX's property map shows a collection of locations hugging the vulnerable coasts of Oahu, Maui, and Kauai.

It is difficult to know which real estate asset class will be most negatively impacted in the shortest period of time by global warming: class-A office buildings in New York City, grocery-anchored shopping centers in Florida, single family homes in the Southeast, or commercial buildings in Hawaii. However, we can likely conclude that these are the categories that are most likely to experience problems over a reasonable investment horizon. Now let us consider some REITs less likely to be negatively impacted by the fallout of climate change.

First there is Weyerhaeuser (WY), the largest private owner of timberland in North America. The company is considered a green company, 100 percent of its output is certified by the Sustainable Forestry Initiative, and it is the only forestry company in the Dow Jones Sustainability Index. In other words, as retail and institutional investors increase their focus on owning carbon-neutral portfolios, WY's valuation should be a beneficiary. Some factors of global warming may actually be good for the forestry business.

As CO_2 increases in the atmosphere, some research suggests that trees will grow more quickly as well as reach sizes that are fire resistant in a shorter number of years.[17] A little more than 40 percent of the company's timber lands are in northern US states and Canada, where warmer temperatures may also lead to a longer growing season for the forests it owns there. Wood may also gain share from other building materials. Cross Laminated Timber (CLT) is increasingly being used to replace concrete and steel as the structural elements of multistory towers. Forming CLT out of plywood uses only a tiny fraction of the energy required to produce steel; results in faster, cleaner, and quieter erection of new buildings; and is surprisingly safe in the event of fire.

The world's largest CLT tower was recently completed in Brumunddal, Norway, which is eighteen stories tall.

GHG emissions are not all good for WY of course—a shorter winter in the North will allow more pests such as borer beetles to infest trees, more severe forest fires are obviously not a positive, and the company's timber stands in the US Southeast will likely be impacted by more regular incidences of extreme heat and severe storm events. There are a few other timber REITs of size including Rayonier, PotlatchDeltic, and CatchMark Timber (RYN, PCH, CTT). These firms are likely to benefit from many of the same climate change impact effects as Weyerhaeuser.

Moving on, there is an unusual REIT that is particularly well positioned for a future where GHG emissions are more heavily regulated and taxed. This is Hannon Armstrong Sustainable Infrastructure (HASI). The company's core business is to work with municipal governments, corporations, and the military to reduce the carbon footprint of targeted buildings. These include projects to install solar PV panels, retrofit aging HVAC and water systems, and upgrade insulation and lighting. HASI provides the lending capital for these ventures and takes a security interest in the buildings or facilities being upgraded. Usually the client receives an immediate reduction in annual energy costs greater than the expense of servicing the loan to HASI, and after about a decade the debt is paid off and the new equipment is owned free and clear. This is a scalable business as recent clients have significant numbers of large buildings such as the city of Harrisburg, Pennsylvania; the US Marine Corps base at Parris Island in South Carolina; and companies with large, flat-roofed buildings ready for solar PV such as Target Corporation. To qualify as a REIT, a large part of Hannon Armstrong's balance sheet has to be composed of mortgages and/or land. Of course, its core business generates mortgages, and the company also buys the land on which utility-scale solar farms are built, which adds long-term assets with a measure of earnings yield.

Next we consider Corporate Office Properties Trust and Easterly Government Properties (OFC, DEA). These two companies primarily lease office buildings to the federal government and the military. Few of their properties are on the water, and the bulk of them are located in the area around Washington, DC. While many presidential administrations talk about shrinking the US government and/or the military, it never seems to happen. If the government is going to provide monetary incentives to harden any buildings against more severe storms, those that house large numbers of federal employees will undoubtedly be at the top of the list.

Let us summarize this section, taking an overall look at REITs most obviously exposed to, or best insulated from, a rising impact of climate change on our nation's economy and overall real estate values. The following chart breaks down $100 billion of market capitalization of REITs into a hot category likely to be negatively impacted by rising temperatures (to be avoided or shorted) and cold REITs prepared to shrug off these changes or even thrive because of them (to be owned):

Table 5.4.   Market Capitalization and Dividend Yield of Selected REIT Stocks[18]

Hot	Market Cap in $B	Yield in %	Cold	Market Cap in $B	Yield in %
BXP	20.1	2.9	WY	20.7	4.9
SLG	6.8	4.2	RYN	3.7	3.8
VNO	12.1	4.2	PCH	2.8	3.9
INVH	15.8	1.8	CTT	0.5	5.1
CPT	10.7	2.9	HASI	1.9	4.6
REG	11.3	3.5	OFC	3.3	3.7
ALEX	1.8	3.1	DEA	1.5	4.9
Average	11.2	3.2	Average	4.9	4.4

As you can see, one can construct a pair trade portfolio of hot versus cold REITs that capture both large- and small-cap names engaged in a diverse portfolio of real estate businesses while actually picking up net dividend yield. Committing capital to such an investment scheme (as with the one offered for banks earlier in this chapter) makes a bet that the southern coastal parts of the United States will underperform over the next ten to twenty years. To be clear, investors should understand that this set of long and short stocks also embeds other major secular "bets." Several of these names to be avoided are also confronted with existential business threats of being disintermediated by the impact of internet commerce, delivery drones, and AI on location-based businesses such as grocery stores, soft goods retail, and the demand for fancy/expensive/impress-the-clients class-A office space.

In contrast, the cold names to be owned are overweight in the forestry and government sectors of the economy. While these areas are less than "exciting," they certainly are two industries that have exhibited relatively stable growth over time. Not exciting does not mean devoid of risk. At some point if the federal government does not raise taxes, it will have to shrink. It is possible that some alternative to wood (nanotechnology?) will be discovered to displace it in building construction.

We conclude this chapter with some summary points:

- Financial services companies are experts at managing risk and allocating capital to the highest return endeavors. Such a core competency should assist the industry as the impacts of climate change mount.
- However, companies in this sector operating in the wrong parts of the nation will struggle while those along the northern tier may thrive.
- Most specifically in real estate, value is determined by location, and global warming will alter these values.
- Organizing the portion of an equity portfolio in this sector using a geographical mindset is likely to generate outperformance over time.

Chapter Six

Infrastructure

Building Arks in a Flood

Many traditional industries will face major threats from the rising impacts of climate change, with the legacy petrochemical sector arguably most at risk. In contrast, the renewable power field represents an area for increased investment, especially as many of the companies in the space are now more robust with larger revenue bases and market capitalizations than a decade ago. Another area likely to see improving business trends are firms operating in the infrastructure sector.

Now that we have considered the potential negative impacts of global warming on the southern and coastal regions of our nation, the call to action is clear: many waterfront cities will have to be defended from rising ocean levels and storm surges with seawalls, pumping stations, raised roadbeds, dams, and the like. Much damage will take place despite this process of climate hardening, requiring rebuilding and retrofit after destructive weather events. Sadly, some areas will not be economically salvageable, requiring yet more infrastructure spending to expand housing stock and transportation grids in urban regions more protected from high water and severe temperatures.

At least in the United States, many projects undertaken to protect against climate change will be on structures that are aging and at the end of their expected lives. Choosing to initiate similar efforts may be more difficult in countries such as Japan, Germany, and China, where infrastructure spending has been robust and many major projects have only recently been completed. While we have allowed our infrastructure to crumble, other nations have been investing in the future.[1] One need only travel and compare the high-speed trains of Japan, the motorways of Germany, and the port facilities of China to see firsthand how far the United States has been falling behind. It should come as no surprise that our spending on infrastructure as a percentage of GDP has been in gradual decline for decades.[2]

In 2017, the American Society of Civil Engineers (ASCE) awarded D+, D, or D- grades to the nation's dams, inland waterways, levees, roads, and schools, as well as its aviation, transit, drinking water, and wastewater systems. It further estimated that the United States needs to spend more than $4.5 trillion on infrastructure by 2025.[3] We have put off these repairs for years, but as climate change inflicts more damage on aging systems, the time for spending will be forced upon us. Spending on projects across the nation will likely ramp up at a rate that will significantly outpace other regions of the world. If we do not rise to this challenge, the cascading negative impacts of failing infrastructure will lead to a dramatic reduction in US economic output. To cite one example of the magnitude of the issue before us, the ninety thousand dams in our nation now have an average age in excess of fifty-six years, and more than fifteen thousand have been identified as having a high-hazard potential compared to ten thousand in 2005.[4] Large numbers of dams built prior to 1970 are in need of repair or rehabilitation, and many were not engineered for the sorts of severe storm events that are becoming increasingly common.

Table 6.1. Top 25 US MSAs (Metropolitan Statistical Areas) by Population Size in 2018[5]

1	New York City-Newark	14	Detroit-Warren
2	Los Angeles-Long Beach	15	Seattle-Tacoma
3	Chicago-Naperville	16	Minneapolis-St. Paul
4	Dallas-Ft. Worth	17	San Diego-Chula Vista
5	Houston-The Woodlands	18	Tampa-St. Petersburg
6	DC-Arlington	19	Denver-Aurora
7	Miami-Fort Lauderdale	20	St. Louis, MO-IL
8	Philadelphia-Camden	21	Baltimore-Columbia
9	Atlanta-Sandy Springs	22	Orlando-Kissimmee
10	Boston-Cambridge	23	Charlotte-Concord
11	Phoenix-Mesa	24	San Antonio-New Braunfels
12	San Francisco-Oakland	25	Portland-Vancouver
13	Riverside-San Bernadino		

For many companies represented in the stock markets, the neglect of our infrastructure networks over the last decades represents a revenue opportunity. The era 2020 to 2040 may come to be the greatest period of infrastructure spending as a percentage of GDP in US history.

A quick look at the accompanying list of MSAs shows that ten of the top twenty-five city areas in the United States are situated on the ocean, with their downtowns built adjacent to a waterfront where only a small increase in sea levels could have an outsized impact on property damage, infrastructure impairment, and economic activity. Another three are sited along the fall lines of tidal river systems that would suffer similar problems with rising oceans levels. Of the remainder, four additional MSAs are located on large interior rivers or the Great Lakes shorelines that are subject to flooding in periods of heavy, sustained rain and/or extreme weather events. Of course, our cities are where they are because moving freight by water is so dramatically more energy efficient than the use of land transportation. Now the problem is that trends triggered by climate change will force our nation to make painful choices for these cities regarding spending to protect or relocate current critical infrastructure.

INFRASTRUCTURE PROJECTS
AND CLIMATE CHANGE = THINKING BIG

The bulk of Washington, DC's economic activity takes place along a relatively flat plain on either side of the Potomac River, which rises and falls daily with the tides: much of our nation's capital is built on a former swamp. Massive economic decisions impacting the entire country are concentrated in buildings such as the US Capitol, the Pentagon, the Federal Reserve, the FCC, the Supreme Court, Amazon's new headquarters in Crystal City, and the White House. Rising tidal surges would arguably only flood some of these buildings but could cause regular havoc for transportation links in the area, including local highways, Ronald Reagan Airport, and the Metro subway system. Future high tides/storm surges on the Potomac would be devastating if they were to coincide with severe rain events that trigger flash flooding in DC, such as the recent storm that took place in July 2019.[6]

One option to keep DC working (to the extent it does) is to build seawalls along the entire northern and southern banks of the Potomac.

This would be prohibitively expensive, and of course such a massive production and installation of concrete would generate large secondary plumes of GHG emissions. A more cost-effective option would be to build a storm surge barrier downstream where the river narrows at Forts Washington and Hunt. This project would be on a much smaller scale than the giant *Maeslantkering* structure already in place to protect the coastal city of Rotterdam. Similar decisions may have to be taken over time to protect cities such as Philadelphia and Baltimore, though with an occasional disruption to their significant port operations.

On the other side of the spectrum of what can be feasibly protected is the San Francisco–Oakland urban conglomeration. San Francisco Bay is technically a drowned river valley that empties into the Pacific Ocean through the iconic Golden Gate. Despite its famous hills, the region's two major airports, skyscraper downtowns, refinery, sports stadiums, port facilities, and several of its major highways are sited in low-lying areas along the bay. As sea levels rise and winter storms become more severe, efforts to "harden" the most at-risk areas are already underway. However, building effective seawalls to protect in excess of a trillion dollars of public infrastructure and private property would be a daunting and economically ruinous project. Still, it is difficult to imagine that we will allow one of the most dynamic economic engines of the nation—and increasingly, of the world—to be disrupted by what will be relatively small increases in sea levels.

The obvious solution can be summed up in four words: The Golden Gate Dam. Using the infrastructure already in place for the famed bridge, a dam could be constructed across the narrows between San Francisco and Marin County. This would be no ordinary dam. It would have to be able to sustain great tidal and potential earthquake forces.[7] To be clear, such a dam project would be a massive environmental catastrophe wiping out scores, if not hundreds, of endemic species that thrive in the salty to brackish water of San Francisco Bay. However, a sad fact of the human experiment is that when the choice comes down to migrating fish or protecting a trillion dollars of infrastructure, the salmon are going to lose.

Economically the Golden Gate Dam would create winners and losers. Significant port trade would migrate from SF/Oakland to Seattle and Long Beach/Los Angeles (a trend that has already been in place for decades), many Dungeness crab fishermen would have to relocate, and tour boats would no longer be able to sail tourists under the picturesque red bridge. However, these impacts would be massively outweighed as California's intensifying drought problems would be alleviated with the creation of the world's largest artificial, freshwater reservoir. Water flows currently earmarked for fish species protection would be diverted to agriculture in the Central Valley as well as to the aqueducts that lead to the parched city of Los Angeles. Excess summertime water flows could even be pumped over the top of the dam to tankers ready to ship cargoes to parts of the world experiencing ever-worse droughts as the planet warms.

The above scenario is not something I would like to see take place: a pronounced decline in GHG emissions and new carbon-capture technology would be dramatically preferable. However, it seems unlikely that the global political will exists to make such rapid changes. Building one dam would cost much less than attempting to construct scores of miles of earthquake-resistant seawalls to protect hundreds of billions of dollars of real estate. The above discussion in this chapter is meant to highlight the massive opportunities for investing in infrastructure stocks that will prevail in coming years. We will now move on to consideration of those companies poised to benefit.

PROJECT MANAGERS

Let us start with engineering project management companies that would benefit from a boom in large infrastructure projects to protect our coastal cities: these include Jacobs Engineering, Emcor, AECOM, Stantec, Arcadis NV, Fluor, WSP Global, and Tetra Tech (J, EME, ACM, STN, ARCVF, FLR, WSPOF, TTEK). These eight companies each employ tens of thousands of people, have a combined market capitalization in excess of $40 billion, and are involved in a large percentage of any major infrastructure project underway across the Western world.

That these stocks are not particularly well known to individual investors is due primarily to their operating as consultants, managers, and project engineers for others, be it federal or state governments or large industrial concerns and real estate companies. This will likely prove to be a positive in an era of a massive increase in infrastructure spending as these firms can easily scale up their operations to record more billable consulting hours and contract to engage in larger cost-plus construction projects.

In contrast, suppliers of inputs for large infrastructure projects such as earthmover equipment, concrete producers, and pipe and wire manufacturers will have to invest up front to increase production so as to supply rising demand. In addition, an obvious source of funds to pay for giant infrastructure projects to deal with the impact of climate change would be imposing taxes on the firms emitting GHG gases. Construction/engineering project management firms are responsible for little CO_2 output. However, companies producing asphalt, concrete, and more are large emitters, and their products will likely be impacted by GHG taxes or costly cap and trade regimes. Such government policies would raise manufacturing costs. It will be difficult to pass all of these increases along to customers, resulting in lower profit margins for producers of infrastructure project inputs. Thus, the engineering project managers stand to be the most clear-cut winners of rising infrastructure spending to combat the impacts of climate change.

Five of the stocks in this group are headquartered in the United States, while Arcadis is based in the Netherlands and WSP and Stantec are Canadian. The bulk of their revenues are from OECD nations, with the United States representing a majority of their bookings. Most large industrial companies have their own engineers on staff, and the federal government has the Army Corps of Engineers. However, infrastructure projects of increasing size and complexity are generally more than can be handled in house, and an outside firm is generally brought in as a consultant to design and/or construct roads, power plants, waterworks, bridges, dams, electrical grids, airports, and more. Rising sea levels, more intense storm events, and longer droughts are all challenges for our civilization. Of course, these trends are also revenue opportunities for project engineering management companies. Best positioned of these firms will likely be those with scale, a focus on the United States, and relatively small exposure to carbon-intense industries.

Jacobs Engineering is the largest firm in the group, and the only one listed in the S&P 500 Index. It has more than seventy thousand employees worldwide, and a market cap greater than $12 billion. The company lists improving the resiliency of coastal cities as one of its five primary core competencies, with the majority of its revenues being reimbursable/fixed price work on buildings or infrastructure for government entities in the United States.[8] While a Dallas-based company, it recently held its 2019 Investor Day in Miami to highlight its resiliency bona fides in what is arguably the major US city most gravely threatened by the impacts of climate change. The company divested its Energy, Chemicals and Resources Segment for $3.3 billion in April 2019, which will at least partially insulate Jacobs from a downturn in investment in carbon-intense energy and chemical industries. JEC should be on the list of stocks investors focused on climate change will want to consider owning.

Next is AECOM, which generates about 75 percent of its revenues from the United States, and more than half of its business is sourced from government entities. While it has more employees than Jacobs at eighty-seven thousand, its market cap is smaller at a bit more than $7 billion. In June 2019, the company announced it would spin off its government services business into a separately traded company. The remaining "core" AECOM will be that much more focused on planning, building, and repairing infrastructure instead of simply managing already completed projects. The company already exited its non-core oil and gas businesses along with construction management of gas-fired power plants. Thus, AECOM is positioned, as with Jacobs, to be less exposed to a decline in the hydrocarbon space.

Moving on, we have the $4.7 billion market cap EMCOR Group with its thirty-three thousand employees and almost all of its business derived from US sources. More than 60 percent of EME's revenues are derived from mechanical and electrical construction operations, with the remainder from building and industrial services contracts. EMCOR is particularly well positioned for a national electrical grid requiring upgrades for managing fluctuating power flows produced by wind and solar rather than those dominated by the burning of hydrocarbons.

Tetra Tech, with a similar market cap, looks to be somewhat less attractive in an era of climate change. While its business is also focused on the United States and 45 percent of its revenues are from federal, state, and local government entities, it has more exposure to the oil and gas industry, and its annual report lists a downturn in investment in this area as a major risk factor to its business. Similarly, Stantec has significant exposure to the legacy energy complex and about a third of its revenues are from Canada, which is not surprising for a company based in Edmonton, a center of that nation's oil and gas industry. In the same category is Fluor with 45 percent of its recently reported revenue backlog from the energy and chemicals segment. While these three companies are well positioned to benefit from greater infrastructure spending to both replace and "climate harden" systems that keep the economy humming, they are likely to encounter at least some slowdown in their overall business if we move relatively rapidly away from new investment in the use of hydrocarbons.

WSP is a solidly diversified geographic play if the United States turns out to be a laggard in future infrastructure spending. The bulk of its business is generated in Europe, Asia, and its home market of Canada. The company has only a small exposure to the energy complex, with a major focus on transportation. Finally, smallest of the group with a market cap of "only" a bit more than $1.5 billion is Arcadis NV. If sea levels are to rise, the company expects many will turn to it for help, as "our water management capabilities, originating from our Dutch heritage of living with the sea, are world-renowned and are now applied in many coastal areas around the world to increase urban resilience."[9] As they say in the Netherlands: "It ain't bragging if it's true."

To conclude this segment, the construction/engineering project managers are extremely well positioned for the rising impacts of climate change. Be it new seawalls, updated power grids, or strengthening old dams, these companies have the expertise and bandwidth to ramp up their businesses in a profitable manner as the waters rise and storms become more severe. The poor condition of many infrastructure systems in the United States makes the upside that much more likely for those stocks in the space with a domestic focus.

CONSTRUCTION MATERIALS

Next we will evaluate some of the companies that supply the raw materials for major road, dam, and building projects. As discussed, a combination of more severe storm events, rising sea levels, and deteriorating transportation and water control networks in the United States should result in better-than-expected demand for construction materials over the next twenty years. While there are several smaller companies in this space, we will concentrate on the largest competitors. Margins in this industry are not particularly high, so big players with economies of scale are likely best positioned for a growth in demand.

In addition, for building materials as with many other products, it is likely that enactment of government policies of taxing GHG emissions or cap and trade regimes would benefit the largest companies. They are best positioned to invest in technologies to measure and reduce the carbon intensity of their manufacturing methods. In such a scenario, the largest companies would likely see higher profit margins and rising market shares compared to smaller competitors who may be forced to exit the market or put themselves up for sale at less than optimal prices. The scope of potential industry consolidation is significant: LafargeHolcim, the world's largest supplier of concrete, has less than a 3 percent global market share.[10]

Vulcan Materials and Martin Marietta Materials (VMC, MLM) are two similar companies that command a combined market cap in excess of $30 billion. Vulcan generates 75 percent of its revenues and almost all of its profits from the sale of aggregates across the United States. This construction material is a catch-all phrase for gravel, crushed stone, and sand used to form roadbeds and are the most mined materials in the world. Its next largest product line is asphalt, which covers the foundation of aggregate to finish a road.[11] The mining, quarrying, preparation, and transportation of these relatively low-value construction materials require large amounts of energy and release significant GHG emissions. Taxation of these releases would force Vulcan to raise its prices and significantly increase the cost of road building for its customers. Positively, the company reduced its emissions by 50 percent from 2013 to 2018 and hopes to become ever more efficient in this area.[12]

Martin Marietta is similar to Vulcan, but with a lower reliance on the sale of aggregates and significant concrete, cement, and specialty chemical businesses. For both of these companies, the rebuilding of aging transportation infrastructure is already a driver of top-line growth. Accelerating requirements to raise roadbeds or relocate roads inland in the face of rising sea levels and more extreme storm events represents large opportunities for VMC and MMC.

Also well positioned for an increase in infrastructure spending are companies that primarily supply cement and concrete to the market such as CRH plc, Cemex, LafargeHolcim, and HeidelbergCement (CRH, CX, HCMLY, HDELY), which have more than $60 billion in combined market capitalization. None of the largest suppliers to the US market are based domestically, but most can be traded on the NYSE or NASDAQ by investors considering the impact of climate change.

CRH, based in Ireland, is a huge international company with almost ninety thousand employees and more than $25 billion in annual revenues in 2018. It has a full listing on the NYSE, and more than two-thirds of its business is generated in the Americas (primarily the United States), where it is the region's number-one supplier of building materials. Remaining revenues are principally sourced across western Europe. Of course, the manufacture and delivery of concrete and cement generate large amounts of GHG emissions, and CRH measures and reports its emission figures in this regard. It is actively working to reduce its CO_2 output per ton while incorporating larger amounts of recycled materials into its product stream over time.

Cemex, based in Mexico, has half the employees of CRH and a much smaller market capitalization. More than 80 percent of its sales are from cement and ready-mix concrete, with 60 percent of its operating profits from Latin America, 25 percent from the United States, and the remainder primarily from Europe. While infrastructure needs will grow south of the Rio Grande as sea levels rise, it is not clear that the emerging markets of the Western Hemisphere will experience the same level of increase in spending as is likely in the United States. Thus, Cemex, while worth considering for a climate change investor, may not be the top pick in its peer group.

LafargeHolcim of Switzerland is not only the world's largest supplier of concrete but also a major producer of cement, aggregates, and asphalt. As with CRH, it has been working to reduce its GHG emissions, reported a 25 percent decline released per ton of cement produced since 1990, and has a 2030 goal of a 40 percent reduction.[13] While certainly well positioned for growth in global infrastructure spending, Lafarge generates less than a quarter of its business in the Americas and so is not as poised to benefit from my prediction of a greater surge in infrastructure spending in the United States. The company may also be less attractive to American investors as its ADR is illiquid. To build a significant position would likely require a brokerage account allowing trading in Switzerland or Paris. HeidelbergCement of Germany is similar to LafargeHolcim in terms of having an illiquid ADR, a smaller US footprint, and a European focus.

Except for Jacobs Engineering, none of these recommended infrastructure stocks positioned to benefit from climate change and its impacts are components of the S&P 500. To make room for these names in a portfolio, we need to identify a blue-chip industrial sector to be avoided as the earth warms. After all, to take overweight positions in J, CRH, VCN, MLM, EME, and ACM, investors working to maintain a balanced portfolio will need to consider what *not* to own. So, what to avoid?

DEFENSE STOCKS: SOMETHING HAS TO GIVE

US defense companies can be considered the ultimate anti-infrastructure stocks. After all, they manufacture products designed to blow things up. A recommendation to *not* own these names may seem unusual in a book exploring a world likely to become less stable and more violent as climate change disrupts traditional agriculture, extractive industries, trade flows, and zones of urban population. Many expect that such trends will lead to greater conflict, and that the planet will become a less peaceful place in the face of global warming, However, this does not necessarily mean that defense spending will rise in the face of several undeniable facts regarding the financial health of the United States and its ability to maintain its current level of military outlays:

* As already mentioned, the nation has significantly underinvested in its infrastructure over the last few decades. It is becoming imperative that federal spending in this space rise significantly in the near future to simply maintain what has already been built. The impacts of climate change (higher sea levels and storm surges, increased severe weather events, more intense heat waves, etc.) will strain our existing infrastructure and further accelerate the amount of government expenditures that must be directed toward maintaining, relocating, and/or hardening the systems that undergird our entire economy.
* The US government is amassing an ever-larger national debt that now exceeds 100 percent of GDP (106 percent in 2019 and likely going higher). As a percent of annual output, the federal debt has doubled since 1990 and is now higher than it was in 1947 soon after the end of the World War II.[14] These levels are already on the borderline of what is sustainable. This means that rising levels of infrastructure

spending will force us to make painful choices regarding what areas of government outlays will have to be reduced.

- Entitlement reform of the runaway Social Security and Medicare systems is nowhere on the horizon, and increased life expectancy of the baby boom generation, if maintained, will result in the need for massive financial infusions to keep these programs funded.
- US defense spending is massive and out of proportion to our global share of GDP at over 35 percent versus 25 percent, respectively. In 2017, our nation's military spending was more than *twice* the *combined* annual defense expenditures of potential rivals China, Russia, and Iran.[15] The defense budget continues to rise and is arguably unsustainable.

At some point in the near future, US defense spending will have to decline due to one or a combination of the following events: a rise in the rate of interest to service the national debt, the requirement to recapitalize the Social Security and Medicare programs, a need to increase infrastructure spending (at least partially due to climate change), a decision to move ahead with a "Green New Deal" to retool our energy industries, a decision to implement a "Medicare for All" health care program, or a major economic recession.

While most defense-oriented stocks in the S&P 500 also sell weapon systems to allied foreign governments, it is unlikely that this area will represent a large area of revenue growth in the future. These nations are resistant to US entreaties to spend more on their militaries, and like this country, they have significant government deficits and aging populations draining pension and health care systems. In addition, just as with the United States, they will also need to increase spending to harden infrastructure and convert to green energy systems as the impacts of climate change intensify (examples include the UK, France, Italy, Canada, Australia, and Japan).

In addition, most companies in the S&P 500 with a major defense component have civilian aerospace as their other major business segment. Moving people and freight at high speeds in a metal tube hurtling through the sky is currently a carbon-intense means of transportation. Rising GHG emission taxation and/or cap and trade regimes will make air travel more expensive and reduce demand. Battery-powered plane engines are now in development, but it is not expected that they will be practicable for more than one-to-two-hour flights. It is also not clear if it will be feasible to economically ramp up high-octane biofuel output. Thus, petroleum-based aviation fuel is likely the primary motive power that will be used for air travel for at least the next decade.

As climate change–driven infrastructure spending and government deficits constrain defense spending in the United States at the same time that the cost of GHG emissions rise, many companies dependent on military contracts and production of commercial aircraft are likely to see declines in revenues. This offers investors a target of what to avoid (or even short) as they invest more in the infrastructure space. S&P 500 Index component stocks in the defense space that look poorly positioned to weather this coming storm include Huntington Ingalls, General Dynamics, Lockheed Martin, Textron, and TransDigm Group (HII, GD, LMT, TXT, TDG).

Huntington Ingalls is arguably the most negatively exposed stock in the defense sector to the impacts of global warming. The company's primary business is building and maintaining warships for the navy and coast guard at its docks in Newport News, Virginia, and Pascagoula, Mississippi. The US military is effectively the sole source of revenues for Huntington Ingalls. A clear risk for this company is that rising sea levels and increased severe storm events will impact the navy's bases more seriously than those of the other major military services. An example of this trend is that since 2008, the giant Norfolk Naval Shipyard in Virginia has experienced nine major flood events that have been intensifying in severity.[16] Billions of dollars have been allocated to build seawalls and elevate equipment at such facilities. However, to retrofit and protect the more than forty bases our navy has just in the United States will cost much, much more as sea levels rise. As these costs increase, they will undoubtedly chip away at the portion of the navy's budget that can be spent on building new ships and result in lower profits per share for HII.

Rising seas will also directly impact Huntington Ingalls as its two main facilities are, of course, right on the water. Its 550-acre Newport News facility is located just across a stretch of Chesapeake Bay from the previously mentioned Norfolk Naval Base. The company's eight-hundred-acre shipyard in Pascagoula is also in an area that has been experiencing increasing flood events particularly due to more powerful hurricanes with heavier rainfall. What is clear is that Huntington Ingalls will have to spend higher amounts to insure and protect its facilities from rising water levels and will suffer greater interruptions in business operations when storm events close the transportation links to its facilities. What is not clear is if the US government will reimburse this private corporation for such costs.

With a market capitalization north of $100 billion, Lockheed Martin is a company dedicated to producing aerospace components and systems. In 2018, 70 percent of its revenues came from the US government, of which the vast majority was from the Defense Department. Most of the rest of its sales are military systems to foreign nations friendly to the United States.[17] The company's annual sales are greater than $50 billion. To put this in context, Lockheed's annual revenues are greater than the *combined* 2018 military spending of Israel, Switzerland, Vietnam, Sweden, Mexico, and Indonesia.[18] The company is the lead contractor in the production of particularly expensive combat systems such as the F-35 fighter and the new hypersonic SR-72 aircraft (able to achieve speeds in excess of 4,000 mph), which have such high price tags that they could easily be in the first wave of programs to be cut or scaled back as the Defense Department has to tighten its belt.

General Dynamics, with a market capitalization about half that of Lockheed, has several diversified business units. However, its primary customer is the US government (in excess of 75 percent of sales). Of its expected 2019 revenues of $39 billion, almost $30 billion was expected to come from its four Defense divisions (Marine Systems, Information Technology, Combat Systems, and Mission Systems).[19] Any reduction in the amount our nation spends on defense, and/or a reduction in General Dynamics' market share of that spending, would be painful for GD shareholders. The remaining revenue base of the company comes from its aviation unit, which would suffer in a world where GHG emissions become more expensive due to government policies.

Textron is much more a commercial company that happens to have a defense arm. Only about a quarter of its revenues are from the US government, and more than 35 percent are international in nature. Of course, a decline in US defense spending would be a headwind for Textron. In addition, the bulk of its total sales are derived from its airplane (Beechcraft, Cessna, Hawker) and Bell helicopter brands. These could experience diminished demand if taxation of GHG emissions becomes onerous over time, and increases the cost of air travel. Such a change would be particularly painful for Textron as its aircraft offerings are primarily small in nature, designed for only a limited number of passengers, and in many cases, aimed at purely recreational and/or luxury market segments. Logic would dictate that these are the areas of civilian aviation that would be most negatively impacted by rising taxation on the carbon intensity of travel. The same logic holds for General Dynamics' aviation unit Gulfstream, famous for its deluxe corporate jets designed to get CEOs to and from Davos.

Similar to Textron in terms of revenue breakdown is TransDigm, which manufactures proprietary aerospace components and electrical systems. About one-third of the company's revenues are from defense contracts, with the remainder from the commercial airline industry. As TransDigm's nondefense sales are primarily focused on top-fifty global airline customers, it is at least somewhat better positioned for a decline in demand for air travel due to rising GHG emission taxation than Textron's focus on smaller aircraft.[20] As a large percentage of TransDigm's sales are also for replacement parts for aircraft already in service, TDG is one of the best insulated companies in the sector to handle a decline in US defense spending as well as new taxation on air travel.

A few comments regarding Boeing (BA). The famous aircraft company certainly has significant exposure to shrinking US defense contracts as well as rising costs of commercial air travel due to taxation of GHG emissions. However, it is not included in the list of names to avoid at this time as its stock has been under significant pressure due to problems with its flagship 737 aircraft. One hopes that the large number of competent engineers at Boeing will be able to solve this issue, and the stock will eventually recover. Until that takes place, I would recommend limiting an underweight on defense stocks to the ones already described.

All investment allocations have risks, and this buy infrastructure/short defense recommendation certainly has them. A scenario in which an extended conflict in the Middle East draws the United States into active fighting while limiting exports of petroleum through the Persian Gulf would support the price of defense stocks against a general market decline. This could also cause losses for a portfolio of buy green energy/short hydrocarbon energy stocks as advised in previous chapters. However, such a scenario is becoming less likely: as the United States is expected to become a net energy exporter in 2020 and has been increasingly retreating from its role of "global policeman" under recent successive presidents, it becomes ever more difficult to see our nation fighting a long conflict to secure the flow of hydrocarbons for Germany, China, and India. In contrast, the science seems clear that we will be increasingly forced to move toward renewable power, more spending on infrastructure, and less on defense.

To conclude this chapter:

- There is a strong case to be made for a coming boom in infrastructure spending due to the rising impacts of climate change.
- This increase is likely to be particularly large in the United States, where maintenance of roads, dams, bridges, and wastewater systems has been neglected to the point that major structures are beginning to fail and threaten the basic workings of the economy.
- The best way to invest to capture the upside of this trend is to focus one's attention on the stocks of the larger engineering project managers with a domestic focus to their business. Also of interest should be the large construction materials companies such as road aggregate and concrete suppliers.
- Offsetting these holdings would be an avoidance (or even shorting) of major defense companies, particularly those building the most exorbitantly expensive military systems and/or also dependent on aviation.

Chapter Seven

Transportation

The Decline and Fall of the Internal Combustion Engine

We now move on to consider the impact of climate change on the transportation sector which will have both winners and losers. Companies in this space will have to be nimble to manage the coming changes. In terms of energy consumption, the biggest change for this industry in the next two decades will be a major shift away from hydrocarbon-burning engines toward battery-powered vehicles.

AUTO/LIGHT TRUCK MANUFACTURERS, DEALERS, AND PART SUPPLIERS

As already discussed, many countries are cajoling, taxing, and forcing consumers and manufacturers away from ICE vehicles toward ones running electric motors, which will increasingly be charged by renewable energy sources. This trend will help a few companies in the automotive industry but will create many significant losers. Most large car manufacturers are already producing hybrids and/or fully electric-powered models. GM and Volkswagen (GM, VWAGY) have recently announced that they will be phasing out hybrid gas/electric vehicles to produce only pure EVs while Toyota and Ford (TM, F) will continue to develop and sell hybrids as core offerings in their product line.[1] It is difficult this early in the game to handicap which competitors will succeed as EVs take over the roads.

What we can predict is that the adoption rate of EVs will continue at a high speed and will likely accelerate due to a number of factors. Assembling electric cars is not as labor intensive nor as complex as the manufacture of traditional petroleum-burning vehicles. It takes up to 40 percent fewer hours to assemble an electric versus a traditional fuel-burning vehicle. Fears of a reduction in overall workforce levels due to the move to EVs is one of the major reasons for the United Auto Workers strike that began in September 2019.[2] The rise of EVs is sure to lead to significantly more labor unrest at automakers in the next few years.

However, at this time, the savings of not having to install a complicated ICE is more than offset by the expense of the batteries required to power an EV. The cost and fuel efficiency of a traditional petroleum-burning system has been relatively stable, but the price of lithium ion batteries has been declining quickly and their energy density has been improving. It is likely that in just a few years an EV will actually be cheaper than the same models powered by a gasoline or diesel engine. In addition, fuel cell technology, while still prohibitively expensive, has also been falling in price and may be ready for mass-consumer adoption in a decade or so.

The imposition of legal restrictions on sales of ICE vehicles and imposition of GHG emission tax regimes will accelerate the evolution of the light vehicle fleet around the world. At the end of the day, the move toward EVs is not due solely to climate change. After all, batteries can always be charged with electricity generated by coal, gas, or oil-fired generator plants. In addition, EVs are becoming increasingly popular due to their falling prices, high performance, and lower maintenance requirements. However, the rise of the battery-powered car is being driven by government policies and the choices of environmentally conscious consumers. As already discussed, the majority of investment around the world into new electric generation is being directed into the rollout of renewable technologies which will ensure that the electrification of the auto fleet will be good for the environment over the next few decades.

Not everyone will want to drive an EV even as they become "cheap." Some drivers enjoy making a lot of noise in a muscle car and/or cruising around in an extra-large vehicle. Others engage in many long-distance drives, or do not park in a dedicated space (garage or driveway) where overnight or worktime charging can take place. However, charging technology is getting much faster with Porsche/BMW's new prototype system adding one hundred miles of range to an EV in ten minutes.[3] A firm called Tritium has new "pumps" that add in excess of 215 miles of range in the same amount of time and has started selling units to VW and Ford.[4] Excellent 4/5 passenger EVs with three-hundred-plus-mile range are becoming increasingly available at reasonable price points. Tesla's new Cybertruck is offered with up to a five-hundred-mile range. Within a short number of years there will be few rational reasons left to own a "gas guzzler."[5]

I am not going to speculate as to how quickly fully autonomous vehicles will be offered for commercial sale except to assume that 1) this is likely to start within the next decade; 2) such vehicles will be common on the road by 2040; and 3) this shift will accelerate the move toward EVs.[6] Autonomous vehicles will be more energy efficient: they will not overaccelerate at green lights, will not exceed the posted speed limit, and will not weave, speeding up and down, in an attempt to move ahead a few car lengths in slow traffic. More efficient driving will extend the cruising range for a given amount of energy utilized and so make battery-powered vehicles that much more feasible. In addition, as vehicles become more autonomous, they will become safer, which means they can be lighter and thus more fuel efficient and will add another factor to the feasibility of EVs.

The most obvious losers from the trend toward EVs and autonomous vehicles are auto dealership stocks such as Asbury Automotive, AutoNation, Group 1 Automotive, Lithia Motors, and Sonic Automotive (ABG, AN, GPI, LAD, SAH). Sadly, the days of having to haggle with a salesman and waiting for him to "take a price to his manager" will not soon be over. However, that does not mean the companies in this space are a good long-term investment. The major problem here is that EVs require less maintenance compared to ICE vehicles. This is because an

Table 7.1. Lithia Motors, Inc., Business Mix[7]

	Revenues	Gross Profit
New Vehicle Sales	53%	19%
Used Vehicle Sales	32%	19%
Parts & Service	11%	35%
F&I (Finance & Insurance)	4%	27%

ICE vehicle requires a much more complicated motor and drivetrain with many more moving parts that are prone to failure. In addition, EV's regenerative braking systems last much longer than traditional friction-based ones. This is a problem for auto dealerships because maintenance is where they generate their profits.

As you can see from the accompanying chart for Lithia Motors, the parts and service business generated only 11 percent of the company's revenue stream but 35 percent of its gross profits. Yes, you are correct: the bill from your dealer's auto shop seems entirely too high. Also, as you can see from the F&I profit margins, you don't really want to go into that little room to see the Finance Manager who is going to try to get you to buy an extended warranty or a "clear coat." As Lithia only had a gross profit margin of 15 percent and a net profit margin of 2.2 percent in 2018, one can see how a decline in auto service requirements could be devastating for the auto dealership business model. Faced with less repair work, firms like Lithia could try to increase their profits by raising costs on used vehicle sales, but that would lead to market share loss to the private sales channel. Padding new car sales with higher prices/profits would result in howls of protest from automakers. Finally, attempts to widen margins on financing and insurance would push more business to direct sales from banks and insurers.

Next in line for trouble are the stocks of the retail store chains offering automotive parts for DIY users and small repair shops such as Advance Auto Parts, AutoZone, and O'Reilly Automotive (AAP, AZO, ORLY), which impressively had more than $60 billion in market capitalization in early 2020. In its most recent annual report, Advance Auto Parts lists thirty-five major categories of products sold in its stores.[8] Fleets of EVs on the road would negatively impact sales for sixteen of these categories, including:

- motor oil
- air filters
- transmission fluid
- oil filters
- antifreeze
- fuel filters
- ignition components and wire
- starters and alternators

- clutches and drive shafts
- exhaust systems and parts
- batteries and battery accessories
- belts and hoses
- brakes and brake pads
- engines and engine parts
- radiators and cooling parts

In its long list of risk factors spelled out in its 2018 10-K, Advance Auto Parts does address EVs. It notes that its business could be negatively impacted by *"technological advances, such as battery electric vehicles, and the increase in quality of vehicles manufactured,* because vehicles that need less frequent maintenance or have lower part failure rates will require less frequent repairs using aftermarket parts and, in the case of battery electric vehicles, do not require oil changes" (italics in the original).[9] Of course, the company's lawyers also made sure to include a brief note that Advance Auto Parts "may be affected by global climate change or by legal, regulatory, or market responses to such change."[10]

Moving on, we come to the companies that supply parts directly to the major auto manufacturers. These include Aptive, BorgWarner, Delphi Technologies, Magna International, Continental AG, and Dana Inc. (APTV, BWA, DLPH, MGA, CTTAY, DAN). These companies manufacture a large range of different parts, many of which will remain in demand no matter what the motive power pushing a car down the road. As the evolution of the auto fleet to EVs will play out over the next few decades, the auto parts companies will have significant time to shift away from producing ICE components, as demand declines. Managing the speed of this change to maximize profits will represent an existential challenge for many auto parts companies over the next decade.

We can certainly see that companies in this space are suffering disruption due to the move toward electrification of the auto fleet. Continental AG of Germany has had an extremely difficult time since the start of 2018 with both its stock and earnings under significant pressure. In August 2019, the company announced it would dramatically cut its investment in ICE parts, as its CFO stated, "that although the auto industry would continue to use conventional internal combustion engines for many years, it was becoming difficult to justify the high cost of improving components to make gasoline and diesel engines less polluting."[11] The head of Continental's powertrain division was even more blunt: "The future is electric. We are convinced of this."[12] BorgWarner, based in the Detroit suburbs, will also be forced to make tough decisions in this near future as the company currently generates more than half its revenue stream from its "Engine" reporting segment, which primarily produces parts related to traditional gas and diesel combustion systems.[13]

MOTORCYCLES: WHITHER THE HOG?

Next, we take a short detour to discuss the future of motorcycles. As emitting GHG becomes more expensive, we should expect more consumers will elect to purchase two-wheelers that transport one or two passengers with much less energy than an automobile. Most manufacturers in this space are large foreign diversified companies not dependent solely on motorcycles, including Honda, Yamaha, Kawasaki, and BMW (HMC, YAMCY, KWHIY, BMWYY). Then there is the American icon Harley-Davidson (HOG). As we all know, riding a Harley is not just about getting from point A to B. The point is looking cool and making enough noise that everyone looks up to check you out as you roar past. These bikes come off the assembly line with massively overpowered engines (600–1900cc's) able to produce up to 80 decibels of engine sound—and that is before many owners spend good money to install after-market mufflers that make their "hogs" even louder. How many readers even realize that all motorcycles sold in the United States come with a horn that can be sounded rather than revving an engine to get the attention of other drivers? Obviously, electrification is a problem for the company as it confronts a future of silent motorcycles.

The typical Harley-Davidson owner is a white, overweight, American male averaging just slightly under fifty years of age who uses his bike primarily for (loud) leisure driving.[14] The company admits that a world of quiet motorcycles represents a grave threat. In its 2018 annual report, the company states that the distinctive sound of its bikes is one of the reasons it is able to charge premium prices and that the "company must make product advancements to respond to changing consumer preferences and market demands while maintaining the unique look, sound and feel associated with Harley-Davidson products, and development of electric vehicles will present challenges to the Company's ability to maintain such look, sound and feel."[15]

Several manufacturers are now selling all-electric "e-bikes" ranging from basic models like the Vespa Elettrica with a sixty-mile range and a $7,000 price tag to the Lightning LS-218, which can accelerate from a standing start to 60 mph in two seconds, top out above 200 mph, but costs almost $40,000. Harley-Davidson has decided to join the move to electric motorcycles with its new LiveWire model, with a starting price of $29,799. Harley's marketing line for the new e-bike: "The Loudest Sound You Hear Will Be Your Heart Racing."[16] Will a silent bike at a premium price appeal to Hog enthusiasts? We will soon find out, but I believe the next ten to twenty years will be painful ones for HOG owners.

ELECTRIC CAR MANUFACTURES

No chapter on this subject would be complete without at least some discussion of the phenomenon that is Tesla, Inc. (TSLA). However, anything written today regarding the investment case for the company will likely be well out of date within weeks due to the mercurial nature of the firm's CEO, its volatile share price, and the extreme passions the stock generates among equity traders. What can be said with assurance is that the company manufactures cars that have achieved a cultlike following among owners, the stock's valuation commands a price-to-revenue ratio dramatically higher than its larger competitors, and that it is surfing the cutting (or bleeding) edge of the evolution of the terrestrial transportation fleet to EVs.

Questions about Tesla's future are significant. Can the company achieve its goal of selling a few million cars and trucks per year by 2025? If so, it will cause serious disruption to the auto manufacturing industry: proving the feasibility of a direct-sales (no dealership middleman) model as well as accelerating the move to EVs more rapidly than many forecasters expect. Or, will investors tire of providing debt financing to a loss-making company as its loose-cannon CEO is forced to resign by the SEC? While I own the stock personally, root for Tesla, drive a Model 3, own a Powerwall, ordered a cybertruck for my wife, and wish Mr. Musk great success, TSLA seems too speculative to represent a core investment for climate-change investors at this time.

NIO Inc. (NIO) is a speculative pure-play investment in the consumer EV space. Based in Shanghai and with a listing on the NYSE, its cars are currently on sale in China, and plans to start selling vehicles in the United States in 2020. The company currently offers two different sized electric SUVs (the ES8 and the ES6) as well as the super-cool EP9 roadster that is billed as the fastest EV in the world. With more than a $3 billion market cap in early 2020, and accelerating losses, it is even money that NIO will be a big winner, or go under just in the time between when these words are written and this book gets published.

MEDIUM/HEAVY TRUCK MANUFACTURERS

Most consumers drive their cars and light trucks within a limited range on a daily basis, which makes them eligible for replacement with EVs. The same is often true for heavier trucks used for local area deliveries, and logistics support with a home base where they could be charged overnight. Most major truck manufacturers are actively at work on this evolution. PACCAR (PCI) is rolling out hybrid, EV, and hydrogen fuel cell models in its Peterbilt, DAF, and Kenworth truck model lines. Competitors such as Mercedes, AB Volvo, Navistar, and Oshkosh are launching similar new offerings. Tesla has also showcased a new all-electric Class 8 semitrailer with autopilot technology and a planned range of five hundred miles on a single charge. Production is promised for late 2020, and thousands of orders with accompanying 10 percent deposits from customers such as Walmart, Pepsi, and FedEx have already been received by the company. Such a new product launch will certainly force legacy competitors to take notice. Truck manufacturers who fail to deliver competitive non-ICE engine models in the next few years will likely find themselves in real financial jeopardy.

Most clearly under pressure to adapt are the parts suppliers for trucks such as Cummins (CMI), which focuses on manufacturing heavy duty engines and affiliated components. This company, with more than $20 billion in market capitalization and sixty thousand employees, is at risk of serious disruption with the end of the oil age. While the company is investing in EV technology, only $7 million of its $23,771 million in sales in 2018 were from the Electrified Power segment. Remaining CMI revenues were almost entirely derived from the legacy ICE business.[17] A short excerpt from the risk factors of Cummins' annual report is a clear expression of the challenges facing the company as the industry evolves:

> We are investing in new products and technologies, including electrified powertrains, for planned introduction into certain existing and new markets. Given the early stages of development of some of these new products and technologies, there can be no guarantee of the future market acceptance and investment returns with respect to these planned products. The increased adoption of electrified powertrains in some market segments could result in lower demand for current diesel or natural gas engines and components and, over time, reduce the demand for related parts and service revenues from diesel or natural gas powertrains. Furthermore, it is possible that we may not be successful in developing segment-leading electrified powertrains and some of our existing customers could choose to develop their own electrified or alternate fuel powertrains, or source from other manufacturers, and any of these factors could have a materially adverse impact on our results of operations, financial condition and cash flows.[18]

In other words, if Cummins moves too fast into electrification technology, its earnings will get crushed. Or, if it moves too slowly, its earnings will get crushed. And even if it gets the pace of change just right, margins in its business may still be pressured.

COMMERCIAL AIRLINES

We have already discussed the challenges of climate change for aviation manufacturing stocks in a previous chapter, specifically as relating to their exposure to the defense industry. Certainly, commercial aviation is at risk as well if GHG emissions are increasingly taxed in many of the more populous nations of the world. Aircraft are much faster than cars and trains at transporting a person from point A to point B, but they require a greater consumption of energy to perform the task. As an example, flying a passenger on a three-hundred-to-five-hundred-mile intercity trip requires more than three times as much energy as riding a Greyhound bus.[19] While airlines represent a tiny fraction of total passenger miles each year, they are responsible for 12 percent of CO_2 emissions from all transportation sources.[20] In addition, aircraft travel at high altitudes utilizing current technology promotes global warming in ways that are particularly potent, including NO_2 in exhaust that impacts ozone (O3) levels, and contrails that promote the formation of heat-trapping cirrus clouds.

The simple solution to reduce GHG emissions from aircraft is, of course, a carbon tax. Increase the cost of the airline ticket to more accurately capture its externalities, and demand will drop. A large percentage of plane trips are discretionary in nature and taken solely for vacations or to visit family and friends. Similarly, much business travel is cost sensitive as well. This is especially true when considering executives sitting near the front of the plane in business, first, or (as Virgin Atlantic calls it), upper class. The larger these more expensive seats, the less energy efficient they are per passenger. Many business trips would not take place if the traveler was informed that, due to cost, they would have to fly coach.

Even without such taxation in place, some consumers are starting to avoid air flight simply due to its impact on the planet. In Sweden, *flygskam* or "flight shame" has led to a measurable shift in passengers now electing to take long-haul train rides to get to their holiday destinations. That of course leads to *tagskryt* or "train bragging." The Swedish teenager and climate activist Greta Thunberg took a sixty-five-hour round-trip train to address the 2019 World Economic Forum in Davos, Switzerland, where she implored attendees to act to reduce global warming.[21] As her audience arrived at the conference in upward of 1,500 private jets, it is unclear if her message fell on deaf ears.[22]

While carbon taxation schemes may accelerate the pace of evolution to EVs when it comes to cars, buses, and trains, there is as of yet no hybrid or electric aircraft engine powerful enough to push a commercial airliner into the sky. Aircraft makers are working on developing such propulsion systems, but it is not clear that current battery technology in use can provide the required energy density. Thus, ground transportation (for example, smaller EVs made with lighter materials replacing large, heavy ICE SUVs) will increasingly become greener and more energy efficient than hydrocarbon-powered airline travel over much of the next decade. Some in the aviation industry hold out hopes of utilizing biofuels made from plants or used cooking oil. Ramping up such production is not necessarily going to be cost effective or feasible due to supply constraints.

Thus, airline stocks are going to be at risk if there is an imposition of any sort of Green New Deal or other government policies that tax or make GHG emissions more expensive. So which airlines would be most harmed by such a change? The answer: those with a focus on short-haul flights, that utilize older aircraft, and operate with lower load factors. Due to the large amount of fuel that must be expended to get a commercial airplane up to speed and into the sky, shorter flights are more energy intensive per passenger mile than longer-range trips.[23] This can be partially offset with the use of newer aircraft that are built with lighter carbon composite materials, more efficient wings, and even special paints that reduce friction as the plane moves through the air. Load factor is also important. It takes little extra fuel to get a 90 percent full 737 into the air than one where only 70 percent of the seats are in use, but the former will be a significantly more energy efficient trip on a per passenger basis.

The International Council on Clean Transportation produces an annual report ranking US airlines by energy efficiency. The most recently released report yields the following data:

Table 7.2. 2016 Fuel Efficiency Rankings for Major US Domestic Airlines[24]

1. Alaska (ALK)	6. United (UAL)
2. Frontier	7. American (AAL)
3. Spirit (SAVE)	8. Allegiant (ALGT)
4. Hawaiian (HA)	9. Delta (DAL)
5. Sun Country	10. Virgin American

Note: Frontier and Sun Country are private, and Virgin America was acquired by ALK in December 2016.

These rankings have been relatively stable over the last several years, though Alaska Air is likely to fall in the scorecard due to its recent $2.6 billion purchase of last-place Virgin America. At a recent Investor Day, Alaska spent some time discussing how the newly combined company's load factors have slipped versus industry averages after the merger as well as initiatives it is undertaking to close this gap.[25] Such efficiency rankings are already important as an indicator of profitability for airlines due to the large expense of aviation fuel as a component of overall operating costs. If any sort of GHG taxation were imposed here in the United States, the cost of fuel would rise and the ICCT's rankings would become even more helpful in determining which stocks will be winners in the marketplace. All things held equal, those airlines with poor energy efficiency would be forced to raise ticket prices the most, and/or accept the greatest declines in operating margins. Due to their lower energy efficiency, business and first-class ticket prices would have to rise that much more than ones for coach seats in a country with GHG taxes. Such a change would push many business travelers to the back of the plane or even to the option of engaging in teleconferencing rather than heading to the airport. As business and first-class tickets are higher-margin products for airlines, such GHG taxation could be the difference between profits and bankruptcy for many carriers.

Eventually we are likely to see commercial aircraft utilizing improved battery technology or hydrogen fuel cells. However, most believe this technology is still a decade away, and when it is rolled out, it is expected to only be applicable for shorter (one-to-two-hour) flights. This will flip the current dynamic as long flights will become "dirtier" while journeys such as those from New York to DC, or LA to San Francisco, will be greener. Until that time, airlines will have to deal with a need to burn high-octane fuel to power their planes regardless of the costs imposed by both government and the market.

To wrap up this chapter, we can summarize some major points:

- The phasing out of the internal combustion engine will be wrenching to many companies in the transportation space. Auto parts, and auto dealer businesses will be most directly hurt by this change in technology.
- It is too early to know which auto manufacturers will be successful in navigating the change to EVs. However, it is likely that those that do not make significant investments to keeping up with the pack will underperform over time.
- While electric motorcycles may be great for the rest of us, they are not a good thing for Harley-Davidson.

- Similarly to passenger vehicles, medium and heavy truck makers will have to evolve to survive. Too fast, and they die. Too slow, and they die. It is clear that the risks in this business have increased.
- The commercial airline business in the US may suffer in coming years. If green governmental regulatory policies are enacted, the cost of a plane ticket may soar leading to a major retrenchment in the industry.

Chapter Eight

Utilities
Pivoting without a Net

While the transportation industry must deal with the painful switch from petroleum-powered vehicles to ones using batteries, electric utilities hope to reap a potential windfall as demand increases. An EV or two, plugged in each night in millions of residential garages, sounds like a fabulous opportunity for electric utilities. After all, the industry is in the business of selling electricity, and what could be better for utility stocks than selling all the juice needed to get millions of cars to and from work, the grocery store, and kids' soccer practices?

In addition, electrification is also expected to take place in the demand for space and water heating. This is because improving efficiency of heat pumps has led to this technology being economically superior to burning natural gas, propane, or heavy oil onsite in many temperate parts of the country where it rarely gets extremely cold.[1] An imposition of carbon taxation is forecast to drive heat pump share above 50 percent by 2050.[2] Of course, global warming also means that over time there will be fewer areas of the United States that are colder than "temperate", while more hot days will increase the use of air conditioning. The Electric Power Research Institute forecasts that the share of electricity in final energy used in the United States will rise from 21 percent in 2018 to 36 percent in 2050 without carbon taxes, and as high as 50 percent if such taxes are imposed.[3]

Such a transition in space heating represents an opportunity for some utilities, but a major threat for others. Some of the companies addressed in this chapter solely generate and distribute electricity and are optimistic about this change. However, others are also in the business of delivering natural gas to customers. Heat pumps may not impact industrial customers' demand, but they could lead to a major drop in use of this hydrocarbon for space heating among residential and commercial users. For power utilities with as many gas customers as electric ones (or even more), a change in the way Americans heat a room or a hot water tank could easily become a net negative.

However, all is not sunny for the business of electric distribution. While total demand for electricity may rise, impacts of climate change and an evolution to alternative energy production represent serious challenges for companies engaged in the production and delivery of power. Consider the basic business model of an electric utility:

- The utility receives a license to operate as a monopoly provider in a certain geography with oversight from a local public utility commission (PUC).
- The utility proposes investment projects in electric generation plant and distribution systems. The PUC approves these along with a rate structure to be charged to customers for delivered electricity, which guarantees the utility a certain reasonable return on its capital investment.
- As demand grows over time, the utility proposes to the PUC that it make use of its retained earnings and borrowing capacity to build additional power projects. These are approved along with adjusted price schedules designed to maintain the company's returns on its larger base of invested capital.

The first negative impact of climate change on this utility business model is that consumers are installing home solar PV systems faster than they are switching to buying EVs. Most PUCs require their regulated utilities to purchase excess power generated from these residential systems under "net metering" agreements. Utilities like buying extra power when needed from massive IPPs under long-term, stable wholesale pricing agreements. Buying small, intermittent amounts of electricity from millions of residential generating systems at constantly shifting periods of the day is significantly more complicated and less profitable. It requires a utility to upgrade its grid infrastructure to handle two-way power flows with greater peaks of demand and supply at many transformer and transmission hub points.

As you can imagine, a monopoly company earning guaranteed rates of return is not happy to hear that thousands of new competitors are being allowed to start selling into its grid network at times of their choosing. This has led to the utilities fighting net metering in myriad ways. State legislators are lobbied, PUC regulatory-capture becomes that much more important, and court challenges are mounted. In many areas, utilities have been able to cap the amount of net metering allowed at a laughably low (2 or 3 percent) level of peak system generation. They also buy consumers' excess solar power at wholesale rates (while selling to the same at retail rates), and make the paperwork required to hook into the system as onerous as possible. At the same time, the companies push major public relations campaigns touting their dedication to consumer choice, a sustainable future, and grid modernization.

Such efforts by utilities have only been partially successful in most states. Of course, once consumers install a home PV system, they tend to buy much less power as they generate a significant percentage of what they need onsite. In other words, each new solar panel array on a home represents a deterioration of a utility's geographic franchise. Lower revenues from these customers result in utilities needing to charge traditional (nonsolar) customers that much more to maintain the increasingly complex grid network. As wealthier customers generally have had the capital to invest in home solar power systems, the poorer residents of a utility end up having to shoulder the burden of maintaining the grid for their wealthier neighbors. Utilities have been able to convince PUCs to approve monthly grid connection fees to their customers, but these revenues often fall short of what is needed to avoid subsidizing those choosing to go green.

In addition, the average consumer is out of the house in the middle of the day, and so uses little electricity. This is when a residential solar PV system is generating the most power, and its output during this period can be sold into the grid. These are the same hours when overall demand is highest and prices peak. The more customers selling into the grid during the middle of the day, the less need the utilities have to operate their peaker plant capacity, which is generally turned on only when demand is greatest. The average utility management team wants to build lots of big capital-intensive plants and sell as much power as possible through a basic grid infrastructure to generate the maximum amount of operating profits. Home solar with net metering clearly interferes with this business model.

These problems are magnified as consumers install home battery systems as well. The software running such a battery can be set to have the solar panels charge the system in the morning while cheap power from the grid is used to run the home. Then, the battery switches on to run the home in the middle of the day when grid prices rise and all midday solar power flows to the grid. This maximizes monetary returns to the consumer. As solar panels and batteries become more efficient and cheaper, homes in sunny areas will be able to "cut the cord" entirely and go off the grid, or become net suppliers of electricity.

Businesses are also going green, and that can be a negative trend for utilities as well. For example, with current technology, big box stores that install rooftop solar panels along with other investment efforts such as switching to LED lighting can reduce their electric power demand by 30 percent.[4] Declining equipment prices and rising retail electric power rates have made such investments ever more economically feasible. Once again, the result is less demand at peak hours, reduced need to build large new power plants, and a customer base that wants to sell as well as buy power requiring an upgraded grid infrastructure. Raising prices to support this investment in the grid only creates greater incentives for both residential and commercial customers to install more solar panel systems while switching to more efficient lighting and appliances.

Utilities in many states have been forced by PUCs to roll out green tariffs or green power products that offer customers the option of choosing power plans in which the electricity they buy is either primarily or completely generated from renewable sources. Historically, these options cost more, but commercial and consumer customers have been increasingly willing to pay a premium for going "green" at the same time that the cost of renewable power has been falling. As previously mentioned, tax and accounting rules led to most utility-scale alternative electricity generation projects to be built by IPPs.

Next, the overall US economy has become significantly more efficient when it comes to the use of energy. Since 1990 the United States has been able to double its GDP while increasing its energy usage by only 20 percent, and from 2000 to 2018 the economy grew by more than 40 percent while energy consumption increased by less than 3 percent.

This trend is likely to accelerate as increasing numbers of Americans come to believe in global warming, make green choices, install smart electronics (that turn off when not in use), and demand similar actions from government and corporations. Such efficiency gains could theoretically overwhelm any demand growth to come from electrification of vehicles and space heating. The imposition of carbon taxation could also significantly reduce demand as this would raise the cost of electricity generated through coal and gas burning and push customers to be significantly more efficient with their use of power.

Table 8.1.   US Energy Consumption and Real Gross Domestic Product[5]

	Energy Consumption in Quadrillion BTUs	GDP in Billions of Chained 2012 US Dollars
1990	84,485	9,366
1995	90,991	10,630
2000	98,776	13,131
2018	101,236	18,638

We also have the direct positive impact of climate change on utilities in that higher temperatures mean more electricity demand for air conditioning. This is likely to be overwhelmed by declining demand for space heating in milder winters, the cost of more severe storms, rising incidences of flooding, and increasingly destructive forest fire seasons that damage electric utility infrastructure. Getting a PUC to approve sufficient rate increases on consumers to pay for all grid repairs after a major hurricane and/or flood is that much more difficult when those same consumers have suffered massive damage to their homes and businesses.

A harbinger of a climate change future is the recent experience of Entergy (ETR), the major utility based in New Orleans, which suffered close to $1 billion in damage from hurricanes Katrina and Rita in 2005. Insurance covered only a small portion of the financial loss, and revenues plummeted as thousands of rate-payers evacuated their flooded homes.[6] The company issued bonds to finance repairs and suffered negative publicity when it was allowed to push through rate increases on many relatively poor customers in the disaster area. These storm restoration charges for Katrina were finally eliminated in 2018.[7]

Of course, *additional* storm restoration charges have been imposed on customer bills to pay for repairs in the wake of hurricanes Gustav, Ike, and Isaac, which will continue to be imposed on Entergy customers through 2026.[8] Luckily, 2019's Hurricane Barry did less damage than was initially feared and did not lead to additional levies on customer utility bills. However, if severe windstorms continue to pummel Entergy's market area, a likely eventual outcome is fewer solvent customers and a PUC forcing the utility (and its equity holders) to shoulder an increasing burden of repair costs. Many flood-prone neighborhoods and industrial areas may be abandoned altogether, leaving the utility with expensive infrastructure that no longer has any economic use.

An even more stark example of the direct impacts of climate change is the cautionary tale of California's PG&E (PCG), which filed for bankruptcy in 2019 under a mountain of lawsuits blaming the company's equipment for starting fires in the drought-ravaged state. Many in the press have announced that this was the first "climate change bankruptcy."[9] At first this economic disaster seemed counterintuitive as PG&E was far ahead of most utilities in being green. After all, more than 85 percent of its power mix in 2017 came from GHG-free sources (52 percent renewables and 34 percent nuclear, with only the remaining 15 percent from natural gas), and C-suite officers' compensation was partially driven by how effectively they could get customers to reduce electricity consumption.[10]

The whole story is, as with anything in California, complex. Certainly PG&E was moving quickly toward the state's goal of being at 60 percent renewable power in 2030, and has almost a quarter of all residential solar net-metering connections in the United States. However, the state's largest utility neglected to mind the basics of its business and took a shockingly lax attitude toward equipment safety. In 2014 the company was convicted in federal court, not only for repeated safety violations of its gas pipelines that led to a fatal explosion, but also for obstruction of justice in the resulting investigation. Now a corporate felon on parole, PG&E failed to perform basic safety management of its electric grid. This negligence caused more than 1,500 fires in recent years (more than one per day), leading to scores of deaths, billions of dollars of damage, entire towns being burned to the ground . . . and the company's recent bankruptcy filing.[11]

While the story of PG&E certainly highlights the dangers of climate change, the biggest lesson for the utility industry and its investors may be that even while the business is becoming riskier and more complex, managing current plant and equipment is just as important as any shift toward renewable energy for long-term success.

DIFFERENT PATHS: XCEL, NEXTERA, AND DUKE

So, what is an electric utility to do? It may hope for market growth due to the electrification of transportation and space heating to take place, but it also has to watch as wildfires and increasing storm severity attack its assets. At the same time, its business model is disrupted by consumer solar PV systems and IPPs building utility-grade renewable projects in their market areas that produce power more cheaply than its legacy coal and gas plants. One option for many large utilities has been to expand elsewhere. Due to complicated federal law, utilities can set up unregulated subsidiaries able to take advantage of tax and accounting rules to profitably build large alternative energy projects outside the parent company's market areas.[12] Other utilities have decided to stick to their knitting, continue to burn coal and gas, and try to restrict renewable competition through government lobbying and lawfare.

Recently, as the cost of generating solar and wind power has declined to levels where it is cheaper than the use of hydrocarbons, some carbon-intense utilities have decided it is time to pivot to a future powered by green energy . . . or else. Xcel Energy (XEL) is a traditional electric utility with regulated businesses stretching across eight states including Michigan, Colorado, and Texas and a focus on burning coal. In late 2018 it announced that it would deliver 100 percent carbon-free electricity to its customers by 2050 and have reduced its GHG emissions by 80 percent by 2030.[13] The company believes that the costs of erecting solar and wind generation units are now so cheap that it will be profitable to build them, despite existing legal hurdles, and retire aging coal plants early. It calls this its "Steel for Fuel" strategy, in which it invests in large amounts of steel (to build wind turbine farms, and solar arrays) on which regulator-allowed rate structures will provide for a reasonable rate of return on investment.[14]

Plans such as Xcel's may be successful for investors as long as the company can successfully complete alternative utility-scale projects at low prices, there is sufficient customer support for a switch to green power, and the overseeing PUC is willing to approve rates that justify the new construction projects. For Xcel, so far, so good, as the stock significantly outperformed the average utility in the year after announcing its plan to decarbonize. However, any imposition of carbon taxation remains a significant risk as the company has a relatively high carbon intensity compared to other electric utilities. Of its 2018 power generation, 33 percent was from coal, and 29 percent from natural gas.[15]

Well ahead of Xcel in green energy is the nation's utility with the highest market capitalization, NextEra Energy (NEE). No discussion of electric utility stocks and climate change would be complete without an examination of NextEra as it is the world's largest generator of energy from solar and wind sources. These assets are held in the company's NextEra Energy Resources (NEER) segment acting as an IPP, where it produces its renewable electricity in several western and northern states—with a focus on generation in California and Texas.

NEE also owns Florida Power and Light (FPL), one of America's largest regulated utilities with operations encompassing the southern half of the state. While NextEra's profitable alternative energy sales have disrupted regulated competitors operating in other geographic regions, the company has worked hard to keep the same from happening in Florida. FPL has lobbied, sued, and used red tape, usually successfully, to slow down or block net metering for residential solar projects, restrict consumers from entering into solar equipment lease contracts, and avoid having to offer green tariffs programs. Thus, it has been able to avoid many grid upgrade expenses and having to invest in new renewable power generation in the state. In 2018, three-quarters of the electricity FPL sold was generated by burning natural gas, 1 percent was from solar, and the rest was from legacy nuclear and coal plants . . . and its customer base had one of the lowest rates of home solar PV systems in the nation.

However, as its Florida network of hydrocarbon plants age and the cost of power from utility-scale solar has plummeted, NextEra has begun to build a number of these projects in the state. Of course, first it had to get the rules changed. Florida's Solar Base Rate Adjustment Rule of 2017 allows utilities to increase their billing rates to all customers to recover the costs of new PV projects as long as said projects come in under a cost cap that was agreed to by the Florida PUC. The cap is, of course, higher than current solar PV installation costs.[16] Other rules have, to date, successfully kept most IPPs from building generation capacity in FPLs' territory, allowing the regulated utility to "disrupt itself" at guaranteed positive rates of return.[17]

While FPL is a larger operating segment with $11.8 billion in revenues in 2018 compared to $4.8 billion at NEER, the alternative power unit generates larger profits that have been growing at a rapid pace compared to the regulated business with its guaranteed but low returns on capital.[18] This certainly makes NEE appear to be an intriguing investment for climate change investors, and the NextEra model appears to be an attractive one:

- Build IPP alternative power plants out of its regulated geography where green tariffs and state renewable mandates ensure strong demand and allow for high profit margins.
- Get local PUCs to support reimbursement for utility-scale alternative projects in its regulated markets as construction prices have come down far enough to make such payments legal.
- While running a PR campaign that the utility is working to bring its customers a "sustainable future," spend considerable funds lobbying the local PUC and the State House and work the courts to keep competitors out—be they IPPs with green energy projects or consumers hoping to install residential solar panel systems.

The biggest risks of owning NEE stock in a climate change portfolio is that 1) it still has significant hydrocarbon-fueled energy production assets that would fall in value with the imposition of carbon taxation; and 2) FPL's geography in southern Florida is problematic as hurricanes become stronger and coastal areas flood more often. These risks can be mostly offset with a pair trade of a long position in NEE with an underweight or short position in a utility stock with a more carbon-intensive business and a similar Southeastern geographic exposure.

This description fits the nation's second most valuable utility, Duke Energy (DUK), which has regulated electricity operations in the Midwest, the Carolinas, and much of Florida not serviced by FPL. Where NEE has built a huge renewables business and three-quarters of its FPL power generation is now from "cleaner" natural gas, Duke still relied on coal for 30 percent of the electricity it generated in its utility footprint in 2018, while renewables such as hydro and solar were less than 2 percent.[19] While Duke also has an unregulated subsidiary that builds solar and wind facilities outside its footprint, "Commercial Renewables," it only represents 2 percent of the company's current revenue stream. This is in stark contrast to NEER's outsized contribution to NextEra's top and bottom lines.

While NEE stock is certainly exposed to the impacts of climate change (storms, sea level rise, etc.) through FPL, Duke has a similar exposure to coastal areas in the Deep South with its business operations in northern Florida and the Carolinas. DUK would also be under significantly more pressure than NEE were carbon taxation imposed on the burning of fossil fuels. The largest risk of a long NEE/short DUK trade is that the former stock has outperformed significantly over the last few years. However, this stock performance has been driven by growth in EPS, which climbed from $6.24 in 2016 to $13.88 in 2018 for NEE compared to a much slower increase of $3.11 to $3.76 at DUK. Also, sell-side analysts covering these stocks forecast an 8 percent annual growth in EPS at NEE over the next five years (2018–2022) versus a bit less than 5 percent at DUK.[20]

OTHER UTILITY STOCKS TO OWN

Hopefully the discussion up to this point in this chapter has made clear the complexities and higher levels of risk involved in investment in the supposedly "boring but safe" utility space in an era of climate change:

- Direct effects of a warmer planet will lead to increased electricity demand for air conditioning.
- This positive is likely to be more than offset by a multitude of ills from more severe storms and rainfall events, to more insidious but still costly "sunny day flooding" due to rising sea levels, and lower worker productivity in hot outdoor locations where utility infrastructure must be maintained.
- Technological improvement lowering the costs and raising the effectiveness of EVs and heat pumps will increase electricity demand to charge EV batteries and warm the air in buildings.

- Similar technological changes are leading to greater adoption of roof-top solar by consumers and businesses that not only reduce revenues for an electric utility but also lead to a multitude of tiny new competitors who each demand the right to sell excess power into the grid. Adoption of heat pumps may also reduce revenues at many utilities that supply natural gas as well as electricity.
- Rapidly falling costs of large-scale renewable power projects are allowing utilities to build or buy green power flows at increasingly low costs where the uncertainty of future costs of fuel (gas, coal, oil) are removed.
- However, this change presents utilities with the risk that many of their legacy hydrocarbon-burning facilities will have to be retired years before their capital costs have been depreciated, leading to financial losses. Falling renewable power costs also increase the chances of the imposition of carbon taxation, which would also lower the value of legacy generation plants as well as reduce demand due to the need to pass through such taxes to customers.

Putting this all together, we can assume that the best positioned electric utilities stocks in the United States over the next decade will be those that are 1) geographically farther north in regions that should suffer less harm from the direct impacts of climate change; 2) do not have outsized natural gas pipeline delivery businesses in temperate climates that will be threatened by increased penetration of heat pumps; and 3) are less dependent on hydrocarbon-fueled electric generation capacity (especially coal), which would become uneconomical to operate in a scenario where GHG emission taxation is imposed. So if a climate change investor chooses to invest in the electric utility space beyond NEE, which other stocks in the S&P 500 best fit the above criteria?

Four stocks stand out as potentially being well positioned:

1. CMS Energy (CMS) is an $18 billion market cap company that is primarily focused on regulated utility operations in Michigan with both electric and natural gas distribution. Its generation mix includes 40 percent natural gas, 16 percent nuclear, 11 percent renewables, and 22 percent coal. The firm has reduced carbon emissions by 38 percent since 2005, and its stated goal is to reduce them by 90 percent by 2040, by which time it will have completely phased out coal, and renewables will be 43 percent of its generation mix.[21] The company's natural gas distribution business lowers the company's

overall exposure to coal, and Michigan's winters are severe enough that heat pumps will likely not make much of a dent in that state in the short to medium term.

2. Consolidated Edison, also known as ConEd (ED), is the major energy utility in the New York City area. It owns little in the way of traditional electric generation and is the second largest producer of solar power in the nation. It has also reduced its GHG emissions by almost 50 percent since 2005. Thus, the company is well positioned for enactment of any form of carbon taxation as such costs would mostly impact the owners of hydrocarbon generation assets rather than a company that primarily provides transmission of electricity.

   Certainly, winters in New York are a bit milder than those in Michigan, but it is still cold enough that heat pump adoption will likely be slower than in warmer geographical areas farther south so as to limit the negative impact on ConEd's gas distribution system. Also, ConEd operates in a coastal market area more threatened by sea level rise and severe storm events than CMS Energy (as with Superstorm Sandy). However, one would imagine that New York City's economy and real estate is so valuable that seawalls, dikes, pumps, and possibly major storm surge barriers will be put in place to harden the region against angry seas and so limit the negative impact on the local power utility.

3. Eversource Energy (ES) is similar to ConEd in that it has sold most of its electric generation assets and operates gas and electric distribution systems in a geographical area that stretches from just north of New York City up through Connecticut and Massachusetts into New Hampshire. It has also made significant renewable energy investments in offshore wind projects.

4. Exelon Corp (EXC) is unusual among electric utilities as it relies on nuclear power for more than 60 percent of its generation output. While it seems unlikely that additional nuclear power plants will be built in the United States in the near future due to massive upfront costs and consumer opposition, the ones in service will continue to generate power (hopefully safely) through their planned operating lives and provide their owners with a windfall if carbon taxation is imposed. Of the rest of Exelon's generation fleet, 25 percent is from natural gas, and about 10 percent is from renewables so it has a much smaller carbon footprint compared to many other electric generation

companies. On balance, EXC's footprint (IL, PA, MD, NJ) is less exposed to the direct impacts of a warming climate than companies operating farther south.

Against these potential holdings, here are four electric utility stocks that are components of the S&P 500 Index that are much more negatively positioned for the impacts of climate change:

1. DTE Energy (DTE) is a good pair trade against CMS Energy. Both are based in Michigan, but where CMS is only 22 percent dependent on coal, DTE is at 64 percent. While the latter company wants to move away from coal, its goal is 50 percent "clean energy" (which includes natural gas) by 2030. CMS is already at 67 percent on that metric. Simply put, any imposition of carbon taxation would hurt DTE more, force the company to write down its asset base, and likely lead to the retirement of its coal-burning plants earlier than planned.
2. Evergy (EVRG) is a good pair trade against a long in Exelon. Where Exelon produces in excess of 70 percent of its electricity from carbon-free nuclear power and renewables, more than 70 percent of Evergy's generation is from burning hydrocarbons. While coal plants with 2.2 GW of output are being taken offline, the company will still source 40 percent of its power from coal by the end of 2020, giving it a much higher level of carbon intensity than many of its peers. Evergy's footprint in Kansas and Missouri is also likely to have a similar profile of risk from extreme weather events as Exelon's Illinois-focused operations.
3. FirstEnergy (FE) is a good pair trade against a long in Consolidated Edison. Where the New York City–based company primarily delivers energy produced by others, FirstEnergy supplies its New Jersey/West Virginia/Pennsylvania/Ohio footprint with electricity from its own plants that are almost entirely coal fired. With its generation facilities primarily based in the coal country of West Virginia, it is difficult to see FirstEnergy converting to cleaner forms of electric production even as competing supplies of power from offshore wind and cheap Marcellus Shale natural gas become increasingly inexpensive. While ConEd certainly has more direct exposure to greater storm events and rising sea levels, FirstEnergy has some of

the same risks in its footprint along the Jersey Shore and eastern Pennsylvania.

4. Finally, Entergy is an attractive pair trade against Eversource. While, as discussed, Eversource owns almost no electric production and only delivers power to its customers, Entergy still owns a large fleet of fossil fuel–generating plants burning gas, oil, and coal. In addition to Entergy being more exposed to any sort of carbon taxation, plans are in the works to bring more green hydroelectric power to Eversource's New England footprint from Hydro-Quebec, which seeks a market for its excess power production.[22] Thus, any imposition of carbon taxation on electricity flows would likely have little impact on price and demand of electricity delivered by Eversource to its customer base. Entergy, of course, is also based in a difficult geography for the impacts of climate change. Rising sea levels, more intense hurricanes, and severe rainfall events will be of particular concern in the company's footprint along the low-lying coast of Louisiana and east Texas. Global warming will also become a drag on Entergy's outdoor workforce maintaining transmission line infrastructure as higher summer temperatures reduce employee productivity.[23]

Most investors in electric utility stocks are focused on yield. As such, a comparison of the dividends of these eight stocks just reviewed is of importance. The four "long" names mentioned—CMS, ED, ES, EXC—have an average dividend yield of 2.82 percent, while the four "short" names—DTE, EVRG, FE, ETR—yield a slightly higher 2.93 percent at the time of this writing.[24] However, giving up a few basis points of yield in return for a higher level of safety against the negative impacts of climate change is likely a reasonable trade-off in terms of equity portfolio construction. Needless to say, the electric utility model is likely to experience significant disruption over the next two decades, which will offer both risks and opportunities for investors in the space.

To wrap up this chapter, we can summarize some major points:

• Utilities will see both opportunities and risks from climate change, the mass adoption of EVs and heat pumps, as well as likely government actions related to GHG emissions.

- Companies with a head-start shifting to renewable power supplies are better positioned than those which still depend on coal for large portions of their revenue stream.
- Companies supplying power along the Gulf Coast and in the Southeast are likely to be more challenged than those based farther north.

Chapter Nine

A Grab Bag from Pandora's Box

When discussing the concept of this book with colleagues in the professional investment management industry, I often received unsolicited ideas regarding stocks thought to be well positioned due to the effects of climate change.[1] Of late, there have also been several newspaper and financial magazine articles that offer similar ideas regarding "sure thing" stocks to buy for a warming planet. This chapter will attempt to delve into a few of these investment ideas. Some have merit; others do not.

PHARMACEUTICALS

Many press articles discuss how pharmaceutical companies will benefit from warmer temperatures spreading outward from the equatorial regions. The argument here is that vector-borne tropical diseases (such as malaria, Zika, Lyme disease, dengue fever, etc., transmitted via mosquitos or ticks) will become more prevalent. *Voila*, more vaccine and antibiotic revenues for big pharma! Morgan Stanley even published a major report attempting to discuss those drug companies best positioned to benefit financially from this spread of . . . well . . . human death.[2]

The problem with the logic here is that sadly, global warming is expected to make us poorer. Wealthy nations can spend a lot on health care. Impoverished ones . . . not as much. Not only will we need to spend more on dams, seawalls, new power plants, and hardening transportation systems, but as a species we will experience more droughts, catastrophic storms, violence, wars, and heat stroke. The World Health Organization's recent report on this overall subject makes for some truly depressing reading.[3] In an extreme case of catastrophic climate change, we are likely to see the carrying capacity of the human race on our little planet fall dramatically from its current level in excess of seven and a half billion.

Where does that leave pharmaceutical stocks? It is true that growth in vaccines to combat tropical diseases becoming more prevalent in the developed world would be a positive for these companies. However, this change is unlikely to be large enough to move the needle for a giant company like Pfizer or Merck. The forecasting firm Technavio predicts that the total global vaccine market will grow to generate more than $47 billion in revenue per year in 2022.[4] That may sound like a lot, but it represents less than 4 percent of the $1.2 trillion of revenues recorded by the pharma industry in 2018—a figure incidentally that has steadily grown each year since 2001 when the total was only $390 billion.[5]

When you combine this data with a consideration that many fast-growing vaccine businesses have nothing to do with warmer weather or mosquitos (such as those to fight HPV, shingles, etc.), you can see that global warming will have little positive top-line impact for pharma companies peddling shots to slow the spread of malaria, Zika, or chikungunya. In addition, vaccines are by no means the highest margin sort of drug sold by these companies. Got something to combat erectile dysfunction, breast cancer, or peanut allergies? That's where the margins are.[6] In contrast, vaccines just aren't that profitable, and antibiotics (to combat Lyme disease, cholera, etc.) have even lower gross margins for manufacturers.

It is more likely that the impacts of climate change will stress government spending and reduce what can be allocated to medical care. This will be especially true for older patients (age sixty-five and up) who, as of 2016, each burned through more than $11,000 per year on average on health care spending compared to less than $3,000 for younger members of the US population (forty-four and younger).[7] Perhaps we will find a way to continue spending an ever-larger percentage of global GDP each year on pharmaceuticals. However, this seems unlikely even without the spread of the perils of global warming.

From time to time there will be a biotech company that executes an IPO with a chemical compound or medical process that may hold promise in fighting a major tropical disease. If you believe this firm is one of the few whose proposed medication will prove to be both effective and able to jump through the FDA's many hoops, acquire some shares quickly . . . for it will soon be bought out, consumed by the ravenous maws of one of the pharmaceutical industry's giants.

AGRICULTURAL CHEMICAL COMPANIES

Many also discuss how global warming will lead to greater stress on traditional agricultural land and help companies that sell genetically modified seeds along with fertilizer products. Perhaps this will be the case. But there are many uncertainties between the onset of the wrath of flood and drought across what was formerly fertile land, and rising profits for the sellers of seeds, insecticides, and fertilizer. First of all, many farmers will simply disappear (along with the populations they support) as arable acres cease to be economically productive.This will be particularly pronounced in the highly populated regions closer to the equator. Thus, there will be fewer customers to buy seeds, fertilizer, and pesticides. The problem is also that the largest companies in this space are not stand-alone agricultural specialty companies, but are instead huge chemical firms where sales to farmers are a relatively small percentage of total revenues.

Monsanto, the company that leads many market share rankings in selling proprietary seeds and agrichemicals, was bought by the German industrial giant Bayer (BAYRY) in 2018. Recent lawsuits involving Monsanto's weed killer, Roundup, may make this the most financially destructive merger in world history. Syngenta of Switzerland was also a strong "stand-alone" player in the agrichemical space, but it too was acquired—by ChemChina. The current Chinese ambassador to Switzerland recently complained that this was a terrible deal, and China would love to sell the company back.[8]

When Dow and DuPont listened to their investment bankers and announced that they would merge in a deal valued at $120 billion in late 2015, the plan was for the new entity to move around assets and spin out a new Dow, a new DuPont, and Corteva (DOW, DD, CTVA), an agricultural seed and chemical company. The merger of Dow and DuPont created a massive player in the space, with its agriculture segment generating $14 billion of revenues in 2018 or around 17 percent of the combined firm's total sales.[9] Against the backdrop of a fabulous 50 percent rally in the S&P 500 Index since the merger was announced, the three new stocks are now trading independently with a combined market capitalization of . . . only $100 billion as of early 2020. So while the deal was a disaster for Dow and DuPont shareholders, investors focused on climate change now at least have a new pure-play stock in CTVA in which to consider investing.

While the amount of arable land may decline resulting in a rising total demand for inputs to get greater food yield out of each remaining usable acre (a big set of "ifs"), there are clearly several problems with being bullish on the agrichemical space due to the impacts of climate change:

• The number of customers may consolidate to be replaced by a smaller group of large, sophisticated buyers demanding volume discounts (e.g., industrial-scale agribusinesses).
• Most agrichemical businesses are part of much larger diversified chemical companies.
• Most chemical products require the burning and/or conversion of large amounts of hydrocarbons resulting in significant GHG emissions, which are likely to be taxed in ever more jurisdictions over time. Higher prices for most products tend to reduce demand, though food is a product where there is relatively low-price elasticity—in other words, most consumers will only curtail their purchases of food slightly unless prices rise significantly.

For those intent on investing in this space, there are a few pure-plays. The most prominent is FMC Corporation (FMC) with a large market cap and a recent windfall as it was allowed to buy significant portions of the crop protection business the US government forced DuPont to divest when it merged with Dow. Rising temperatures mean fewer freezes in temperate developed nations to kill off pests and weeds that threaten crops. FMC is well positioned for this trend, with its recent revenue breakdown being 57 percent from insecticides, 31 percent from herbicides, and 7 percent from fungicides.[10] A risk here is that the company has a geographically balanced sales mix with 25 percent of its sales from North America, 24 percent from Asia, 28 percent from Latin America, and 23 percent from EMEA.[11] Thus, FMC's customer base may shrink over time as areas at lower latitudes experience a decline in land under cultivation due to droughts, floods, severe storms, and more caused by climate change.

Next there is the new Corteva, whose sales are reasonably evenly split with a slight overweight toward its Seed business versus that of Crop Protection products. Climate change will not only spur demand for pest control, but will also offer changes in demand for modified seeds. Crops will need to be able to thrive in hotter climates with often drier or wetter conditions than are optimal for traditional varieties of plants that have been cultivated. As with FMC, Corteva has a sales mix that is diversified by geography.

While we are on this subject, it is worth considering mining companies that extract, process, and then deliver nitrate-based fertilizer to farmers' fields. The biggest player in this space used to be Potash Corporation of Canada (POT).[12] In 2018 it chose to merge with Agrium, another fertilizer company, though one that primarily produced its products through the use of the combustion and conversion of natural gas. The new company, Nutrien (NTR), based in the lovely Canadian city of Saskatoon, is a giant in the industry with close to $20 billion in annual sales and ready access to low-cost potash mineral deposits and natural gas to source its products.[13] Nutrien has a significant focus in North America, but deliveries have been rising to the massive agricultural markets of China and India, providing a strong case for growth over the next two decades even before taking into account a potential decline in food production in places such as Egypt, Australia, Pakistan, and the Philippines, driven by climate change.

Yes, the mining of potash and manufacturing of nitrogen and phosphate-based chemical fertilizers leads to the emission of significant GHG gasses. However, people have to eat, and additional fertilizer is one of the few sure-fire ways to increase crop yields. Carbon taxation may lead to Nutrien having to pay more to produce its products, pass on some of those costs, and increase the price of agricultural products. However, most consumers in the developed world spend a relatively small amount of their total income on food and, once again, people have to eat.[14]

LITHIUM AND COBALT

Clearly governments are nudging, pushing, and forcing a large number of industries to move toward the use of lithium ion batteries for EV transportation, electric energy storage, and potentially even short-haul commercial airplane flights. Many in the press say that "lithium is the new oil."[15] The technology is advancing quickly both in terms of energy density per battery cell and the ability to recycle components to make new batteries after their expected seven to ten years of use. Entrepreneurs are also finding many novel and profitable ways to use existing units for years after they become a decade old.[16] These batteries also require large inputs of cobalt and lithium. So, who stands to benefit from this trend? Tesla is well positioned, but as discussed in a previous chapter, it is not clear that this is a company with a management team that will produce profits (or even stay out of jail).

Several Asian companies offer opportunities in this space. The problem is that investing in the stocks of many of these firms requires a brokerage account in China or South Korea which is relatively difficult to open for US-based investors. Those with such access may want to consider Samsung SDI and LG Chem in Korea (006400.KS, 051910. KS) or BYD and Contemporary Amperex Technology in China (1211. HK, 300750.SZ). Companies in this space offering some level of liquid trading opportunities on US markets, such as Panasonic and Toshiba (PCRFY, TOSBF), are, for better or worse, part of large industrial conglomerates where lithium batteries are only a small percentage of total sales.

One other option is to buy shares in EnerSys (ENS), a smaller-cap stock based in the United States that makes both traditional lead-acid batteries as well as lithium ion ones primarily for use in the broadband, telecom, alternative energy storage, and industrial markets. Lithium ion battery demand is growing much faster, but the lead-acid market share remains significantly larger.[17] A major risk with EnerSys is that it is attempting to "disrupt" its own business as it transitions away from lead-acid batteries to the newer lithium technologies. So far it has been successful in this endeavor, but such corporate evolutions are notoriously difficult to execute.

If one can't easily invest in the larger makers of lithium batteries, at least there is an option to invest in Albemarle Corp (ALB), which is a specialty mining and chemical company based in North Carolina, with its biggest segment being lithium products at 36 percent of sales for the twelve months ending in June 2019.[18] The company is working to increase the size of this business while maintaining its other major segments (bromine and catalysts) as cash cows to produce investment capital for lithium expansion. The risk here is that while demand for components of EV batteries is rising quickly, Albemarle's catalysts business is still close to one-third of its revenues and is focused on sales to the hydrocarbon industry. An investment in ALB is a bet that the company will be able to smoothly transition away from the oil age. While the stock has dramatically outperformed the S&P 500 Index since the start of the new millennium, it has performed poorly more recently in the face of oversupply of its primary product.[19]

Smaller, cheaper, more of a pure-play on lithium and a less well-known idea in this space is Livent Corp (LTHM), which was spun out of FMC in 2018. Livent generated more than 85 percent of its revenue from the sale of lithium compounds in 2018 with energy storage being by far the largest end use for its products. This spin-off was designed to allow FMC's lithium business to catch an emerging growth stock valuation. However, the deal was badly timed for investors (though not the investment bankers). LTHM stock fell from almost $19 a share soon after the spin-off to less than $8 in late 2019 on the back of excess global mining output coupled with lower than expected demand from China's slowing economy. Certainly an investment in Livent still has risk, but an investor bullish on the growth of EV fleets and alternative energy storage around the world should consider at least a small position in LTHM stock.

Another interesting option is that investors can combine bullishness in fertilizers *and* lithium mining in the Chilean company Sociedad Quimica y Minera de Chile, known as "SQM," which has a full NYSE listed stock (SQM). In the most recent trailing twelve months, lithium sales generated 45 percent of the company's gross profit, and fertilizers represented an additional one-third.[20] Of course, SQM stock has also been bruised by the emerging glut of lithium production coming online, though the price of the metal appears to be finding a bottom. Over time, higher prices for lithium, more government pressure to switch away from hydrocarbons in transportation, and continued expected improvement in battery technology should lead to at least one more heroic bull market in lithium miners such as SQM, LTHM, and ALB in coming years.

Finally, there is an Exchange Traded Fund, the Global X Lithium & Battery Tech ETF (LIT) that owns most of the names mentioned in this section, including those traded only in Asia (Taiwan, South Korea, China), which are difficult for most US investors to buy directly. Its 0.75 percent annual expense ratio is higher than for many other ETFs but may be reasonable for a fund that provides its holders with diversification across several geographic trading markets. It should be noted that as of the middle of 2019, four of the fund's top ten holdings were ALB, SQM, ENS, and TSLA, which are simple purchases for any US investor with a discount brokerage account.[21]

Sadly, there are few ways to play a growth in demand in cobalt. The largest producer is the Swiss mining giant Glencore (GLNCY). However, this element is a tiny fraction of what the company hauls out of the earth for sale on a yearly basis. This is because most cobalt is found as a by-product of nickel and copper mining. The giant copper mining company, Freeport-McMoRan (FCX), has also become a major producer of cobalt for this reason. One of the few places where high-grade cobalt ore is found is in the Democratic Republic of Congo, and the mining region has been wracked by civil war, armed invasions, and human rights abuses for more than a decade. While there are a few illiquid investments in this area, the risks are high enough for US investors that they will not be discussed here.

HYDROGEN FUEL CELLS

What if we didn't have to use lithium ion batteries to store green power? What if we could just power our cars, trains, trucks, and airplanes with the most common element in the universe, hydrogen? That is the promise of fuel cells that convert chemical energy (usually from combining hydrogen and oxygen) into electricity . . . and some water. The basic technology has been around since the mid-1800s, and the problem of commercialization has primarily been around price.

Ballard Power Systems (BLDP), based in British Columbia but traded on the NASDAQ since the mid-1990s, has been a leader in fuel cells. At one point during the peak of its hype, the stock rose above

$100 a share, but it has languished below $6 for the last decade while still commanding a market cap in excess of $1 billion. Fuel cell electric buses powered by Ballard technology and refueled from its hydrogen filling stations are now at work in nations as diverse as Denmark, Latvia, China, and the UK. Perhaps the era of the fuel cell is finally at hand. More likely is that this technology is still at least a decade away from significant commercial utilization and taking over from batteries powered by lithium. Other competitors in this space include Hydrogenics (HYGS), FuelCell Energy (FCEL), and Plug Power (PLUG). These are all clearly speculative investments at this time, but ones that should be monitored by an investor cognizant of the increasing impacts of climate change on the capital markets.

GEOTHERMAL POWER

Electricity created from geothermal sources is another form of reliable green power that has been commercially proven. Of course, this is only feasible in regions close to tectonic plate boundaries where human efforts can drill down far enough to make use of the planet's internal heat. Water is pumped down a bore shaft to a heat source where it is converted to steam used to run electric generators or supply space heating. The United States is the leader in the field in terms of total power produced, but commercial plants are in operation in nations as diverse as New Zealand, Chile, Italy, and Japan. The famous Blue Lagoon tourist attraction in Iceland is actually the effluent runoff from the Svartsengi geothermal power station: now that is great rebranding! It is estimated that geothermal power could meet 3 to 5 percent of global demand by 2050 and 10 percent by 2100 in the presence of appropriate carbon taxation and/or economic incentives.[22] The US Department of Energy also recently issued a roadmap for a massive increase in domestic geothermal energy production by 2050 through streamlining approval processes and better use of existing technology.[23]

Unfortunately, the only clear way to play the growth of geothermal power is through the stock of Ormat Technologies (ORA), based in Nevada with more than a $3 billion market capitalization. The company is profitable and has a recent history of steady, if unremarkable, top-line growth. Ormat's primary business is managing its own electric power plants around the world, but it also generates about one-third of its sales selling generating equipment to others who are in the midst of constructing new geothermal facilities.

CONCLUDING POINTS

I am absolutely sure that there will be readers of this book who believe some fabulous stock ideas perfectly positioned for the impacts of climate change have been missed. How about biodiesel and Renewable Energy Group (REGI)? How about harnessing the tides with Ocean Power Technologies (OPTT)? Sadly, many of these ideas are just a bit too small and/or speculative at this time. Additional investment opportunities will be created as human ingenuity is put to the test of protecting our civilization from the fallout of anthropogenic global warming. For now, let us conclude with a few points:

• Climate change is likely *not* going to be good for pharmaceutical stocks, even those with some nifty new vaccines in the development pipeline.
• Climate change is likely *not* going to be good for agrichemical/seed business due to a) less arable land on the planet over time, b) most major players in this space are units of giant chemical conglomerates that will be negatively impacted by imposition of GHG emission taxes raising the cost to buyers of their final products. However, due to the inelasticity of food demand, the small number of pure-play stocks in this space may make for good investments.
• Lithium supply growth has recently outstripped growth in demand. Over time it is likely that increased sales of EVs and alternative energy storage systems will push up sales and prices of both lithium ion batteries and their components. This trend will bolster share prices of companies in the space.
• Fuel cells are an interesting technology. Investments in the space remain speculative at this time, and performance may lag the markets for many years until safety, price, and refueling infrastructure is better developed.
• The outlook for growth in the hydrothermal space is bright, and the one pure-play stock, ORA, has significant potential for climate change investors.

Chapter Ten

The Rest of the World

Just as this book argues that investors should overweight and underweight select industrial sectors in their US equity portfolios due to climate change, the same is true when directing capital in international stock markets. The impact of global warming will increase political instability, war, famine, and the migration of refugees. An investor who elects to avoid stocks of companies in dirty industries that release massive amounts of CO_2 and instead buy those in greener companies will help reduce the impact of climate change catastrophes on our species.

There is no reason the same investor can't also ethically choose to own stocks from those nations best positioned to survive and adapt to global warming while avoiding those, sadly, most likely to see their economics severely damaged by the impact of global warming. In many cases the countries best positioned to outperform in a changing climate are also the ones that have imposed carbon taxation programs, utilize a larger percentage of renewable power sources, are moving faster to electrify their vehicle fleet, and are putting greater effort into protecting their forests, fisheries, and other aspects of the environment. Choosing to boycott investing in nations that lag in these areas may help spur them to greater implementation of green policies.

To start this global tour with an eye for investing in an era of climate change, we will consider two case studies.

CASE STUDY: OLIVE OR PINE
TREES—SPAIN AND ITALY VERSUS THE NORDICS

Let us consider the choice between an investment in the ETFs of Spain and Italy (EWP and EWI) versus the same amount used to purchase a basket of ETFs for Denmark, Norway, Sweden, and Finland (EDEN, ENOR, EWD, and EFNL). While the two Mediterranean countries have much larger populations and GDPs than the Nordic nations, the impacts of global warming are likely to lead to underperformance for the stock markets of Italy and Spain.

The most obvious impact is that the northern rim of the Mediterranean is becoming hotter and drier. As Spain's climate comes to more resemble that of Morocco and that of the Atlas Mountains today serves as a template for the future of the Alps, there are huge implications for stock market investors. The economies of Spain and Italy are now being stressed by intense annual summer heat waves that negatively impact tourism, spark more intense forest fires, cause crop failures, and increase summer energy demand for indoor cooling.

Of even greater concern is what is taking place along the southern and eastern shores of the Mediterranean where higher temperatures and declining rainfall are turning many densely inhabited areas to desert. Similar climate change impacts are taking place to the south of the Sahara as well. This has forced millions to flee northward and for seaborne migrants to wash up on the coasts of Spain and Italy—not all of them alive. Both nations now manage crowded refugee camps and deport tens of thousands of these "economic" refugees.

Many scientists now argue that the vicious Syrian Civil War was at least partially a result of global warming and warn that it is the first of many climate change conflicts to come.[1] The fighting in Syria drove millions of refugees to Europe, and the number of asylum applicants across the EU more than doubled to one hundred thousand per month in 2015. This inflow of impoverished migrants placed enormous strain on the political and social institutions of the EU as well as those of its constituent nations. The combined population of Egypt, Algeria, Libya, and Morocco is ten times that of prewar Syria. The policy planners of Italy and Spain must pray often for good harvests and peace among their neighbors to the south. How long until we see an even larger wave of climate refugees heading across the Mediterranean toward southern Europe? In contrast, while global warming will certainly have negative impacts in the Nordic nations over the next ten or twenty years, there will be positive aspects as well. Farmers will enjoy longer growing seasons, with increased agricultural yields and the ability to sow new crops such as corn and soybeans.[2] Forest fires will be more severe, but acceleration in tree growth will be an offsetting positive for the forestry industry. And while Spanish and Italian businesses will have to spend more on air conditioning going forward, heating costs will fall for those in the Nordic region. Impoverished climate refugees heading from Africa toward the wealthier and cooler north will reach Spain and Italy long before they arrive at the Danish border. It seems unlikely that the Schengen Agreement allowing for the free flow of people among its European signatory nations will survive another major influx of refugees. For better or worse, the Nordic nations are somewhat insulated from the impact of such an exodus from the south compared to Spain and Italy.

As the impacts of global warming intensify, at least in wealthier nations, we are likely to see GHG emission taxation rates rise and an intensification of efforts to switch to the use of alternative energy sources. While Spain and Italy have made great strides ramping up the use of renewables in the last decade, they are still well behind the Nordics on this measure. Thus, as this conversion takes place, businesses in those two Mediterranean nations will have to bear the costs of higher inputs to produce their goods and services.

In addition, while the countries being compared in this case study are relatively rich in the context of global rankings, the GDP/capita in the Nordics is about twice that of the Spanish and Italian average.

Table 10.1.　2016 Electricity Production Share from Renewable and Nuclear Power Sources[3]

	Renewables	Nuclear	Total
Italy	37%	0%	37%
Spain	38%	21%	59%
Denmark	61%	0%	61%
Finland	44%	33%	77%
Sweden	57%	40%	97%
Norway	97%	0%	97%

The GINI Index (a measure of income distribution across a population) also indicates that the Nordic nations have some of the highest levels of economic equality in the world. Logically, more affluent countries with a population that is generally homogeneous and where wealth is relatively evenly dispersed will be better able to manage the costs of mitigating the effects of climate change compared to those that are poorer, harbor minority groups with separatist leanings, and where most wealth is concentrated in the hands of a few.

Finally, as the costs of global warming rise, Italy and Spain have stock markets more heavily tilted toward those industries that will be most injured. Compared to those of the Nordics, the ETF's for these two nations have higher weightings for utilities and energy and less in the way of health care, technology, and consumer staples. While Sweden, Norway, and Finland do have larger weightings in the energy-hungry industrials sector, these nations consume relatively small amounts of fossil fuels and instead rely on nuclear, hydro, and wind to power their economies. To the extent that the output of this sector is sold abroad, the Scandinavians are effectively exporting green energy, and their products would be largely shielded from CO_2 taxation. So, for a variety of reasons we can expect a basket of holdings of EWD, EDEN, ENOR, and EFNL will likely outperform one composed of EWP and EWI over
• time.

Table 10.2.   Sector Weightings for Six Country ETFs[4]

	Spain	Italy	Sweden	Denmark	Norway	Finland
ETF Ticker	EWP	EWI	EWD	EDEN	ENOR	EFNL
Financials	38.5%	30.9%	26.9%	10.9%	23.5%	10.8%
Utilities	20.8%	17.4%	0.0%	4.5%	0.0%	4.2%
Industrials	13.6%	11.1%	34.8%	24.3%	4.0%	27.1%
Communications	8.1%	3.9%	5.9%	0.0%	11.6%	5.4%
Energy	6.6%	19.0%	1.9%	1.0%	30.3%	5.0%
Consumer Discretionary	4.8%	13.6%	6.8%	2.5%	0.0%	3.1%
Information Technology	4.4%	0.0%	11.6%	2.4%	1.8%	18.7%
Heath Care	2.8%	1.8%	0.0%	39.0%	2.0%	2.8%
Materials	0.0%	0.0%	2.3%	7.6%	0.0%	17.6%
Consumer Staples	0.0%	0.0%	7.6%	7.0%	15.6%	2.3%
Real Estate	0.0%	0.0%	0.0%	0.0%	1.5%	0.0%

We should certainly take no pleasure when considering Italy and Spain having to suffer drought, killing heat, and being forced to decide the future of millions of desperate people arriving on their doorsteps. However, ethically, there is no reason that investors should shy away from considering such factors as climate change and political risk in advance and allocating their capital accordingly.

CASE STUDY: THE LUCKY COUNTRIES OF AUSTRALIA AND CANADA

At first glance these nations appear to be quite similar to the global investor. They have similar cultures, legal systems, population sizes, political orientations, levels of equality, GDP per capita, and language. These are huge countries with vast empty lands, rich natural resources, and a concentration of their citizens into a handful of cities.

Table 10.3. Australia and Canada—So Very Similar[5]

	Population (M)	Population per sq km	GDP per Capita (US$000)	Urban Population	GINI Index
Canada	36.7	4	46.7	81.40%	34
Australia	24.6	3.2	48.5	85.90%	35

With such similarities, it is not surprising that ETFs of these two nations, the EWA and the EWC, have moved in lockstep and exhibited remarkably similar performance characteristics over the last five, ten, and twenty years. However, this trend may be set to diverge in an era of global warming. Australia is considered to be the most ecologically fragile of all the inhabited continents.[6] Only Antarctica is drier, and only Africa is hotter, and due to climate change, Australia is becoming progressively drier and hotter. Much of the giant nation has been in drought since the start of the millennium, and scientists expect rainfall to continue to decline over the century. In contrast, rather than being too hot, Canada has been too cold. Climate change is making the Great White North warmer and wetter with milder winters and more rain.[7]

While heat has encouraged most Australians to live along the southern coast of the continent, the population still resides much closer to the equator than does Canada's. Sydney and Perth are at latitudes 34 and 32 degrees, while Toronto and Vancouver are at 43 and 49. For comparison, Tijuana and Baghdad are at 33 degrees. Australians generally live as close to the South Pole as possible. As temperatures rise and bush fires rage, there is no place to retreat—except perhaps to the island of Tasmania. After a record-breaking heat wave in early 2018, Australia suffered its hottest month on record to start 2019. Cities such as Sydney and Melbourne are experiencing ever more days over 100 degrees Fahrenheit each year, and 110-degree days are becoming annual occurrences. These heat waves are not solely experienced in the air: upward of half of the coral in the famous Great Barrier Reef has died since 2016 due to "bleaching" from warmer ocean water.

In contrast to Australia, Canadians live as close to the equator as possible, with 90 percent residing within one hundred miles of the US border. While climate change will certainly have some negative impacts, a Canada that is progressively warmer and wetter will also reap some advantages. The agriculture and forestry industries are increasingly experiencing longer and more productive growing seasons. There has also been some amelioration of the killing cold of the long Canadian winter, which was the cause of almost 5 percent of total deaths in the nation over the last century.[8]

In addition, while Canada may benefit this century from global warming, compared to Australia, it is also dramatically greener when it comes to energy production and is positioned to rapidly reduce its GHG emissions. Some 23 percent of Canadian total energy production now comes from non–fossil fuel sources compared to only 2 percent in Australia.[9] This dichotomy is even more extreme in terms of electricity, where Canada derives more than 80 percent from non–fossil fuel generation. More rain, less snow, and warmer temperatures are all positives for the growth of Canadian hydro, wind, and even solar power production, and the nation is already the world's second largest exporter of electricity behind Germany. At the same time, a hotter climate reduces the 81 percent of residential and 63 percent of commercial and industrial total energy demand that goes to space and water heating, which is still mostly provided by the burning of fossil fuels.[10]

Australia only generates 17 percent of its electricity from renewable sources.[11] The largest source of this production is from hydropower, which is imperiled by declining rainfall. Hotter prevailing conditions are also a negative for Australia's solar power production as PV panel output declines above the standard test temperature of 25 degrees Celsius (77 Fahrenheit), while at the same time increasing the demand for space cooling.

Many Americans naively perceive Canada as a land of tundra, moose, and polar bears, but it is actually an advanced technologically competitive economy with significant automotive, computer, industrial equipment, and aircraft industries. In comparison, Australia's exports are primarily from intensive GHG extractive industries: oil, coal, natural gas, iron, aluminum, gold, and agricultural commodities.

Table 10.4. 2018 Australian and Canadian Top 10 Exports by Category[12]

Australia	% of Total Exports	Canada	% of Total Exports
Fossil Fuels	34.6	Fossil Fuels	22
Ores	23.5	Vehicles	13.5
Gems/Precious Metals	6.3	Machinery/Computers	7.7
Meat	4	Gems/Precious Metals	4
Inorganic Chemicals	3.2	Wood	3.2
Cereals	1.9	Plastics	3
Machinery/Computers	1.9	Electrical Machinery	3
Aluminum	1.5	Aircraft/Spacecraft	2.4
Electrical Machinery	1.3	Aluminum	2.2
Technical Apparatus	1.3	Paper	1.8
Top 10 as a % of exports	79.5	Top 10 as a % of exports	62.8
Top 10 in US$B	201.8	Top 10 in US$B	281.7
Percent of GDP	14%	Percent of GDP	15%

Considering the composition of its exports and the sources of its energy supply, it is clear that Australia's economy is more exposed to a world shifting away from unfettered fossil fuel use and untaxed GHG emissions. Output of energy intensive industries is clearly at risk. Exports of meat, grains, and wool are also threatened by a hotter and drier climate, and land utilized for agriculture has declined by more than 20 percent since 1980.[13] In contrast, Canadian farmers have been expanding their efforts northward, and total cropland has increased by more than 20 percent over the same period.[14] While the rising prevalence of forest fires and beetle infestation are negatives, Canada's wood and paper industries may see net benefits from a warmer and wetter climate, which has resulted in an increase of vegetation growth across the nation that is visible from space.[15]

Finally, while much of Australia becomes an increasingly harsh desert, Canada is experiencing the start of an economic boom in its lands above the Arctic Circle. Declining sea ice in the summer is allowing more ships to transit the northwest passage, and port facilities are being built to service what are expected to be Canada's fastest growing regions—Nunavut and the Yukon.

In conclusion, several impacts of climate change have converged so that Canada's economy is likely to outperform Australia's over the next two decades. These include warmer temperatures, changes in rainfall, upfront capital costs to shift to green energy sources, and composition of exports. In general, overweighting the Canada ETF (EWC) and underweighting or even shorting the Australian ETF (EWA) is likely to generate positive equity performance over time. While Australia has been known as "the lucky country," that luck may be running out.

Table 10.5.   Sector Weightings of EWA (Australia) versus EWC (Canada)[16]

	EWA	EWC
Financials	36.4%	38.6%
Materials	19.3%	10.3%
Health Care	8.9%	1.2%
Real Estate	7.5%	7.0%
Energy	6.2%	20.0%
Industrials	6.1%	9.4%
Consumer Discretionary	5.6%	4.2%
Consumer Staples	5.2%	4.5%
Utilities	2.1%	2.4%
Communication	1.5%	3.0%
Information Technology	0.6%	5.0%

However, a few comments should be made regarding the composition of these two traded funds. One fact that may catch the reader's eye is the large weighting of the energy sector in the EWC at 20 percent and how it roughly matches that of the materials sector in the EWA. A "naked long" of the Canadian ETF certainly exposes an investor to a loss were its energy stocks to fall in value due to an imposition of carbon taxation and/or a more rapid shift to renewable power. However, what would hurt Canada's energy stocks would likely be similarly painful to

Australian materials companies engaged in the energy-hungry business of mining, extracting, and shipping coal, iron ore, and aluminum. Another option to hedge this risk for an investor of the EWC is to consider shorting a few Canadian energy stocks already highlighted earlier in this book as some of the most carbon intense in the world, such as Suncorp Energy, Canadian National Resources, and Husky Energy (SU, CNQ, and HUSKF).

OTHER NATIONAL PAIR-TRADE IDEAS

The analysis of Spain and Italy versus the Nordic nations and Australia versus Canada yields a set of criteria to evaluate other nations around the world:

- Countries closer to the poles are likely to be advantaged versus those at lower latitudes.
- The same logic holds for those with higher GDP/capita and more well-distributed wealth.
- Nations made up of island archipelagos are particularly at risk due to rising sea levels as well as storm surges caused by intensifying weather events.
- States that are landlocked, or less focused on seaborne commerce, will likely be relatively advantaged.
- Efficient users of energy and those that have shifted away from fossil fuels will find the costs of GHG emissions taxation easier to bear.
- National stock markets with heavy sector weightings in information technology, health care, and communications will be advantaged versus those dominated by energy, materials, and industrials.

Applying these metrics to other national stock markets yields several additional pair trade opportunities for those concerned about rising impacts and costs of climate change.

A few of these pair trades listed in Table 10.6 may initially raise eyebrows but hopefully become logical with a bit of explanation. Consider Mexico/Brazil and Israel/Turkey: Mexico certainly has a hot climate, but its centers of population and industry are away from the coastline in areas that rarely suffer hits from hurricanes. In contrast, Brazil is even

Table 10.6. Additional National Pair Trades

Long/ETF Ticker	Short/ETF Ticker
Mexico/EWW	Brazil/EWZ
China/MCHI	India/INDA
Chile/ECH	Philippines/EPHE
Switzerland/EWL	South Africa/EZA
Russia/ERUS	Indonesia/EIDO
New Zealand/ENZL	Singapore/EWS
Argentina/AGT	Thailand/THD
Germany/EWG	Japan/EWJ
Israel/EIS	Turkey/TUR

hotter as it straddles the equator, and its population is concentrated along the coast where it will be impacted by rising sea levels.[17] Drought is a major problem in the nation's most populous states of São Paolo, Rio de Janeiro, and Minas Gerais. Yes, Mexico has been suffering droughts as well, but they have not been in the regions of its largest cities (Puebla, Guadalajara, Monterrey, and of course, Mexico City). Finally, Brazil's economy is significantly more exposed to extractive industries than Mexico's, which has benefited from long-term manufacturing job growth from the United States in the wake of NAFTA going into effect in 1994.

Israel may also seem a strange choice at first for climate change investors due to its reputation as a desert land surrounded by implacable enemies. However, the Jewish state has several surprising advantages to cope with an era of global warming. First, its stock market has one of the world's highest exposures to the tech sector, with its market cap in excess of 30 percent. The nation's "start-up" culture is likely to continue generating new companies that go public at high valuations. Israel is also a leader in desalination technology so as to sustain the nation's water needs in a scenario of greater drought across the Mediterranean basin. Solar energy project growth is rapid, and new offshore natural gas fields are being brought online. Turkey's stock market has a higher carbon intensity, with more than 50 percent of its market capitalization in the industrial, consumer staples, materials, and energy sectors. By this measure, Israel is less than 18 percent.[18]

To conclude this chapter:

- The effects of climate change and efforts to mitigate them will be unevenly distributed around the world. Some nations are likely to be sorely tested as they experience truly horrific cascading tragedies of sea level rise, collapsing food production, more destructive storms, and an increase in violence and war. In contrast, a few countries may actually reap some small net positives from global warming—at least for a time.
- Poorer nations closer to the equator are likely to be more negatively impacted by a changing climate even though in many cases they have emitted little in the way of the industrial gasses that caused the problem in the first place.
- Clearly, this is a glaring case of the unfairness of life, and one can hope that the better-off nations of the world share their technology and wealth in an attempt to even out the costs borne by societies around the world.
- Certainly, individual investors should consider doing their part to reduce global suffering by reducing their own carbon footprints and making charitable donations to applicable nonprofit organizations. However, there is no reason that such an investor should feel ethically obliged to continue directing capital toward companies, industries, or even nations where returns are expected to decline, or become negative, due to the impact of climate change.

Conclusion

In late September 2019, as I was finishing up the draft manuscript of this book, I attended my twenty-fifth Harvard Business School class reunion. The festivities were, simply put, a ton of fun. After a quarter century, most of the members of the class of 1994 have found some level of success in the world, accepted a measure of humility, and have come to focus significant time on family and nonprofit interests. Thus, it was a great atmosphere for me, whose most recent "business accomplishment" was publishing a history book on World War II military strategy.[1]

This being Harvard Business School, a reunion couldn't be all about cocktail parties and a pat on the back from the dean. No, there had to be serious work involved. That meant some of the school's best professors teaching case studies in the large seminar rooms of Aldrich Hall. Of course, the "students" were expecting to be taught at a high level. After all, the twenty-fifth reunion class included the likes of Jeff Harmening, CEO of General Mills; Victor Dodig, CEO of Canadian Imperial Bank of Commerce; Sean Covey, bestselling author and president of FranklinCovey Education; and Ulrich Brechbuhl, the number-three man at the State Department.[2] And that's just a sampling of titles from my *one* section of ninety people out of a class of eight hundred! Also attending the seminars were the groups from the thirtieth, thirty-fifth, and fortieth class reunions—people who have accumulated what Harvard likes to refer to as generational wealth who might be cajoled into donating a building or two to the university.

155

While students tended to treat their professors almost with reverence while they waited to receive their MBAs, they are significantly more comfortable expressing their true opinions at class sessions held at reunion events. I enjoyed watching one exchange in which a "student" interrupted a professor and vehemently disagreed with a point being made regarding economic policy, accentuating his argument with the statement, "And I know something about this issue as I was president of the St. Louis Federal Reserve Bank for a decade." In other words, at reunion events, professors have to bring their A game.

So, what did Harvard Business School decide to teach to its graduates? Not surprisingly to me, a significant portion of the curriculum was dedicated to the impacts of climate change on the global economy and the capital markets. Case studies in the two-day program included the following:

- "The Future of Energy in a Changing Climate" presented by Daniel Schrag, professor of Environmental Science and Engineering. This case focused on current scientific data and climate modeling to extrapolate how quickly the earth would warm in coming decades, the rapid ongoing shift in the energy complex toward renewable power, and how major corporations are planning for these changes. A lively discussion ensued regarding the best strategies and roadmaps for decarbonizing the global economy.
- "Investing in the 21st Century: Risk, Return, and Impact" presented by senior lecturer in business administration Vikram Gandhi. This session concerned the rapid rise of nontraditional investing overlays, including environmental, social, and governance analysis (ESG) that have now grown to cover more than $30 trillion, which exceeds a quarter of all professionally managed assets. A short video was shown with a clip of Al Gore's May 2019 address to Harvard College from which he had graduated fifty years earlier. Gore compared owning fossil fuel stocks today to owning South African equities during the era of apartheid. The former vice president then went on to thunder that the +$36 billion Harvard endowment should divest all ownership of securities from the hydrocarbon industry. We then turned to the "meat" of the session in which topics discussed included how asset managers should quantify these moral metrics and measure the impact of their decision making.

- "Investing in Resilience: Cities, Structures, and Capital" presented by senior lecturer in business administration John Macomber. The basic questions this case asked were: 1) How much risk is there in the coastal real estate and municipal bond markets in the face of climate change; 2) How should banks and insurers consider allocating capital in such a world; and 3) What are the opportunities for investing in hardening buildings and infrastructure against more destructive flooding and storm events?
- "Solar Geoengineering: A 'Real' Option for the Planet" presented by Joseph Lassiter, professor of management practice in environmental management (ret.). A big question was asked in this session: should we consider engaging in intentional industrial-scale efforts to alter the planet so as to slow the warming of the atmosphere? Such an effort would likely make the climate better for many, but would also trigger major flooding and droughts in other parts of the globe. What about other negative side effects of proposed efforts of injecting SO_2 aerosols into the stratosphere, or seeding great swaths of the ocean with iron filings? How should we study and execute real-life trials of this field of science, and how do we establish an international framework for their possible general implementation?

The classrooms holding these events were packed. Many reunion attendees were forced to sit in the aisles and on stairs (and these are people used to getting pretty good seats). Some sessions required the opening of an overflow room, where the presentations were simulcast onto a large screen.

At the end of the long weekend, reunion attendees filtered back to Logan Airport to begin their return journeys to their homes and jobs. One message certainly came through loud and clear: Harvard Business School believes that climate change is increasingly becoming a major factor determining business practices, capital market flows, and how investment dollars will be allocated. A great number of reunion attendees clearly agree. The question now is, do you?

Notes

INTRODUCTION

1. The Fourth National Climate Assessment, see: https://nca2018.global-change.gov/chapter/1/, last accessed October 9, 2019.

2. Ibid.

3. Ibid.

4. Greenhouse gas emissions by gas from "Our World in Data," https://ourworldindata.org/co2-and-other-greenhouse-gas-emissions, last accessed September 23, 2019.

5. Data from the Global Carbon Project, https://docs.google.com/spreadsheets/d/10ZkDgDDOHaZPAKkN_JWVz1d56DDgLVnUOWnSdNX-qTl0/edit#gid=0, last accessed September 23, 2019.

6. The World Bank, https://data.worldbank.org/indicator/EN.ATM.CO2E.KT?view=chart&year_high_desc=true, May 10, 2018.

7. National Oceanic and Atmospheric Administration, https://www.esrl.naa.gov/gmd/ccgg/trends/full.html, last accessed May 21, 2018.

8. Richard Wike, "What the World Thinks about Climate Change in 7 Charts," April 18, 2016, http://www.pewresearch.org/fact-tank/2016/04/18/what-the-world-thinks-about-climate-change-in-7-charts/, last accessed October 19, 2019.

9. Wikipedia, https://en.wikipedia.org/wiki/Climate_change_denial, last accessed May 22, 2018.

10. Governor's Office of Planning and Research, State Government of California, http://www.opr.ca.gov/facts/list-of-scientific-organizations.html, May 22, 2018.

11. Damian Carrington, "BBC Admits 'We Get Climate Change Coverage Wrong Too Often,'" *Guardian*, September 7, 2018, https://www.theguardian.com/environment/2018/sep/07/bbc-we-get-climate-change-coverage-wrong-too-often, last accessed October 9, 2019.

12. Jeff Tsao, Nate Lewis, and George Crabtree, Solar FAQs, Sandia National Laboratory, Albuquerque, New Mexico, 2006, 10, http://www.sandia.gov/~jytsao/Solar%20FAQs.pdf, May 23, 2018.

13. Skeptical Science, http://4hiroshimas.com/#Science, October 9, 2019.

14. National Centers for Environmental Information, NOAA Climate at a Glance: Global Time Series, published September 2019, https://www.ncdc.noaa.gov/cag/, last accessed October 9, 2019.

15. Ibid.

16. National Oceanic and Atmospheric Administration, https://www.climate.gov/news-features/understanding-climate/climate-change-ocean-heat-content, last accessed May 24, 2018.

17. Environmental Protection Agency, https://www.epa.gov/climate-indicators/climate-change-indicators-sea-surface-temperature, last accessed May 24, 2018.

18. Ibid., https://www.epa.gov/climate-indicators/climate-change-indicators-sea-level, last accessed May 22, 2018.

19. Skeptical Science, https://www.skepticalscience.com/sea-level-rise-predictions-intermediate.htm, last accessed May 29, 2018.

20. Maurice Tamman, "Ocean Shock: Lobster's Great Migration Sets Up Boom and Bust," *Reuters*, October 30, 2018, https://www.reuters.com/article/us-oceans-tide-lobster-specialreport/ocean-shock-lobsters-great-migration-sets-up-boom-and-bust-idUSKCN1N420I, also see Robert Lee Hotz, "Climate Change Drives Fish into New Waters, Remaking an Industry," *Wall Street Journal*, December 22, 2018, https://www.wsj.com/articles/climate-change-drives-fish-into-new-waters-remaking-an-industry-11545454860?ns=prod/accounts-wsj, last accessed October 9, 2019.

21. David Appell using IPCC data, https://davidappell.blogspot.com/2013/10/epa-sued-to-stop-pacnw-ocean.html, May 24, 2018.

22. National Oceanic and Atmospheric Administration, https://www.pmel.noaa.gov/co2/story/What+is+Ocean+Acidification%3F, last accessed May 30, 2018.

23. There are many sources showing the correlation between heat and crime. For a few examples see, Jari Tihonen, Pirjo Halonen, Laura Tihonen, Hannu Kautiainen, Markus Storvik, and James Callaway, "The Association of Ambient Temperature and Violent Crime," National Institute of Health, July 28, 2017, https://www.ncbi.nlm.nih.gov/pmc/articles/PMC5533778/, last accessed October 9, 2019, or the Association for Psychological Science, https://www.

psychologicalscience.org/observer/global-warming-and-violent-behavior, and the National Bureau of Economic Research, https://www.nber.org/papers/w20598.pdf.

24. Ibid.

25. Union of Concerned Scientists, https://www.ucsusa.org/global-warming/science-and-impacts/impacts/global-warming-rain-snow-tornadoes.html#.Ww3VsEgvzIU, last accessed May 29, 2018.

26. Fourth National Climate Assessment, https://nca2014.globalchange.gov/report/our-changing-climate/heavy-downpours-increasing#graphic-16693, last accessed May 29, 2018.

27. The World Bank, https://data.worldbank.org/indicator/EN.ATM.CO2E.KT?view=chart&year_high_desc=true, last accessed June 1, 2018.

28. Ibid.

29. The World Bank, https://data.worldbank.org/indicator/EN.ATM.NOXE.KT.CE?end=2012&start=1970&view=chart&year_high_desc=true and https://data.worldbank.org/indicator/EN.ATM.METH.KT.CE?view=map&year_high_desc=true, June 1, 2018.

30. Our World in Data, a project of Oxford University, https://ourworldindata.org/co2-and-other-greenhouse-gas-cmissions#future-emission-scenarios, June 1, 2018.

CHAPTER ONE

1. Data from Yahoo! Finance, https://finance.yahoo.com, last accessed September 30, 2019.

2. Julia Kollewe, "Coal Power Becoming 'Uninsurable' as Firms Refuse Cover," *Guardian*, December 2, 2019.

3. "AXA Accelerates Its Commitment to Fight Climate Change," December 12, 2017, https://www.axa.com/en/newsroom/press-releases/axa-accelerates-its-commitment-to-fight-climate-change, last accessed October 9, 2019.

4. HSBC press release, https://www.hsbc.com/news-and-insight/insight-archive/2018/hsbc-strengthens-energy-policy, last accessed June 12, 2018.

5. Laura Kusisto and Arian Campo-Flores, "Rising Sea Levels Reshape Miami's Housing Market," *Wall Street Journal*, April 20, 2018, https://www.wsj.com/articles/climate-fears-reshape-miamis-housing-market-1524225600?ns=prod/accounts-wsj, last accessed June 13, 2018.

6. Jesse Keenan, Thomas Hill, and Anurag Gumber, "Climate Gentrification: From Theory to Empiricism in Miami-Dade County, FL," Environmental Research Letters, http://iopscience.iop.org/article/10.1088/1748-9326/aabb32, last accessed June 13, 2018.

7. A king tide refers to an especially high tide that only occurs a few times a year. They are natural and predictable events. See https://en.wikipedia.org/wiki/King_tide.

8. California Energy Commission, http://www.energy.ca.gov/title24/2019standards/rulemaking/documents/, last accessed June 12, 2018.

9. Greg Ip, "Business Worries About Climate Intensify, Business Actions to Fix It, Not So Much," *Wall Street Journal*, January 16, 2019, https://www.wsj.com/articles/business-worries-about-climate-intensify-their-actions-less-so-11547643600?mod=hp_featst_pos2, last accessed September 30, 2019.

10. Jennifer DePinto, Fred Backus, and Anthony Saluto, "Most Americans Say Climate Change Should Be Addressed Now—CBS News Poll," CBS News, September 15, 2019.

11. Cary Funk and Meg Hefferon, "Many Republican Millennials Differ with Older Party Members on Climate Change and Energy Issues," http://www.pewresearch.org/fact-tank/2018/05/14/many-republican-millennials-differ-with-older-party-members-on-climate-change-and-energy-issues/, last accessed July 7, 2018.

12. Brian Kennedy, "Most Americans Say Climate Change Affects Their Local Community, Including Two-Thirds Living Near Coast," http://www.pewresearch.org/fact-tank/2018/05/16/most-americans-say-climate-change-affects-their-local-community-including-two-thirds-living-near-coast/, last accessed July 7, 2018.

13. Michon Scott, "National Climate Assessment Map Shows Uneven Impact of Future Global Warming on U.S. Energy Spending," https://www.climate.gov/news-features/featured-images/national-climate-assessment-map-shows-uneven-impact-future-global, last accessed October 1, 2019.

14. Mark Muro, David Victor, and Jacob Whiton, "How the Geography of Climate Damage Could Make the Politics Less Polarizing," Brookings Institution, January 29, 2019, https://www.brookings.edu/research/how-the-geography-of-climate-damage-could-make-the-politics-less-polarizing/, last accessed October 1, 2019.

15. Bruce Drake, "How Americans View the Top Energy and Environmental Issues," http://www.pewresearch.org/fact-tank/2015/01/15/environment-energy-2/, last accessed July 7, 2018.

16. See the website for "Fossil Free," a project of 350.org: https://gofossilfree.org/divestment/commitments/, last accessed September 23, 2019.

17. See, http://www.climateaction100.org/, last accessed July 9, 2018.

18. Soh Young In, Ki Young Park, and Ashby H. B. Monk, "Is 'Being Green' Rewarded in the Market?: An Empirical Investigation of Decarbonization and Stock Returns," Stanford Global Project Center Working Paper, April 16, 2018, last accessed September 9, 2018, https://papers.ssrn.com/sol3/papers.cfm?abstract_id=3020304, see also the performance of the "Clean 200" versus

the overall S&P Global 1200 Energy Index, https://www.asyousow.org/report/clean200-2018-q1/, last accessed July 13, 2018.

19. Larry Fink, "A Sense of Purpose," BlackRock Investor Relations, https://www.blackrock.com/corporate/investor-relations/larry-fink-ceo-letter, last accessed July 13, 2018.

20. Ibid.

21. See, "We Mean Business" website, https://www.wemeanbusinesscoalition.org/, last accessed January 14, 2020.

22. Joe Romm, "Shell Oil CEO Stunner: 'My Next Car Will Be Electric,'" August 3, 2017, https://thinkprogress.org/shell-oil-ceo-says-his-next-car-will-be-electric-fdee683b4e36/, last accessed October 9, 2019.

23. Lorenzo Ligato, "9 Companies That Are Changing Their Habits to Save Our Planet," Huffington Post, September 18, 2015, https://www.huffingtonpost.com/entry/we-mean-business-climate-change_us_55e88ec9e4b0b7a9633c4293, last accessed October 9, 2019.

24. See Kimberly-Clark's corporate website section on these matters, https://www.sustainability2022.com/strategy, last accessed October 9, 2019.

CHAPTER TWO

1. Lazard Asset Management, "Lazard's Levelized Cost of Energy Analysis—Version 12.0," November 2018, page 7, https://www.lazard.com/media/450784/lazards-levelized-cost-of-energy-version-120-vfinal.pdf, last accessed October 9, 2019.

2. US Energy Information Administration, "Today in Energy," January 10, 2019, https://www.eia.gov/todayinenergy/detail.php?id=37952, last accessed October 9, 2019.

3. Lazard Asset Management, "Lazard's Levelized Cost of Energy Analysis—Version 12.0," November 2018, page 7, https://www.lazard.com/media/450784/lazards-levelized-cost-of-energy-version-120-vfinal.pdf, last accessed October 9, 2019.

4. Renewable Energy Policy Network for the 21st Century, Renewables 2018 Global Status Report, http://www.ren21.net/gsr-2018/chapters/chapter_05/chapter_05/, last accessed October 9, 2019.

5. See Bloomberg New Energy Finance Outlook 2018, https://about.bnef.com/new-energy-outlook/, last accessed May 1, 2019.

6. Jeremy Taylor, Nathan Cockrell, Alistair Godrich, and Neil Millar, "The Growing Importance of the 'E' in ESG," Lazard Asset Management, https://www.lazardassetmanagement.com/docs/-m0/67480/TheGrowingImportanceOfTheEInESG_LazardResearch_en.pdf.

7. "Business Worries About Climate Intensify, Business Actions to Fix It, Not So Much," *Wall Street Journal*, January 16, 2019, https://www.wsj.

com/articles/business-worries-about-climate-intensify-their-actions-less-so-11547643600?mod=hp_featst_pos2, last accessed September 30, 2019.

8. Kristin Eberhard, "Map: The Future Is Carbo-Priced and the US Is Getting Left Behind," Sightline Institute, https://www.sightline.org/2017/06/06/map-the-future-is-carbon-priced-and-the-us-is-getting-left-behind/, last accessed October 9, 2019.

9. Of the ten largest US metropolitan areas by economic output, eight are adjacent to coal-producing regions or oil- and gas-yielding shale formations. See http://www.visualcapitalist.com/map-economic-might-u-s-metro-area/ and https://www.sourcewatch.org/index.php/File:776px-Shaleusa2.jpg, last accessed October 9, 2019.

10. US Energy Information Administration, "What Is US Electricity Generation by Energy Source?" https://www.eia.gov/tools/faqs/faq.php?id=427&t=3, and Wikipedia entries on solar and wind energy, https://en.wikipedia.org/wiki/Solar_power_in_the_United_States#/media/File:US_Monthly_Solar_Power_Generation.svg, https://en.wikipedia.org/wiki/Wind_power_in_the_United_States#/media/File:US_Monthly_Wind_Generated_Electricity.svg, last accessed October 9, 2019.

11. https://en.wikipedia.org/wiki/Solar_power_in_the_United_States#/media/File:Projected_US_Renewable_Electric_Capacity.jpg, last accessed October 9, 2019.

12. Technically wind power is also solar power as winds are primarily created by the heat of the sun warming the earth. For simplicity's sake, we will split wind and solar into separate categories.

13. See Wikipedia, https://en.wikipedia.org/wiki/Green_New_Deal, last accessed October 9, 2019.

14. See Bloomberg New Energy Finance Outlook 2018, https://about.bnef.com/new-energy-outlook/, last accessed September 30, 2019.

15. Market Cap and yield data as of 9/26/19 from bloomberg.com. Power generation breakdown numbers are from individual company reports.

16. Bjorn Carey, *Stanford News*, September 14, 2012, https://news.stanford.edu/news/2012/september/offshore-wind-energy-091412.html, last accessed October 9, 2019.

17. Ørsted company presentation 11/28/18, page 38, https://orsted.com/-/media/WWW/Docs/Corp/COM/Investor/CMD2018/CMD-Presentation-2018.pdf, last accessed October 9, 2019.

18. This US 50-m Wind Resource map was created by the National Renewable Energy Laboratory for the US Department of Energy with data provided by AWS TruePower, https://www.nrel.gov/gis/assets/pdfs/windsmodel4publ-1-9base200904enh.pdf, last accessed September 26, 2019.

19. Ørsted company presentation, November 28, 2018, page 67–71, https://orsted.com/-/media/WWW/Docs/Corp/COM/Investor/CMD2018/CMD-Presentation-2018.pdf.

20. For US data, see US Department of Energy report of September 9, 2016, https://www.energy.gov/eere/articles/computing-america-s-offshore-wind-energy-potential. For Japan see Linklaters, https://www.linklaters.com/en-us/insights/publications/2018/october/japan-offshore-wind, last accessed October 9, 2019.

21. An ADR, or American Depository Receipt, is a popular product that allows US investors to invest in a foreign equity on a US exchange. A US bank purchases shares in a company's home market, places them in a vault, and sells traded certificates backed by the collateral. See, https://en.wikipedia.org/wiki/American_depositary_receipt, last accessed October 9, 2019.

22. Brookfield company presentation from September 26, 2018, pages 54–55, https://bep.brookfield.com/~/media/Files/B/Brookfield-BEP-IR/events-and-presentations/investor-day/2018/2018-bep-investor-day-presentation-vf.pdf, last accessed October 9, 2019.

23. For a discussion of this, see, Ivan Penn, "The $3 Billion Plan to Turn Hoover Dam into a Giant Battery," *New York Times*, June 24, 2018, https://www.nytimes.com/interactive/2018/07/24/business/energy-environment/hoover-dam-renewable-energy.html, last accessed September 30, 2019.

24. Carbon intensity defined as the emission rate of GHGs relative to intensity of the output rate of an energy source or industrial production process.

25. See, Warren Cornwall, "Hundreds of New Dams Could Mean Trouble for Our Climate," *Science*, September 28, 2016, http://www.sciencemag.org/news/2016/09/hundreds-new-dams-could-mean-trouble-our-climate, last accessed September 30, 2019.

26. See, L. A. W. Banbace, F. M. Ramos, I. B. T. Lima, and R. R. Rosa, "Mitigation and Recovery of Methane Emissions from Tropical Hydroelectric Dams," *ScienceDirect*, June 2007. https://www.sciencedirect.com/science/article/abs/pii/S0360544206002611?via%3Dihub, last accessed September 20, 2019.

27. See NASDAQ's dividend history tracker, https://www.nasdaq.com/symbol/bep/dividend-history, last accessed October 9, 2019.

28. A yieldco, or yield co, is a company set up to own completed operating assets and provide a reasonably predictable dividend payout to its owners. They are usually externally managed and are similar in structure to MLPs and REITs, though these have specific and important differences as to how they are treated by the IRS for taxation purposes. See, https://en.wikipedia.org/wiki/Yield_co, last accessed October 9, 2019.

29. See Northland's 12/17 information matrix, https://northlandpower.com/cmsAssets/docs/pdfs/Northland_Fact%20Sheet_December_2017_012918_V2.pdf, last accessed September 30, 2019.

30. US Department of Energy, https://windexchange.energy.gov/maps-data/321, last accessed October 9, 2019.

31. Azure Power investor presentation of February 13, 2019, page 13, http://investors.azurepower.com/~/media/Files/A/Azure-Power-IR/documents/events/q3-2019-earnings-call/apgl-3q19-earnings-presentation.pdf, last accessed October 9, 2019.

32. Renewables 2018 Global Status Report, http://www.ren21.net/gsr-2018/chapters/chapter_05/chapter_05/, last accessed October 9, 2019.

33. 1,000 kW = 1 MW. US retail electric prices rose from an average of $6.81 per kilowatt hour in 2000 to $10.54 in 2017. See: T. Wang, https://www.statista.com/statistics/183700/us-average-retail-electricity-price-since-1990/, and https://www.statista.com/statistics/201714/growth-in-us-residential-electricity-prices-since-2000/, last accessed October 9, 2019.

34. This Photovoltaic Solar Resource of the United States map was created by the National Renewable Energy Laboratory for the US Department of Energy, https://www.nrel.gov/gis/images/solar/national_photovoltaic_2009-01.jpg, last accessed September 26, 2019.

35. See Sunrun December 2018 investor presentation, page 13, http://investors.sunrun.com/static-files/5576bb84-eb9f-4466-b6b0-1bcc406632fc.

36. National Renewable Energy Laboratory, see page vi, https://www.nrel.gov/docs/fy17osti/68925.pdf, last accessed October 9, 2019.

37. Tom Lombardo, "What Is the Lifespan of a Solar Panel?" Engineering.com, April 20, 2014, https://www.engineering.com/3DPrinting/3DPrintingArticles/ArticleID/7475/What-Is-the-Lifespan-of-a-Solar-Panel.aspx, last accessed September 26, 2019.

38. Calculations from Energysage, https://news.energysage.com/much-solar-panels-save/, last accessed October 9, 2019.

39. See Wood Mackenzie Solar Market Insight of December 2018: https://www.woodmac.com/research/products/power-and-renewables/us-solar-market-insight/, last accessed October 9, 2019.

40. UC San Diego, http://jacobsschool.ucsd.edu/news/news_releases/release.sfe?id=1094, last accessed October 9, 2019.

41. See Sunrun November 2018 investor presentation, page 14, http://investors.sunrun.com/static-files/5576bb84-eb9f-4466-b6b0-1bcc406632fc and Vivint September 2018 investor presentation, page 12, https://s2.q4cdn.com/820306591/files/doc_presentations/VSLR-Investor-Presentation_2018_09.pdf, last accessed October 9, 2019.

42. Company financials, Bloomberg.com, Yahoo Finance.

43. See, Lucas Mearian, "In Shift, More Homeowners Are Buying Solar Panels Than Leasing Them," *Computerworld*, March 8, 2017, https://www.computerworld.com/article/3178342/sustainable-it/tectonic-shift-in-solar-sees-homeowners-now-buying-more-than-leasing-panels.html, last accessed September 30, 2019.

44. See the Better Business Bureau website, https://www.bbb.org/us/ ut/lehi/profile/solar-energy-contractors/vivint-solar-1166-22302389, last accessed September 30, 2019.

45. "Repowering Clean," April 5, 2019, https://www.sunrun.com/sites/default/files/repowering-clean-sunrun.pdf, last accessed October 9, 2019.

CHAPTER THREE

1. Wallace Erickson, Melissa Wolfe, Kimberly Bay, Douglas Johnson, and Joelle Gehring, "A Comprehensive Analysis of Small-Passerine Fatalities from Collision with Turbines at Wind Energy Facilities," *PlosOne*, https://journals. plos.org/plosone/article?id=10.1371/journal.ponc.0107491#ponc.0107491-Loss3, last accessed October 9, 2019.

2. Jon Greenberg, "Donald Trump's Ridiculous Link between Cancer, Wind Turbines," Politiifact, https://www.politifact.com/truth-o-meter/statements/2019/apr/08/donald-trump/republicans-dismiss-trumps-windmill-and-cancer-cla/, last accessed October 9, 2019.

3. "Property Values Not Hurt by Wind Farms," Energy and Policy Institute, April 13, 2014, https://www.energyandpolicy.org/wind-energy-does-not-hurt-property-values/, last accessed October 9, 2019.

4. "The Total Investment Scale of Renewable Energy during the 13th Five-Year Plan Period Will Reach 2.5 Trillion Yuan," China National Energy Administration, January 5, 2017, http://www.nea.gov.cn/2017-01/05/c_135956835. htm, last accessed October 9, 2019.

5. See Bloomberg NEF data for each of the three years: https://about. bnef.com/blog/vestas-reclaims-top-spot-annual-ranking-wind-turbine-makers/; https://www.bloomberg.com/news/articles/2018-02-26/these-four-power-giants-rule-the-world-s-growing-wind-market; https://about.bnef.com/blog/vestas-leads-break-away-group-big-four-turbine-makers/, last accessed October 9, 2019.

6. Alyssa Danigelis, "Global Onshore Wind Turbine Commissioning Declined in 2018," February 15, 2019, Environment + Energy Leader, https://www.energymanagertoday.com/onshore-wind-turbine-commissioning-0181542/, last accessed October 9, 2019.

7. "Global Wind Power Systems Market 2018–2022," April 2018, Technavio, https://www.technavio.com/report/global-wind-power-systems-market-analysis-share-2018, last accessed October 9, 2019.

8. "Offshore Wind Power Market to Reach a Capacity of 94 GW by 2026, at a CAGR of 19.2%," Fortune Business Insights, June 6, 2019, https://www. bloomberg.com/press-releases/2019-06-06/offshore-wind-power-market-to-

reach-a-capacity-of-94-gw-by-2026-at-a-cagr-of-19-2-exclusive-report-by-fortune-business, last accessed October 9, 2019.

9. https://www.vestas.com/~/media/vestas/investor/investor%20pdf/financial%20reports/2017/q4/2017_offshore.pdf.

10. Keith Bradsher, "To Conquer Wind Power, China Writes the Rules," *New York Times*, December 15, 2010, https://www.nytimes.com/2010/12/15/business/global/15chinawind.html, last accessed October 9, 2019.

11. See Goldwind's 2018 results presentation pages 13–14: http://106.38.64.54:8080/goldwind-en/upload/files/20190424093517cjE3TWnj.pdf, last accessed October 9, 2019.

12. Zak Doffman, "China's Spies Accused of Stealing EU Tech Secrets, Just as China and EU Agree Stronger Ties," *Forbes*, April 11, 2019, https://www.forbes.com/sites/zakdoffman/2019/04/11/chinese-spies-accused-of-major-european-ip-theft-just-as-china-and-europe-agree-stronger-ties/#51cc010470f4, last accessed October 9, 2019.

13. Nate Raymond, "China's Sinovel Fined in U.S. Trade Secrets Theft Case," Reuters, July 6, 2018, https://www.reuters.com/article/us-sinovel-windgro-usa-court/chinas-sinovel-fined-in-u-s-trade-secrets-theft-case-idUSKBN-1JW2RI, last accessed October 9, 2019.

14. TPI Composite's June 2019 investor presentation, pages 16–18, http://s21.q4cdn.com/635504763/files/doc_presentations/2019/06/TPI-Investor-Presentation-June-2019.pdf, last accessed October 9, 2019.

15. See for example, Yuzo Waki, "China Pays Dearly for Overinvestment," Nikkei Asian Review, https://asia.nikkei.com/Economy/China-pays-dearly-for-overinvestment, or https://www.tandfonline.com/doi/full/10.1080/1351847X.2016.1211546, or https://www.imf.org/en/Publications/WP/Issues/2016/12/31/Is-China-Over-Investing-and-Does-it-Matter-40121, last accessed October 9, 2019.

16. Solar Energy Industries Association (SEIA), https://www.seia.org/solar-industry-research-data, last accessed October 9, 2019.

17. First Solar 2018 Annual Report, page 12, https://s2.q4cdn.com/646275317/files/doc_event/2019/First-Solar-Inc.-2018-Annual-Report-Web-Posting.pdf.

18. Jinko Solar's 2018 Annual Report, page 58, http://ir.jinkosolar.com/index.php/static-files/cff7be11-1bfc-43fc-910a-1ea6d35c1310, last accessed October 9, 2019.

19. Canadian Solar's 2018 Annual Report, pages 40, 41, 46, 95, 96, 97, http://investors.canadiansolar.com/static-files/f5df404b-6f97-4027-8be3-db-57c5bb35d6, last accessed October 9, 2019.

20. SolarEdge's May 6, 2019, investor presentation, pages 10–11, https://investors.solaredge.com/static-files/2d497b7a-c9c1-4d5e-b49f-48809d20f9aa, last accessed October 9, 2019.

CHAPTER FOUR

1. "How Much Carbon Dioxide Is Produced When Different Fuels Are Burned?," US Energy Information Administration, https://www.eia.gov/tools/faqs/faq.php?id=73&t=11, last accessed October 9, 2019.

2. "Electricity in the United States Is Produced with Diverse Energy Sources and Technologies," US Energy Information Administration, https://www.eia.gov/energyexplained/index.php?page=electricity_in_the_united_states, last accessed October 9, 2019.

3. Nadja Popovich, "How Does Your State Make Electricity?," *New York Times*, December 24, 2018, https://www.nytimes.com/interactive/2018/12/24/climate/how-electricity-generation-changed-in-your-state.html, last accessed September 29, 2019.

4. Source: https://www.tradingview.com/symbols/SP-SPN/components/, last accessed September 29, 2019.

5. "BP Energy Outlook 2018 Edition," page 12, https://www.bp.com/content/dam/bp/en/corporate/pdf/energy-economics/energy-outlook/bp-energy-outlook-2018.pdf, last accessed September 19, 2019.

6. Jess Shankleman and Hayley Warren, "Why the Prospect of 'Peak Oil' Is Hotly Debated," *Bloomberg Businessweek*, December 21, 2017, https://www.bloomberg.com/news/articles/2017-12-22/why-the-prospect-of-peak-oil-is-hotly-debated-quicktake-q-a, last accessed September 19, 2019.

7. "Energy Transition Outlook 2018," DNV-GL, https://eto.dnvgl.com/2018/download, last accessed September 19, 2019.

8. "2020 Vision: Why You Should See the Fossil Fuel Peak Coming," Carbon Tracker Initiative, September 19, 2018, https://www.carbontracker.org/reports/2020-vision-why-you-should-see-the-fossil-fuel-peak-coming/, last accessed September 30, 2019.

9. Ibid.

10. Tim Gould and Christophe McGlade, "Crunching the Numbers—Are We Heading for an Oil Supply Shock?," International Energy Agency, November 16, 2018, https://www.iea.org/newsroom/news/2018/november/crunching-the-numbers-are-we-heading-for-an-oil-supply-shock-1.html, last accessed September 20, 2019.

11. Libby George and Ahmad Ghaddar, "New Rules on Ship Emissions Herald Sea Change for Oil Markets," Reuters, May 17, 2018, https://www.reuters.com/article/us-shipping-fuel-sulphur/new-rules-on-ship-emissions-herald-sea-change-for-oil-market-idUSKCN1II0PP, last accessed October 1, 2019.

12. "Distribution of Oil Demand in the OECD in 2017 by Sector," Statista, https://www.statista.com/statistics/307194/top-oil-consuming-sectors-worldwide/, last accessed September 18, 2019.

13. "List of Countries Banning Fossil Fuel Vehicles," https://en.wikipedia. org/wiki/List_of_countries_banning_fossil_fuel_vehicles#cite_note-14, last accessed October 9, 2019.

14. Echo Huang, "Here's One Number That Shows the Craze for Electric Vehicles in China," *Quartz*, June 11, 2018, https://qz.com/1301725/heres-one-number-that-shows-the-craze-for-electric-vehicles-in-china/, last accessed October 1, 2019.

15. Nico Muzi, "Forty Percent of Europeans Say the Next Car They Buy Is Likely to Be Electric—Poll," *Transport & Environment*, October 1, 2018, https://www.transportenvironment.org/press/forty-percent-europeans-say-next-car-they-buy-likely-be-electric-poll, last accessed September 20, 2019.

16. AAA website, "1 in 5 US Drivers Want Electric Vehicles," https://newsroom.aaa.com/2018/05/1-in-5-us-drivers-want-electric-vehicle/, last accessed October 1, 2019.

17. "Mandatory Renewable Energy Target," Wikipedia, https://en.wikipedia. org/wiki/Mandatory_renewable_energy_target#Targets_by_country, last accessed October 1, 2019.

18. "What Growth in Bioplastics Industry Means for Investors and the Economy," Green dot bioplastics, https://www.greendotbioplastics.com/growth-bioplastics-industry-means-investors-economy/, last accessed October 1, 2019.

19. Chelsea Harvey, "United Airlines Is Flying on Biofuels. Here's Why That's a Really Big Deal," *Washington Post*, March 11, 2016, https://www.washingtonpost.com/news/energy-environment/wp/2016/03/11/united-airlines-is-flying-on-biofuels-heres-why-thats-a-really-big-deal/?noredirect=on&utm_term=.bfd7cbf3389b, last accessed October 1, 2019.

20. Energystar website: https://www.energystar.gov/about/origins_mission/energy_star_numbers, last accessed October 9, 2019.

21. Rina Chandran, "Can Philippine Storm Survivors Hold Major Companies Responsible for Contributing to Climate Change?," Reuters, March 22, 2018, https://www.reuters.com/article/us-philippines-climatechange-lawmaking-a/can-philippines-storm-survivors-hold-companies-to-account-for-climate-damage-idUSKBN1GY04V, last accessed October 1, 2019.

22. International Energy Agency, https://www.iea.org/publications/freepublications/publication/English.pdf, page 3, last accessed October 9, 2019.

23. ExxonMobil's 2017 10-K, pages 108–18, https://corporate.exxonmobil. com/en/company/investors, last accessed October 1, 2019.

24. "Royal Dutch Shell's Oil and Gas Reserves from 2010 to 2018, by Region (in Million Barrels of Oil Equivalent)," https://www.statista.com/statistics/260332/royal-dutch-shells-oil-and-gas-reserves/, last accessed October 1, 2019.

25. Shell Energy Transition Report, April 12, 2018, pages 10 and 37, https://www.shell.com/media/news-and-media-releases/2018/new-report-on-strategy-for-energy-transition.html, last accessed October 1, 2019.

26. "Barrel Breakdown," *Wall Street Journal*, April 15, 2016, http://graphics.wsj.com/oil-barrel-breakdown/, last accessed October 1, 2019.

27. Avaz Nanji, "The 10 Industries Most Distrusted by US Consumers," https://www.marketingprofs.com/charts/2017/32764/the-10-industries-most-distrusted-by-us-consumers, last accessed September 30, 2019.

28. "Marcellus Formation," Wikipedia, https://en.wikipedia.org/wiki/Marcellus_Formation#/smedia/File:Marcellus_Shale_Gas_Play.png, last accessed October 9, 2019.

29. "Northeast Megalopolis, Wikipedia, https://en.wikipedia.org/wiki/Northeast_megalopolis, last accessed October 9, 2019.

30. Cabot Oil and Gas Corporation reports and presentations. See the 2018 third-quarter earnings presentation, and the 2017 10-K, http://phx.corporate-ir.net/phoenix.zhtml?c=116492&p=irol-calendar, http://phx.corporate-ir.net/phoenix.zhtml?c=116492&p=irol-sec, last accessed September 19, 2019.

31. Industry experts note that groundwater pumped for human use is sourced from wells that are drilled at much shallower levels than those where fracking takes place. Proper procedures (if followed) result in no contamination of drinking water. Earthquakes, if they are caused by fracking, are relatively small in magnitude and have done little property damage to date. Methane leakage can be minimized with appropriate monitoring and regulatory fines.

32. Dr. Paul Griffin, "The Carbon Majors Database," Climate Accountability Institute, July 2017, page 6, https://b8f65cb373b1b7b15feb-c70d8ead6ced550b4d987d7c03fcdd1d.ssl.cf3.rackcdn.com/cms/reports/documents/000/002/327/original/Carbon-Majors-Report-2017.pdf?1499691240, last accessed September 19, 2019. (kgCO2e/boe) = kilograms of CO_2 equivalent released per every barrel of oil equivalent produced and burned.

33. Rebecca Elliot, "In Booming Oilfield Natural Gas Can Be Free," *Wall Street Journal*, December 27, 2018, https://www.wsj.com/articles/in-booming-oilfield-natural-gas-can-be-free-11545906601, last accessed September 15, 2019.

34. "Crude Oil vs. Natural Gas—10-Year Daily Chart," Macrotrends, https://www.macrotrends.net/2500/crude-oil-vs-natural-gas-chart, last accessed September 15, 2019.

35. Based on 2017 revenues in US$. See, "List of Largest Oil and Gas Companies by Revenue," https://en.wikipedia.org/wiki/List_of_largest_oil_and_gas_companies_by_revenue#frb-inline, last accessed September 15, 2019.

36. "What Are Tar Sands?," Union of Concerned Scientists, February 23, 2016, https://www.ucsusa.org/clean-vehicles/all-about-oil/what-are-tar-sands, last accessed September 30, 2019.

CHAPTER FIVE

1. Mark Muro, David Victor, and Jacob Whiton, "How the Geography of Climate Damage Could Make the Politics Less Polarizing," Brookings Institution, January 29, 2019, https://www.brookings.edu/research/how-the-geography-of-climate-damage-could-make-the-politics-less-polarizing/, last accessed October 1, 2019.

2. Company reports and Bloomberg.com as of June 27, 2019. P/E ratio is on average analyst-estimated 2019 earnings. Note "PR" for Popular is for Puerto Rico, which is a territory rather than a state, last accessed September 18, 2019.

3. Kevin Loria, "Galveston, Texas: Galveston Set Another Record for Most Flooding Days in 2017, along with Boston; Sabine Pass, Texas; and Atlantic City and Sandy Hook in New Jersey," *Business Insider*, June 12, 2018, https://www.businessinsider.com/sea-level-rise-high-tides-sunny-day-flooding-coastal-cities-2018-4#galveston-texas-galveston-set-another-record-for-most-flooding-days-in-2017-along-with-boston-sabine-pass-texas-and-atlantic-city-and-sandy-hook-in-new-jersey-6, last accessed October 1, 2019.

4. Climate Central, April 19, 2019, https://www.climatecentral.org/gallery/graphics/how-your-city-state-and-country-is-warming, last accessed October 1, 2019.

5. See the website Current Results: https://www.currentresults.com/Yearly-Weather/USA/FL/Tampa/extreme-annual-tampa-high-temperature.php, last accessed October 1, 2019.

6. US Census Bureau, https://www.census.gov/library/visualizations/2019/comm/num-pop-change-county.html, last accessed October 1, 2019.

7. Mike Maciag, "After Years of Explosive Growth, Migration to the West and the South Slows," Governing.com, April 18, 2019, https://www.governing.com/topics/urban/gov-census-migration-south-west.html, last accessed October 1, 2019.

8. Company Reports and Yahoo! Finance as of April 27, 2019.

9. Kim Stanley Robinson, *New York 2140* (New York: Orbit, 2017). Note, in a shameless plug: I published fiction depicting a New York City turned into a modern-day Venice by global warming a full two decades ago. See James Ellman, *Risk Capital* (Tiburon, CA: Seacliff Publications, 1998).

10. Yes, there are indeed insurance companies that sell insurance to reinsurance companies as well. This is known as retrocession.

11. GC Securities Proprietary Database, https://www.gccapitalideas.com/2018/03/08/chart-catastrophe-bond-issuance-and-capital-outstanding-2/, last accessed September 25, 2019.

12. See the Florida Office of Insurance Regulation website: https://www.floir.com/, last accessed October 9, 2019.

13. See www.climatecentral.org: https://ss2.climatecentral.org/#12/40.7298/-74.0070?show=satellite&projections=0-K14_RCP85-SLR&level=5&unit=feet &pois=hide, last accessed September 15, 2019.

14. See the Nareit website: https://www.reit.com/data-research/reit-indexes/reits-sp-indexes. The S&P 500 market cap was $22.9 trillion in May 2019, and real estate was 2.9 percent of the total. Last accessed October 1, 2019.

15. See Invitation Home's July 2019 Nareit conference presentation, page 8, https://www.invh.com/Cache/1500121118.PDF?O=PDF&T=&Y=&D=&FI D=1500121118&iid=4426247; See Camden's June 3, 2019, Investor Presentation, page 14, https://investors.camdenliving.com/Cache/1001253190.PDF?O =PDF&T=&Y=&D=&FID=1001253190&iid=103094, last accessed October 1, 2019.

16. See Regency Center's May 2, 2019, investor presentation, page 6, http://investors.regencycenters.com/static-files/85585786-ec34-4408-986b-e938b8d46d07, last accessed October 1, 2019.

17. Steven Higgins and Simon Scheiter, "Atmospheric CO_2 Forces Abrupt Vegetation Shifts Locally, But Not Globally," *Nature*, June 27, 2012, https://www.nature.com/articles/nature11238, last accessed October 1, 2019.

18. Data sourced from Bloomberg.com, last accessed 9/25/19.

CHAPTER SIX

1. See The World Bank's 2007 to 2018 national rankings for infrastructure and logistical competence: https://lpi.worldbank.org/international/global/201 8?sort=asc&order=Logistics%20competence#datatable, last accessed October 1, 2019.

2. Congressional Budget Office report of October 18, page 4, https://www.cbo.gov/system/files/2018-10/54539-Infrastructure.pdf, last accessed October 1, 2019.

3. See the American Society of Civil Engineers' "2017 Infrastructure Report Card": https://www.infrastructurereportcard.org/the-impact/economic-impact/, last accessed October 1, 2019.

4. Ibid., https://www.infrastructurereportcard.org/cat-item/dams/.

5. Wikipedia 2018 estimates: https://en.wikipedia.org/wiki/List_of_metropolitan_statistical_areas, last accessed October 1, 2019.

6. Jason Samenow, Ian Livingston, and Jeff Halverson, "How and Why the D.C. Area Was Deluged by a Month's Worth of Rain in an Hour Monday," *Washington Post*, July 8, 2019, https://www.washingtonpost.com/weather/2019/07/08/washington-dc-flash-flood-how-why-area-was-deluged-by-months-worth-rain-an-hour-monday/, last accessed October 1, 2019.

7. Another option that would preserve current historic structures but require much more concrete would be to build four dams running from Tiburon, California, in the north to Angel Island to Alcatraz Island to Fort Mason in San Francisco. Such a series of dams would have the advantage of being built through significantly shallower water than the Golden Gate, and a road across the top of this network could improve north-south traffic flow. The shoreline of Sausalito along Richardson Bay could then be converted to port facilities to take the place of those in Oakland and San Francisco.

8. See Jacobs Engineering's 2019 investor day presentation, page 18: http://s1.q4cdn.com/838591571/files/doc_presentations/2019/02/Jacobs-Investor-Day-Deck-2019.02.19-_FINAL.PDF, last accessed October 2019.

9. Arcadis Annual Integrated Report 2018, page 16, https://www.arcadis.com/media/A/D/3/%7BAD3625A8-E667-4A03-9071-72EB7AE03426%7DArcadis%20Annual%20Integrated%20Report%202018-spreads.pdf, last accessed October 1, 2019.

10. This figure excludes the Chinese market. 2018 LafargeHolcim annual report, page 21, https://www.lafargeholcim.com/annual-interim-reports?field_year_tid_i18n_exposed=1233, last accessed October 1, 2019.

11. Vulcan Materials' 2018 annual report, part 1, page 6: https://www.sec.gov/Archives/edgar/data/1396009/000139600919000021/vmc-20181231x10k.htm, last accessed October 1, 2019.

12. Ibid., 14.

13. LafargeHolcim 2018 annual report, page 46, https://www.lafargeholcim.com/annual-interim-reports, last accessed October 1, 2019.

14. Kimberly Amadeo, "National Debt by Year Compared to GDP and Major Events," *Balance*, July 27, 2019, https://www.thebalance.com/national-debt-by-year-compared-to-gdp-and-major-events-3306287, last accessed October 1, 2019.

15. Nan Tian, Aude Fleurant, Alexandra Kuimova, Pieter Wezeman, and Siemon Wezeman, "Trends in World Military Expenditure, 2018," Stockholm International Peace Research Institute, April 2019, page 2, https://sipri.org/sites/default/files/2019-04/fs_1904_milex_2018_0.pdf, last accessed October 1, 2019.

16. Nicolas Kusnetz, "Rising Seas Threaten Norfolk Naval Shipyard, Raising Fears of 'Catastrophic Damage,'" NBC News, November 19, 2018, https://www.nbcnews.com/news/us-news/rising-seas-threaten-norfolk-naval-shipyard-raising-fears-catastrophic-damage-n937396, last accessed October 1, 2019.

17. Lockheed Martin's 2018 Form 10-K, Part I, page 9, https://www.lockheedmartin.com/content/dam/lockheed-martin/eo/documents/annual-reports/2018-annual-report.pdf, last accessed October 1, 2019.

18. Tian et al., "Trends in World Military Expenditure, 2018."

19. See General Dynamics "2Q19 Highlights and 2019 Outlook," July 24, 2019, page 7, https://s22.q4cdn.com/891946778/files/doc_financials/2019/q2/2Q19-GD-Earnings-Highlights-and-Outlook.pdf, last accessed October 1, 2019.

20. See TransDigm's Analyst Day presentation of June 28, 2018, https://www.transdigm.com/investor-relations/presentations/, last accessed October 1, 2019.

CHAPTER SEVEN

1. Mike Colias, "GM, Volkswagen Say Goodbye to Hybrid Vehicles," *Wall Street Journal*, August 12, 2019, https://www.wsj.com/articles/gm-volkswagen-say-goodbye-to-hybrid-vehicles-11565602200?mod=hp_lead_pos7, last accessed September 30, 2019.

2. Chester Dawson, Keith Naughton, and Gabrielle Coppola, "'They Don't Need Us Anymore': Auto Workers Fear Electric Unrest," Bloomberg.com, https://www.bloomberg.com/news/articles/2019-09-27/-they-don-t-need-us-anymore-auto-workers-fear-electric-unrest?cmpid=BBD092719_BIZ&utm_medium=email&utm_source=newsletter&utm_term=190927&utm_campaign=bloombergdaily, last accessed October 1, 2019.

3. Ryan Whitwam, "BMW, Porsche Demo Super-Fast Electric Car Charger," *ExtremeTech*, December 17, 2018, https://www.extremetech.com/extreme/282364-bmw-porsche-demo-super-fast-electric-car-charger, last accessed September 30, 2019.

4. David Stringer, "Fastest Electric Car Chargers Are Waiting for Batteries to Catch Up," *Bloomberg*, April 3, 2019, https://www.bloomberg.com/news/articles/2019-04-03/fastest-electric-car-chargers-waiting-for-batteries-to-catch-up, last accessed October 10, 2019.

5. Full disclosure: I drive a 310-mile range, dual-motor, all-wheel drive Tesla Model 3 with a 4.4 second 0–60 mph. It is an amazing vehicle. The current price of such a car on the company website is slightly less than $48,000, which falls to around $40,000 when gas savings are taken into account. This makes it cheaper than many comparable small luxury offerings from competitors such as BMW, Jaguar, Mercedes, Audi, Lexus, or Infiniti. The Tesla accelerates faster, has more nimble handling, is much quieter, and of course was significantly cheaper than the Maserati Ghibli driven by my wife (she of the large carbon footprint).

6. Autonomous self-driving cars may lower operating costs, allow the elderly to continue "driving," and result in higher auto ownership penetration rates (cheaper insurance, fewer accidents requiring repair, ease of use, etc.).

Or the technology may be expensive and lead to most people renting such transportation by the ride (as with Uber or Lyft) rather than buying a car. This discussion is outside the scope of this work.

7. Lithia Investor Presentation, July 2019, page 15, http://www.lithiainvestorrelations.com/LAD_Q219_InvestorPresentation.pdf, last accessed September 30, 2019.

8. Advance Auto Parts Form 10-K for 2018 page 3, http://www.annualreport.advanceauto.us/2018/AAP_2018_Form-10K.pdf, last accessed September 30, 2019.

9. Ibid., 6.

10. Ibid., 12.

11. William Boston, "Auto Supplier Continental Slams Brakes on Engine Parts Amid Shift to Electric," *Wall Street Journal*, August 7, 2019, https://www.wsj.com/articles/auto-parts-giant-continental-slams-brakes-on-engine-parts-amid-shift-to-electric-11565165087?emailToken=99843d4f2bb3c036fee663da12dc2bd2nJRl43m6XJZ+flAIDGdvGGEqPbXRsZJRjHsrOn8uPiM2PY GAqEzT6bbun2nzXIgpQP7AVWskwJB1Em/BKhjH0JaJ7STL7y2xetBnGbz-Rck625likiYD0wHeFG58Wxii0fIsDdRCnMvJcuF2IcAfH4g%3D%3D&reflink=article_email_share, last accessed September 30, 2019.

12. Ibid.

13. BorgWarner201810-K,page5,https://www.borgwarner.com/docs/default-source/investors/annual-reports/2018-bwa-annual-report.pdf?sfvrsn=25428c3c_8, last accessed September 30, 2019.

14. Claire Suddath, "Harley-Davidson Needs a New Generation of Riders," *Bloomberg Businessweek*, August 23, 2018, https://www.bloomberg.com/news/features/2018-08-23/harley-davidson-needs-a-new-generation-of-riders, last accessed October 10, 2019.

15. Harley-Davidson 2018 10-K, pages 4, 11, https://investor.harley-davidson.com/static-files/e0705aa3-25a7-409f-a8fc-5487789a6a71, last accessed September 30, 2019.

16. Harley-Davidson website: https://www.harley-davidson.com/us/en/motorcycles/future-vehicles/livewire.html, last accessed September 30, 2019.

17. Cummins 2018 10-K, page 31, http://investor.cummins.com/static-files/dd263f2c-186c-4791-8ccb-8cbc2384d447, last accessed September 30, 2019.

18. Ibid., 17.

19. Irene Kwan, "Planes, Trains and Automobiles: Counting Carbon," International Council on Clean Transportation, September 19, 2013, https://theicct.org/blogs/staff/planes-trains-and-automobiles-counting-carbon, last accessed September 30, 2019.

20. Air Transport Action Group, https://www.atag.org/facts-figures.html, last accessed October 10, 2019.

21. Douglas Broom, "Sweden Has Invented a Word to Encourage People Not to Fly. And It's Working," World Economic Forum, June 5, 2019, https://www.weforum.org/agenda/2019/06/sweden-has-invented-a-word-to-encourage-people-not-to-fly-and-it-s-working/, last accessed September 30, 2019.

22. Quentin Fottell and Jacob Passey, "Nearly 1,500 Private Jets to Land at Climate Change–Focused Davos Summit," *New York Post*, January 23, 2019, https://nypost.com/2019/01/23/nearly-1500-private-jets-to-land-at-climate-change-focused-davos-summit/, last accessed September 30, 2019.

23. "Air Travel Is Surging. That's a Huge Problem for the Climate," *Vox*, January 13, 2019, https://www.vox.com/energy-and-environment/2019/1/11/18177118/airlines-climate-change-emissions-travel, last accessed September 30, 2019.

24. U.S. Domestic Airline Fuel Efficiency Ranking, 2015–2016, The International Council on Clean Transportation, December 2017, https://theicct.org/sites/default/files/publications/US-Airline-Ranking-2015-16_ICCT-White-Paper_14122017_vF.pdf, last accessed September 29, 2019.

25. See the Alaska Airlines 2018 Investor Day Presentation, https://alaskaairgroupinc.gcs-web.com/static-files/94dea078-6b34-4db7-837a-452723220c5b, last accessed September 29, 2019.

CHAPTER EIGHT

1. For a map of temperate regions of the world see, https://en.wikipedia.org/wiki/K%C3%B6ppen_climate_classification, last accessed September 30, 2019.

2. "U.S. National Electrification Assessment," April 2018, Electric Power Research Institute, see pages 31–32, http://mydocs.epri.com/docs/PublicMeetingMaterials/ee/000000003002013582.pdf.

3. Ibid., see 39.

4. "Infographic: U.S. Businesses Need More Renewable Energy from the Grid," World Resources Institute, May 17, 2017, https://www.wri.org/resources/data-visualizations/infographic-us-businesses-need-more-renewable-energy-grid, last accessed October 10, 2019.

5. "Primary Energy Overview," Eia.gov, https://www.eia.gov/totalenergy/data/monthly/pdf/sec1_3.pdf, last accessed October 10, 2019, and "Real Gross Domestic Product (GPD) of the United States of America from 1990 to 2018 in billion chained (2012) U.S. dollars," July 19, 2019, https://www.statista.com/statistics/188141/annual-real-gdp-of-the-united-states-since-1990-in-chained-us-dollars/, last accessed October 10, 2019.

6. Rod Walton, "Ten Years After: How Entergy New Orleans Survived Hurricane Katrina," *Electric Light & Power*, August 24, 2015, https://www. elp.com/articles/2015/08/ten-years-after-how-entergy-new-orleans-survived-hurricane-katrina.html, last accessed October 10, 2019.

7. Greg LaRose, "Entergy Louisiana Customer Bills Lower as Katrina-Rita Recovery Debt Is Paid Off," *Times-Picayune*, August 2, 2018, https://www. nola.com/news/business/article_be41687e-9a56-5016-b962-23d80b891606. html, last accessed October 10, 2019.

8. "Storm Restoration FAQ," Entergy corporate website, https://www. entergy-louisiana.com/storm_costs/, last accessed October 10, 2019.

9. Russell Gold, "PG&E: The First Climate-Change Bankruptcy, Probably Not the Last," *Wall Street Journal*, January 18, 2019, https://www.wsj.com/ articles/pg-e-wildfires-and-the-first-climate-change-bankruptcy-11547820006, last accessed January 18, 2019.

10. See PG&E website "Delivering Low-Emission Energy," https://www. pge.com/en_US/about-pge/environment/what-we-are-doing/clean-energy-solutions/clean-energy-solutions.page, last accessed October 10, 2019.

11. Russell Gold, Katherine Blunt, and Rebecca Smith, "PG&E Sparked at Least 1,500 Califonia Fires. Now the Utility Faces Collapse," *Wall Street Journal*, January 13, 2019, https://www.wsj.com/articles/pg-e-sparked-at-least-1-500-california-fires-now-the-utility-faces-collapse-11547410768, last accessed October 10, 2019.

12. The Public Utility Holding Company Act (PUHCA) prevents utility companies from subsidizing unregulated businesses with profits from guaranteed-return regulated revenue streams. This law precludes utilities from setting up IPP subsidiaries that sell power to that same utility as inflated inter-company pricing could be used to subsidize the IPP operations.

13. "Xcel Energy Aims for Zero-Carbon Electricity by 2050," Xcel Energy corporate website, December 4, 2018, https://www.xcelenergy.com/company/ media_room/news_releases/xcel_energy_aims_for_zero-carbon_electricity_ by_2050, last accessed October 1, 2019.

14. See Xcel Energy's Carbon Report of February 2019, https://www.xcelenergy.com/staticfiles/xe/PDF/Xcel%20Energy%20Carbon%20Report%20 -%20Feb%202019.pdf, last accessed October 10, 2019.

15. Xcel Energy website, "Our Power Supply," https://www.xcelenergy. com/energy_portfolio/electricity/power_generation, last accessed October 10, 2019.

16. Emma Foehringer Merchant, "Developers Struggle to Find a Way in as Florida's Utility-Scale Solar Market Shines," Greentech Media, July 18, 2019, https://www.greentechmedia.com/articles/read/a-look-at-floridas-rise-to-the-top-of-utility-scale-solar-rankings, last accessed October 10, 2019.

17. Ivan Penn, "Florida's Utilities Keep Homeowners from Making the Most of Solar Power," *New York Times*, July 7, 2019, https://www.nytimes.com/2019/07/07/business/energy-environment/florida-solar-power.html, last accessed September 30, 2019, and Jerry Iannelli, "Florida Lawmaker Again Files Bill That Would Help Break Monopoly-Solar Stranglehold," *Miami New Times*, January 4, 2019, https://www.miaminewtimes.com/news/bill-would-help-break-floridas-solar-panel-stranglehold-10971356, last accessed September 30, 2019.

18. NextEra 2018 10-K report, page 118, http://otp.investis.com/clients/us/nextera_energy_inc/SEC/sec-show.aspx?FilingId=13234910&Cik=0000753308&Type=PDF&hasPdf=1, last accessed October 10, 2019.

19. Duke Energy 2018 10-K, page 12, https://dukeenergy.gcs-web.com/static-files/949f8829-4535-4cf4-bd11-e15545073562, last accessed October 1, 2019.

20. Data on expected earnings growth from the NASDAQ website as of August 30, 2019. See https://www.nasdaq.com/symbol/duk/earnings-growth and https://www.nasdaq.com/symbol/nee/earnings-growth, last accessed August 30, 2019.

21. CMS Energy 2019 ESG Report, https://s2.q4cdn.com/027997281/files/doc_presentations/2019/06/ESG-2019.pdf, last accessed October 1, 2019.

22. Edward Murphy, "Canadian Hydropower Supplier Says It Has Plenty of Capacity for New England," *Press Herald*, December 6, 2018, https://www.pressherald.com/2018/12/06/canadian-hydropower-supplier-says-it-has-plenty-of-capacity-for-n-e/, last accessed October 10, 2019.

23. I have had the pleasure of attending school and working at jobs in both southern New England and east Texas. Yes, it is hot in August in Boston, but working outside there is a piece of cake compared to laboring in the heat of a Houston summer, which seems to last from late April to sometime in November.

24. Data from Bloomberg.com as of February 12, 2020.

CHAPTER NINE

1. To be fair, just as often, I have received eye rolls, guffaws, and slow shakes of the head when bringing up the subject of this volume with "professional" stock pickers. Of course, most of these men and women spend all their time trying to figure out if next quarter's earnings for a stock will be $1.11 or $1.13. Thus, we shouldn't be surprised that they have little interest in longer-term trends. That, of course, is the opportunity for brilliant investors now in possession of a lawfully purchased copy of this book.

2. Ben Winck, "Morgan Stanley: These 7 Pharma Companies Will Be Critical to Fighting Infectious Diseases Brought on by Climate Change," *Markets Insider*, July 25, 2019, https://markets.businessinsider.com/news/stocks/7-biopharma-companies-most-critical-for-fighting-tropical-diseases-2019-7-1028384776#glaxosmithkline2, last accessed October 10, 2019.

3. "Climate Change and Health," World Health Organization, February 1, 2018, https://www.who.int/en/news-room/fact-sheets/detail/climate-change-and-health, last accessed October 1, 2019.

4. "Vaccine Market Analysis—Technavio Vaccination Report Portfolio and Segmentation Analysis," https://www.technavio.com/research/vaccine-market-analysis, last accessed September 13, 2019.

5. "Revenue of the Worldwide Pharmaceutical Market from 2001 to 2018 (in Billion U.S. Dollars)," Statistica, June 5, 2019, https://www.statista.com/statistics/263102/pharmaceutical-market-worldwide-revenue-since-2001/, last accessed September 13, 2019.

6. See "Pharmaceutical Industry Overview: Trends, Risks, Opportunities & Deals," investmentbank.com, https://investmentbank.com/pharma-industry-overview/, last accessed September 26, 2019.

7. "Here's How Much Your Healthcare Costs Will Rise as You Age," from US Department of Health & Human Services MEPS data, last accessed September 13, 2019, https://www.registerednursing.org/healthcare-costs-by-age/, last accessed October 10, 2019.

8. John Miller, "Chinese Envoy Says Syngenta Takeover Was a Bad Deal: Report," *Reuters*, June 29, 2019, https://www.reuters.com/article/us-swiss-syngenta-china/chinese-envoy-says-syngenta-takeover-was-a-bad-deal-report-idUSKCN1TU0E0, last accessed October 10, 2019.

9. See DowDupont 2018 Form 10–K, page 195, https://s23.q4cdn.com/116192123/files/doc_financials/2018/DOWDUPONT-2018-10-K-Final-02.11.19.pdf, last accessed October 10, 2019.

10. FMC Investor Day Presentation 2018, page 7, https://fmccorp.gcs-web.com/static-files/185261d4-923a-44bf-aad8-9bc858c54f9a, last accessed September 16, 2019.

11. Ibid., EMEA = Europe, Middle East, Africa.

12. For decades its ticker generated knowing chuckles across the investment community. When the company decided to merge with Agrium, the ticker was in high demand (see what I did there), and eventually it landed with a small company called Weekend Unlimited, which sells bongs and pipes and other cannabis-related paraphernalia.

13. You have never truly been cold until you have traveled to Saskatoon in February to sell mutual funds.

14. As of 2015, the populations of several nations actually spent less than 10 percent of consumer expenditures on food: including the United States,

Switzerland, Canada, Singapore, Germany, the UK, Ireland, and Australia as per the World Economic Forum. I am guessing, from unscientific personal experience in visiting the last four of these boozy nations, that this data does not include money spent on alcohol. Alex Gray, "Which Countries Spend the Most on Food? This Map Will Show You," World Economic Forum, December 7, 2016, https://www.weforum.org/agenda/2016/12/this-map-shows-how-much-each-country-spends-on-food/, last accessed September 16, 2019.

15. See for example, Vikram Mansharamani, "Could Lithium Become the New Oil?" *PBS NewsHour*, October 15, 2015, https://www.pbs.org/newshour/economy/lithium-become-new-oil, last accessed September 16, 2019, or Peter Tertzakian, "Lithium May Be the New Oil, But a Double Whammy Looms for the Battery Market," *Financial Post*, July 25, 2017, https://business.financialpost.com/commodities/energy/lithium-may-be-the-new-oil-but-theres-a-double-whammy-looming-for-the-new-energy-source, last accessed October 10, 2019.

16. See for example, "How Electric Vehicle Batteries Are Reused or Recycled," July 23, 2018, Fleetcarma, https://www.fleetcarma.com/electric-vehicle-batteries-reused-recycled/, last accessed September 17, 2019.

17. EnerSys September 2019 Investor Presentation, pages 6 and 35, https://investor.enersys.com/static-files/6c842d43-f5e3-4367-a736-c7aba28d03f5, last accessed September 17, 2019.

18. Albemarle Investor Presentation September 2019, page 4, https://investors.albemarle.com/static-files/75e6a065-d30e-42d8-a05c-b1bc27fddfee, last accessed September 16, 2019.

19. ALB stock rose more than 790 percent from January 3, 2000, to January 2, 2019, compared to a 100 percent increase in the S&P 500 over the same period. However, in the two years ending September 2, 2019, the stock declined by 46 percent compared to a 22 percent gain in the S&P 500. Data as per Yahoo! Finance, last accessed September 16, 2019.

20. SQM Corporate Presentation, August 2019, page 6, http://s1.q4cdn.com/793210788/files/doc_presentations/2019/08/New-presentation_august 2019_website_final.pdf, last accessed September 15, 2019.

21. See the June 30, 2019, LIT fact sheet, page 1, https://cdn.globalxetfs.com/content/files/LIT-factsheet.pdf, last accessed September 15, 2019.

22. See the Wikipedia entry on geothermal power, https://en.wikipedia.org/wiki/Geothermal_power#cite_note-:0-4, last accessed September 17, 2019.

23. "DOE Releases New Study Highlighting the Untapped Potential of Geothermal Energy in the United States," US Department of Energy, May 30, 2019, https://www.energy.gov/articles/doe-releases-new-study-highlighting-untapped-potential-geothermal-energy-united-states, last accessed September 17, 2019.

CHAPTER TEN

1. Colin Kelley, Mohtadi Shahrzad, Mark Cane, Richard Seager, and Yochanan Kushnir, "Climate Change in the Fertile Crescent and Implications of the Recent Syrian Drought," *Proceedings of the National Academy of Sciences*, March 17, 2015, https://www.pnas.org/content/112/11/3241, last accessed October 1, 2019.

2. Lotten Wirehn, "Nordic Agriculture under Climate Change," Land Use Policy, September 2018, see: https://www.sciencedirect.com/science/article/abs/pii/S0264837717308293, last accessed October 10, 2019.

3. Renewables include hydro, wind, solar, geothermal, and biomass. Wikipedia: https://en.wikipedia.org/wiki/List_of_countries_by_electricity_production_from_renewable_sources, and https://en.wikipedia.org/wiki/Nuclear_power_by_country, last accessed October 1, 2019.

4. See the iShares website: https://www.ishares.com/us/products/etf-product-list#!type=ishares&tab=overview&view=list&fr=43522, last accessed April 15, 2019.

5. Michigan State University's globalEDGE website utilizing World Bank data. See: https://globaledge.msu.edu/comparator/home/results?year=&field =SP-POP-TOTL&field=SP-URB-TOTL-IN-ZS&field=EN-POP-DNST& field=NY-GDP-PCAP-PP-CD&field=EG-ELC-PROD-KH&country =155&country=4, last accessed September 30, 2019.

6. For a discussion of Australia's ecological fragility, see chapter 13 of Jared Diamond, *Collapse* (New York: Viking Press, 2005).

7. "New Maps Highlight Changes Coming to Canada's Climate," Prairie Climate Center, http://prairieclimatecentre.ca/2017/10/new-map-series-highlights-changes-coming-to-canadas-climate/, last accessed October 19, 2017.

8. "Cold Deemed Deadlier Than Heat When It Comes to Weather Deaths," May 20, 2015, CBC News, https://www.cbc.ca/news/health/cold-deemed-deadlier-than-heat-when-it-comes-to-weather-deaths-1.3081053, last accessed October 10, 2019.

9. This includes nuclear, hydro, solar, wind, and more. Source: Michigan State University's globalEDGE website utilizing World Bank data. https://globaledge.msu.edu/comparator/home/results?year=&field=SP-POP-TOTL&field=SP-URB-TOTL-IN-ZS&field=EN-POP-DNST&field=NY-GDP-PCAP-PP-CD&field=EG-ELC-PROD-KH&country=155&country=4, last accessed September 30, 2019.

10. National Resources Canada: Energy Fact Book 2018–2019, https://www.nrcan.gc.ca/sites/www.nrcan.gc.ca/files/energy/pdf/energy-factbook-oct2-2018%20(1).pdf, last accessed October 10, 2019.

11. Energy.gov.au, "Australian Energy Statistics, Table O Electricity Generation by Fuel Type 2017–2018 and 2018," https://www.energy.gov.

au/publications/australian-energy-statistics-table-o-electricity-generation-fuel-type-2017-18-and-2018, last accessed October 10, 2019.

12. Data from "World's Top Exports" website: http://www.worldstopexports.com/, last accessed September 30, 2019.

13. "Australia—Agricultural Land (% of Land Area)," Trading Economics, https://tradingeconomics.com/australia/agricultural-land-percent-of-land-area-wb-data.html, last accessed October 10, 2019.

14. Statistics Canada, https://www150.statcan.gc.ca/n1/daily-quotidien/170510/cg170510a002-eng.csv, last accessed October 10, 2019.

15. "Warmer Earth Greener North," NASA, https://climate.nasa.gov/climate_resources/3/graphic-warmer-earth-greener-north/, last accessed October 10, 2019.

16. iShares website: https://www.ishares.com/us/products/239607/ishares-msci-australia-etf, and https://www.ishares.com/us/products/239615/ishares-msci-canada-etf as of April 16, 2019.

17. See Wikipedia, "List of Largest Cities in Brazil": https://en.wikipedia.org/wiki/List_of_largest_cities_in_Brazil, last accessed September 30, 2019.

18. Data from the iShares websites: https://www.ishares.com/us/products/239689/ishares-msci-turkey-etf and https://www.ishares.com/us/products/239663/ishares-msci-israel-capped-etf, last accessed September 30, 2019.

CONCLUSION

1. A shameless plug for my recent book: James Ellman, *Hitler's Great Gamble* (Lanham, MD: Stackpole Books, 2019).

2. It is difficult to say if Mr. Brechbuhl will still be Counselor of the United States Department of State by the time this book is published. The tenure of a job in the Trump Administration is . . . uncertain. He certainly still held the position when this was written. He was identified in a 2019 whistleblower complaint as being one of those on the phone line during President Trump's famous conversation with Ukrainian president Volodymyr Zelensky. He also refused to appear after being subpoenaed by the House Intelligence Committee. Thus, Ulrich has guaranteed himself at least a small footnote in the historical record. See Wikipedia, https://en.wikipedia.org/wiki/Ulrich_Brechbuhl, last accessed September 27, 2019.

Bibliography

AAA. "1 in 5 US Drivers Want Electric Vehicles." https://newsroom.aaa.com/2018/05/1-in-5-us-drivers-want-electric-vehicle/, last accessed October 1, 2019.

Advance Auto Parts Form 10-K for 2018 page 3. http://www.annual-report.advanceauto.us/2018/AAP_2018_Form-10K.pdf, last accessed September 30, 2019.

Air Transport Action Group. https://www.atag.org/facts-figures.html, last accessed October 10, 2019.

Alaska Airlines 2018 Investor Day Presentation. https://alaskaairgroupinc.gcs-web.com/static-files/94dea078-6b34-4db7-837a-452723220c5b, last accessed September 29, 2019.

Albemarle Investor Presentation September 2019, page 4. https://investors.albemarle.com/static-files/75e6a065-d30e-42d8-a05c-b1bc27fddfee, last accessed September 16, 2019.

Amdao, Kimberly. "National Debt by Year Compared to GDP and Major Events." *Balance*, July 27, 2019. https://www.thebalance.com/national-debt-by-year-compared-to-gdp-and-major-events-3306287, last accessed October 1, 2019.

American Society of Civil Engineers' "2017 Infrastructure Report Card." https://www.infrastructurereportcard.org/the-impact/economic-impact/, last accessed October 1, 2019.

Appell, David, using IPCC data. https://davidappell.blogspot.com/2013/10/epa-sued-to-stop-pacnw-ocean.html, last accessed May 24, 2018.

Arcadis Annual Integrated Report 2018, page 16. https://www.arcadis.com/media/A/D/3/%7BAD3625A8-E667-4A03-9071-72EB7AE03426%7

DArcadis%20Annual%20Integrated%20Report%202018-spreads.pdf, last accessed October 1, 2019.

Australian Department of Energy. "Australian Energy Statistics, Table of Electricity Generation by Fuel Type 2017–2018 and 2018." https://www. energy.gov.au/publications/australian-energy-statistics-table-o-electricity-generation-fuel-type-2017-18-and-2018, last accessed October 10, 2019.

"AXA Accelerates Its Commitment to Fight Climate Change." December 12, 2017. https://www.axa.com/en/newsroom/press-releases/axa-accelerates-its-commitment-to-fight-climate-change, last accessed October 9, 2019.

Azure Power investor presentation of February 13, 2019, page 13. http://investors.azurepower.com/~/media/Files/A/Azure-Power-IR/documents/events/q3-2019-earnings-call/apgl-3q19-earnings-presentation.pdf, last accessed October 9, 2019.

Banbace, L. A. W., F. M. Ramos, I. B. T. Lima, and R. R. Rosa. "Mitigation and Recovery of Methane Emissions from Tropical Hydroelectric Dams." *ScienceDirect*, June 2007. https://www.sciencedirect.com/science/article/abs/pii/S0360544206002611?via%3Dihub, last accessed September 20, 2019.

Better Business Bureau. https://www.bbb.org/us/ut/lehi/profile/solar-energy-contractors/vivint-solar-1166-22302389, last accessed September 30, 2019.

Bloomberg NEF data for each of the three years. https://about.bnef.com/blog/vestas-reclaims-top-spot-annual-ranking-wind-turbine-makers/; https://www.bloomberg.com/news/articles/2018-02-26/these-four-power-giants-rule-the-world-s-growing-wind-market; https://about.bnef.com/blog/vestas-leads-break-away-group-big-four-turbine-makers/, last accessed October 9, 2019.

Bloomberg New Energy Finance Outlook 2018. https://about.bnef.com/new-energy-outlook/, last accessed May 1, 2019.

BorgWarner 2018 10-K page 5. https://www.borgwarner.com/docs/default-source/investors/annual-reports/2018-bwa-annual-report.pdf?sfvrsn=25428c3c_8, last accessed September 30, 2019.

Boston, William. "Auto Supplier Continental Slams Brakes on Engine Parts Amid Shift to Electric." *Wall Street Journal*, August 7, 2019. https://www.wsj.com/articles/auto-parts-giant-continental-slams-brakes-on-engine-parts-amid-shift-to-electric-11565165087?emailToken=99843d4f2bb3c036fee66 3da12dc2bd2nJRl43m6XJZ+flAIDGdvGGEqPbXRsZJRjHsrOn8uPiM2PY GAqEzT6bbun2nzXIgpQP7AVWskwJB1Em/BKhjH0JaJ7STL7y2xetBnG-bzRck625likiYD0wHeFG58Wxii0flsDdRCnMvJcuF2IcAfH4g%3D%3D& reflink=article_email_share, last accessed September 30, 2019.

"BP Energy Outlook 2018 Edition," page 12. https://www.bp.com/content/dam/bp/en/corporate/pdf/energy-economics/energy-outlook/bp-energy-outlook-2018.pdf, last accessed September 19, 2019.

Bradsher, Keith. "To Conquer Wind Power, China Writes the Rules." *New York Times*, December 15, 2010. https://www.nytimes.com/2010/12/15/business/global/15chinawind.html, last accessed October 9, 2019.

Brookfield company presentation from September 26, 2018, pages 54–55. https://bep.brookfield.com/~/media/Files/B/Brookfield-BEP-IR/events-and-presentations/investor-day/2018/2018-bep-investor-day-presentation-vf.pdf, last accessed October 9, 2019.

Broom, Douglas. "Sweden Has Invented a Word to Encourage People Not to Fly. And It's Working." World Economic Forum, June 5, 2019. https://www.weforum.org/agenda/2019/06/sweden-has-invented-a-word-to-encourage-people-not-to-fly-and-it-s-working/, last accessed September 30, 2019.

Cabot Oil and Gas Corp reports and presentations. See the 2018 third-quarter earnings presentation, and the 2017 10-K. http://phx.corporate-ir.net/phoenix.zhtml?c=116492&p=irol-calendar, http://phx.corporate-ir.net/phoenix.zhtml?c=116492&p=irol-sec, last accessed September 19, 2019.

Camden's 6/3/19 Investor Presentation, page 14. https://investors.camdenliving.com/Cache/1001253190.PDF?O=PDF&T=&Y=&D=&FID=1001253190&iid=103094, last accessed October 1, 2019.

Canadian Solar's 2018 Annual Report, pages 40, 41, 46, 95, 96, 97. http://investors.canadiansolar.com/static-files/f5df404b-6f97-4027-8be3-db-57c5bb35d6, last accessed October 9, 2019.

Carbon Tracker Initiative. "2020 Vision: Why You Should See the Fossil Fuel Peak Coming." September 19, 2018. https://www.carbontracker.org/reports/2020-vision-why-you-should-see-the-fossil-fuel-peak-coming/, last accessed September 30, 2019.

Carey, Bjorn. "Offshore Wind Energy Could Power Entire U.S. East Coast, Stanford Scientists Say." *Stanford News*, September 14, 2012. https://news.stanford.edu/news/2012/september/offshore-wind-energy-091412.html, last accessed October 9, 2019.

Carrington, Damien. "BBC Admits 'We Get Climate Change Coverage Wrong Too Often.'" *Guardian*, September 7, 2018. https://www.theguardian.com/environment/2018/sep/07/bbc-we-get-climate-change-coverage-wrong-too-often, last accessed October 9, 2019.

CBS News. "Cold Deemed Deadlier Than Heat When It Comes to Weather Deaths." May 20, 2015. https://www.cbc.ca/news/health/cold-deemed-deadlier-than-heat-when-it-comes-to-weather-deaths-1.3081053, last accessed October 10, 2019.

Chandran, Rina. "Can Philippine Storm Survivors Hold Major Companies Responsible for Contributing to Climate Change?" Reuters, May 22, 2018. https://www.reuters.com/article/us-philippines-climatechange-lawmaking-a/can-philippines-storm-survivors-hold-companies-to-account-for-climate-damage-idUSKBN1GY04V, last accessed October 1, 2019.

China National Energy Administration. "The Total Investment Scale of Renewable Energy during the 13th Five-Year Plan Period Will Reach 2.5 Trillion Yuan." January 5, 2017. http://www.nea.gov.cn/2017-01/05/c_135956835. htm, last accessed October 9, 2019.

Climate Central. April 19, 2019. https://www.climatecentral.org/gallery/graphics/how-your-city-state-and-country-is-warming, last accessed October 1, 2019.

Climate Central. https://ss2.climatecentral.org/#12/40.7298/-74.0070?show= satellite&projections=0-K14_RCP85-SLR&level=5&unit=feet&pois=hide, last accessed September 15, 2019.

CMS Energy 2019 ESG Report. https://s2.q4cdn.com/027997281/files/doc_ presentations/2019/06/ESG-2019.pdf, last accessed October 1, 2019.

Colias, Mike. "GM, Volkswagen Say Goodbye to Hybrid Vehicles." *Wall Street Journal*, August 12, 2019. https://www.wsj.com/articles/gm-volkswagen-say-goodbye-to-hybrid-vehicles-11565602200?mod=hp_lead_pos7, last accessed September 30, 2019.

Congressional Budget Office report of 10/18, page 4. https://www.cbo.gov/system/files/2018-10/54539-Infrastructure.pdf, last accessed October 1, 2019.

Cornwall, Warren. "Hundreds of New Dams Could Mean Trouble for Our Climate." *Science*, September 28, 2016. http://www.sciencemag.org/news/2016/09/hundreds-new-dams-could-mean-trouble-our-climate, last accessed September 30, 2019.

Cummins 2018 10-K page 31. http://investor.cummins.com/static-files/dd263f2c-186c-4791-8ccb-8cbc2384d447, last accessed September 30, 2019.

Current Results. https://www.currentresults.com/Yearly-Weather/USA/FL/Tampa/extreme-annual-tampa-high-temperature.php, last accessed October 1, 2019.

Danigelis, Alyssa. "Global Onshore Wind Turbine Commissioning Declined in 2018." February 15, 2019. Environment + Energy Leader. https://www.energymanagertoday.com/onshore-wind-turbine-commissioning-0181542/, last accessed October 9, 2019.

Dawson, Chester, Keith Naughton, and Gabrielle Coppola. "'They Don't Need Us Anymore': Auto Workers Fear Electric Unrest." Bloomberg.com. https://www.bloomberg.com/news/articles/2019-09-27/-they-don-t-need-us-anymore-auto-workers-fear-electric-unrest?cmpid=BBD092719_BIZ&utm_ medium=email&utm_source=newsletter&utm_term=190927&utm_ campaign=bloombergdaily, last accessed October 1, 2019.

Diamond, Jared. *Collapse*. New York: Viking Press, 2005.

DNL-GL. "Energy Transition Outlook 2018." https://eto.dnvgl.com/2018/ download, last accessed September 19, 2019.

Doffman, Zak. "China's Spies Accused of Stealing EU Tech Secrets, Just as China and EU Agree Stronger Ties." *Forbes*, April 11, 2019. https://www.forbes.com/sites/zakdoffman/2019/04/11/chinese-spies-accused-of-major-european-ip-theft-just-as-china-and-europe-agree-stronger-ties/#51cc010470f4, last accessed October 9, 2019.

DowDupont 2018 Form 10-K, page 195. https://s23.q4cdn.com/116192123/files/doc_financials/2018/DOWDUPONT-2018-10-K-Final-02.11.19.pdf, last accessed October 10, 2019.

Drake, Bruce. "How Americans View the Top Energy and Environmental Issues." http://www.pewresearch.org/fact-tank/2015/01/15/environment-energy-2/, last accessed July 7, 2018.

Duke Energy 2018 10-K, page 12. https://dukeenergy.gcs-web.com/static-files/949f8829-4535-4cf4-bd11-e15545073562, last accessed October 1, 2019.

Eberhard, Kristin. "Map: The Future Is Carbo-Priced and the US Is Getting Left Behind." Sightline Institute. https://www.sightline.org/2017/06/06/map-the-future-is-carbon-priced-and-the-us-is-getting-left-behind/, last accessed October 9, 2019.

Electric Power Research Institute. "U.S. National Electrification Assessment." April 2018. See pages 31–32. http://mydocs.epri.com/docs/PublicMeeting-Materials/ee/000000003002013582.pdf, last accessed October 1, 2019.

Elliot, Rebecca. "In Booming Oilfield Natural Gas Can Be Free." *Wall Street Journal*, December 27, 2018. https://www.wsj.com/articles/in-booming-oilfield-natural-gas-can-be-free-11545906601, last accessed September 15, 2019.

Energy and Policy Institute. "Property Values Not Hurt by Wind Farms." April 13, 2014. https://www.energyandpolicy.org/wind-energy-does-not-hurt-property-values/, last accessed October 9, 2019.

Energysage. https://news.energysage.com/much-solar-panels-save/, last accessed October 9, 2019.

Energystar. https://www.energystar.gov/about/origins_mission/energy_star_numbers, last accessed October 9, 2019.

EnerSys September 2019 Investor Presentation, pages 6 and 35. https://investor.enersys.com/static-files/6c842d43-f5e3-4367-a736-c7aba28d03f5, last accessed September 17, 2019.

Entergy. "Storm Restoration FAQ." https://www.entergy-louisiana.com/storm_costs/, last accessed October 10, 2019.

Environmental Protection Agency. https://www.epa.gov/climate-indicators/climate-change-indicators-sea-surface-temperature, last accessed May 24, 2018.

Environmental Protection Agency. https://www.epa.gov/climate-indicators/climate-change-indicators-sea-level, last accessed May 22, 2018.

Erickson, Wallace, Melissa Wolfe, Kimberly Bay, Douglas Johnson, and Joelee Gehrin. "A Comprehensive Analysis of Small-Passerine Fatalities from Collision with Turbines at Wind Energy Facilities." *PlosOne*. https://journals. plos.org/plosone/article?id=10.1371/journal.pone.0107491#pone.0107491-Loss3, last accessed October 9, 2019.

ExxonMobil's 2017 10-K, pages 108–18. https://corporate.exxonmobil.com/en/company/investors, last accessed October 1, 2019.

Fink, Larry. "A Sense of Purpose." BlackRock investor relations. https://www.blackrock.com/corporate/investor-relations/larry-fink-ceo-letter, last accessed July 13, 2018.

Fleetcarma. "How Electric Vehicle Batteries Are Reused or Recycled." July 23, 2018. https://www.fleetcarma.com/electric-vehicle-batteries-reused-recycled/, last accessed September 17, 2019.

Fleurant, Nan Tian, Alexandra Kuimova, Pieter Wezeman, and Siemon Wezeman. "Trends in World Military Expenditure, 2018." Stockholm International Peace Research Institute, April 2019, page 2. https://sipri.org/sites/default/files/2019-04/fs_1904_milex_2018_0.pdf, last accessed October 1, 2019.

Florida Office of Insurance Regulation. https://www.floir.com/, last accessed October 2019.

FMC Investor Day Presentation 2018, page 7. https://fmccorp.gcs-web.com/static-files/185261d4-923a-44bf-aad8-9bc858c54f9a, last accessed September 16, 2019.

Fortune Business Insights. "Offshore Wind Power Market to Reach a Capacity of 94 GW by 2026, at a CAGR of 19.2%." June 6, 2019. https://www.bloomberg.com/press-releases/2019-06-06/offshore-wind-power-market-to-reach-a-capacity-of-94-gw-by-2026-at-a-cagr-of-19-2-exclusive-report-by-fortune-business, last accessed October 9, 2019.

Fossil Free, a project of 350.org. https://gofossilfree.org/divestment/commitments/, last accessed September 23, 2019.

Fottell, Quentin, and Jacob Passey. "Nearly 1,500 Private Jets to Land at Climate Change–Focused Davos Summit." *New York Post*, January 23, 2019. https://nypost.com/2019/01/23/nearly-1500-private-jets-to-land-at-climate-change-focused-davos-summit/, last accessed September 30, 2019.

Fourth National Climate Assessment. https://nca2018.globalchange.gov/chapter/1/, last accessed October 9, 2019.

Funk, Cary, and Meg Hefferon. "Many Republican Millennials Differ with Older Party Members on Climate Change and Energy Issues." Pew Research Center, http://www.pewresearch.org/fact-tank/2018/05/14/many-republican-millennials-differ-with-older-party-members-on-climate-change-and-energy-issues/, last accessed July 7, 2018.

GC Securities Proprietary Database. https://www.gccapitalideas. com/2018/03/08/chart-catastrophe-bond-issuance-and-capital-outstanding-2/, last accessed September 25, 2019.

General Dynamics "2019 Highlights and 2019 Outlook." July 24, 2019, page 7. https://s22.q4cdn.com/891946778/files/doc_financials/2019/q2/2Q19-GD-Earnings-Highlights-and-Outlook.pdf, last accessed October 1, 2019.

George, Libby, and Ahmad Ghaddar. "New Rules on Ship Emissions Herald Sea Change for Oil Markets." Reuters, May 17, 2018. https://www.reuters. com/article/us-shipping-fuel-sulphur/new-rules-on-ship-emissions-herald-sea-change-for-oil-market-idUSKCN1II0PP, last accessed October 1, 2019.

Global Carbon Project. https://docs.google.com/spreadsheets/d/10ZkDgDD OHaZPAKkN_JWVz1d56DDgLVnUOWnSdNXqTl0/edit#gid=0, last accessed September 23, 2019.

Gold, Russell. "PG&E: The First Climate-Change Bankruptcy, Probably Not the Last." *Wall Street Journal*, January 18, 2019. https://www.wsj.com/articles/pg-e-wildfires-and-the-first-climate-change-bankruptcy-11547820006, last accessed January 18, 2019.

Gold, Russell, Katherine Blunt, and Rebecca Smith. "PG&E Sparked at Least 1,500 California Fires. Now the Utility Faces Collapse." *Wall Street Journal*, January 13, 2019. https://www.wsj.com/articles/pg-e-sparked-at-least-1-500-california-fires-now-the-utility-faces-collapse-11547410768, last accessed October 10, 2019.

Goldwind's 2018 results presentation pages 13–14. http://106.38.64.54:8080/goldwind-en/upload/files/20190424093517cjE3TWnj.pdf, last accessed October 9, 2019.

Gould, Tim, and Christophe McGlade. "Crunching the Numbers—Are We Heading for an Oil Supply Shock?" International Energy Agency, November 16, 2018. https://www.iea.org/newsroom/news/2018/november/crunching-the-numbers-are-we-heading-for-an-oil-supply-shock-1.html, last accessed September 20, 2019.

Governor's Office of Planning and Research, State Government of California. http://www.opr.ca.gov/facts/list-of-scientific-organizations.html, last accessed May 22, 2018.

Gray, Alex. "Which Countries Spend the Most on Food? This Map Will Show You." World Economic Forum, September 7, 2016. https://www.weforum. org/agenda/2016/12/this-map-shows-how-much-each-country-spends-on-food/, last accessed September 16, 2019.

Green Dot Bioplastics. "What Growth in Bioplastics Industry Means for Investors and the Economy." https://www.greendotbioplastics.com/growth-bioplastics-industry-means-investors-economy/, last accessed October 1, 2019.

Greenberg, Jon. "Donald Trump's Ridiculous Link between Cancer, Wind Turbines." Politifact. https://www.politifact.com/truth-o-meter/statements/2019/

apr/08/donald-trump/republicans-dismiss-trumps-windmill-and-cancer-cla/, last accessed October 9, 2019.

Griffin, Dr. Paul. "The Carbon Majors Database." Climate Accountability Institute, July 2019, page 6. https://b8f65cb373b1b7b15feb-c70d8ead-6ced550b4d987d7c03fcdd1d.ssl.cf3.rackcdn.com/cms/reports/documents/000/002/327/original/Carbon-Majors-Report-2017.pdf?1499691240, last accessed September 19, 2019.

Harley-Davidson 2018 10-K, pages 4, 11. https://investor.harley-davidson.com/static-files/e0705aa3-25a7-409f-a8fc-5487789a6a71, last accessed September 30, 2019.

Harley-Davidson. https://www.harley-davidson.com/us/en/motorcycles/future-vehicles/livewire.html, last accessed September 30, 2019.

Harvey, Chelsea. "United Airlines Is Flying on Biofuels. Here's Why That's a Really Big Deal." *Washington Post*, March 11, 2016. https://www.washingtonpost.com/news/energy-environment/wp/2016/03/11/united-airlines-is-flying-on-biofuels-heres-why-thats-a-really-big-deal/?noredirect=on&utm_term=.bfd7cbf3389b, last accessed October 1, 2019.

Higgins, Steven, and Simon Scheiter. "Atmospheric CO_2 Forces Abrupt Vegetation Shifts Locally, But Not Globally." *Nature*, June 27, 2012. https://www.nature.com/articles/nature11238, last accessed October 1, 2019.

Hotz, Robert Lee. "Climate Change Drives Fish into New Waters, Remaking an Industry." *Wall Street Journal*, December 22, 2018. https://www.wsj.com/articles/climate-change-drives-fish-into-new-waters-remaking-an-industry-11545454860?ns=prod/accounts-wsj, last accessed October 9, 2019.

HSBC press release. https://www.hsbc.com/news-and-insight/insight-archive/2018/hsbc-strengthens-energy-policy, last accessed June 12, 2018.

Huang, Echo. "Here's One Number That Shows the Craze for Electric Vehicles in China." *Quartz*, June 11, 2018. https://qz.com/1301725/heres-one-number-that-shows-the-craze-for-electric-vehicles-in-china/, last accessed October 1, 2019.

Iannelli, Jerry. "Florida Lawmaker Again Files Bill That Would Help Break Monopoly-Solar Stranglehold." *Miami New Times*, January 4, 2019. https://www.miaminewtimes.com/news/bill-would-help-break-floridas-solar-panel-stranglehold-10971356 , last accessed September 30, 2019.

In, Soh Young, Ki Young Park, and Ashby H. B. Monk. "Is 'Being Green' Rewarded in the Market?: An Empirical Investigation of Decarbonization and Stock Returns." Stanford Global Project Center Working Paper, April 16, 2018. https://papers.ssrn.com/sol3/papers.cfm?abstract_id=3020304, last accessed July 9, 2018.

International Council on Clean Transportation. U.S. Domestic Airline Fuel Efficiency Ranking, 2015–2016. December 2017. https://theicct.org/sites/

default/files/publications/US-Airline-Ranking-2015-16_ICCT-White-Paper_14122017_vF.pdf, last accessed September 29, 2019.

International Energy Agency. https://www.iea.org/publications/freepublications/publication/English.pdf, page 3, last accessed October 9, 2019.

InvestmentBank.com. "Pharmaceutical Industry Overview: Trends, Risks, Opportunities & Deals." investmentbank.com; https://investmentbank.com/pharma-industry-overview/.

Ip, Greg. "Business Worries About Climate Intensify, Business Actions to Fix it, Not So Much." *Wall Street Journal*, January 16, 2019. https://www.wsj.com/articles/business-worries-about-climate-intensify-their-actions-less-so-11547643600?mod=hp_featst_pos2, last accessed September 30, 2019.

iShares. https://www.ishares.com/us/products/etf-product-list#!type=ishares&tab=overview&view=list&fr=43522, last accessed April 15, 2019.

iShares. https://www.ishares.com/us/products/239607/ishares-msci-australia-etf, and https://www.ishares.com/us/products/239615/ishares-msci-canada-etf, last accessed April 15, 2019.

iShares. https://www.ishares.com/us/products/239689/ishares-msci-turkey-etf and https://www.ishares.com/us/products/239663/ishares-msci-israel-capped-etf, last accessed September 30, 2019.

Jacobs Engineering's 2019 investor day presentation, page 18. http://s1.q4cdn.com/838591571/files/doc_presentations/2019/02/Jacobs-Investor-Day-Deck-2019.02.19-_FINAL.PDF, last accessed October 2019.

Jinko Solar's 2018 Annual Report, page 58. http://ir.jinkosolar.com/index.php/static-files/cff7be11-1bfc-43fc-910a-1ea6d35c1310, last accessed October 9, 2019.

Keenan Jesse, Thomas Hill, and Anurag Gumber. "Climate Gentrification: From Theory to Empiricism in Miami-Dade County, FL." Environmental Research Letters. http://iopscience.iop.org/article/10.1088/1748-9326/aabb32, last accessed June 13, 2018.

Kelley, Colin, et al. "Fertile Crescent and Implications of the Recent Syrian Drought." March 17, 2015. Proceedings of the National Academy of Sciences. https://www.pnas.org/content/112/11/3241, last accessed October 1, 2019.

Kennedy, Brian. "Most Americans Say Climate Change Affects Their Local Communities including Two Thirds Living Near Coast." Pew Research Center, May 16, 2018. http://www.pewresearch.org/fact-tank/2018/05/16/most-americans-say-climate-change-affects-their-local-community-including-two-thirds-living-near-coast/, last accessed July 7, 2018.

Kimberly-Clark. https://www.sustainability2022.com/strategy, last accessed October 9, 2019.

Kuristo, Laura, and Arian Campo-Flores. "Rising Sea Levels Reshape Miami's Housing Market." *Wall Street Journal*, April 20, 2018. https://

www.wsj.com/articles/climate-fears-reshape-miamis-housing-market-1524225600?ns=prod/accounts-wsj, last accessed June 13, 2018.

Kusnetz, Nicolas. "Rising Seas Threaten Norfolk Naval Shipyard, Raising Fears of 'Catastrophic Damage.'" NBC News, November 19, 2018. https://www.nbcnews.com/news/us-news/rising-seas-threaten-norfolk-naval-shipyard-raising-fears-catastrophic-damage-n937396, last accessed October 1, 2019.

Kwan, Irene. "Planes, Trains and Automobiles: Counting Carbon." The International Council on Clean Transportation, September 19, 2013. https://theicct.org/blogs/staff/planes-trains-and-automobiles-counting-carbon, last accessed September 30, 2019.

LafargeHolcim annual report, page 21. https://www.lafargeholcim.com/annual-interim-reports?field_year_tid_i18n_exposed=1233, last accessed October 1, 2019.

LaRose, Greg. "Entergy Louisiana Customer Bills Lower as Katrina-Rita Recovery Debt Is Paid Off." *Times-Picayune*, August 2, 2018. https://www.nola.com/news/business/article_be41687e-9a56-5016-b962-23d80b891606.html, last accessed October 10, 2019.

Lazard Asset Management. "Lazard's Levelized Cost of Energy Analysis—Version 12.0." November 2018, page 7. https://www.lazard.com/media/450784/lazards-levelized-cost-of-energy-version-120-vfinal.pdf, last accessed October 9, 2019.

Ligato, Lorenzo. "9 Companies That Are Changing Their Habits to Save Our Planet." Huffington Post, September 18, 2015, https://www.huffingtonpost.com/entry/we-mean-business-climate-change_us_55e88ec9e4b0b7a9633c4293, last accessed October 9, 2019.

Linklaters. https://www.linklaters.com/en-us/insights/publications/2018/october/japan-offshore-wind, last accessed October 9, 2019.

LIT fact sheet, page 1. https://cdn.globalxetfs.com/content/files/LIT-factsheet.pdf, last accessed September 15, 2019.

Lithia Investor Presentation, July 2019, page 15. http://www.lithiainvestorrelations.com/LAD_Q219_InvestorPresentation.pdf, last accessed September 30, 2019.

Lockheed Martin's 2018 Form 10-K, Part I, page 9. https://www.lockheedmartin.com/content/dam/lockheed-martin/eo/documents/annual-reports/2018-annual-report.pdf, last accessed October 1, 2019.

Lombardo, Tom. "What Is the Lifespan of a Solar Panel?" Engineering.com, April 20, 2014. https://www.engineering.com/3DPrinting/3DPrintingArticles/ArticleID/7475/What-Is-the-Lifespan-of-a-Solar-Panel.aspx, last accessed September 26, 2019.

Loria, Kevin. "Galveston, Texas: Galveston Set Another Record for Most Flooding Days in 2017, along with Boston; Sabine Pass, Texas; and Atlantic City and Sandy Hook in New Jersey." *Business Insider*, June 12, 2018. https://www.businessinsider.com/sea-level-rise-high-tides-sunny-day-flooding-coastal-cities-2018-4#galveston-texas-galveston-set-another-record-for-most-flooding-days-in-2017-along-with-boston-sabine-pass-texas-and-atlantic-city-and-sandy-hook-in-new-jersey-6, last accessed October 1, 2019.

Maciag, Mike. "After Years of Explosive Growth, Migration to the West and the South Slows." Governing.com, April 18, 2019. https://www.governing.com/topics/urban/gov-census-migration-south-west.html, last accessed October 1, 2019.

Macrotrends. "Crude Oil vs. Natural Gas—10-Year Daily Chart." https://www.macrotrends.net/2500/crude-oil-vs-natural-gas-chart, last accessed September 15, 2019.

Mansharamani, Vikram. "Could Lithium Become the New Oil?" *PBS News Hour*, October 15, 2015. https://www.pbs.org/newshour/economy/lithium-become-new-oil, last accessed September 16, 2019.

Mearian, Lucas. "In Shift, More Homeowners Are Buying Solar Panels Than Leasing Them." *Computerworld*, March 8, 2017. https://www.computerworld.com/article/3178342/sustainable-it/tectonic-shift-in-solar-sees-homeowners-now-buying-more-than-leasing-panels.html, last accessed September 30, 2019.

Merchant, Emma Foehringer. "Developers Struggle to Find a Way In as Florida's Utility-Scale Solar Market Shines." Greentech Media, July 8, 2019. https://www.greentechmedia.com/articles/read/a-look-at-floridas-rise-to-the-top-of-utility-scale-solar-rankings, last accessed October 10, 2019.

Michigan State University's globalEDGE website utilizing World Bank data. See: https://globaledge.msu.edu/comparator/home/results?year=&field=SP-POP-TOTL&field=SP-URB-TOTL-IN-ZS&field=EN-POP-DNST&field=NY-GDP-PCAP-PP-CD&field=EG-ELC-PROD-KH&country=155&country=4, last accessed September 30, 2019.

Miller, John. "Chinese Envoy Says Syngenta Takeover Was a Bad Deal: Report." Reuters, June 29, 2019. https://www.reuters.com/article/us-swiss-syngenta-china/chinese-envoy-says-syngenta-takeover-was-a-bad-deal-report-idUSKCN1TU0E0, last accessed October 10, 2019.

Muro, Mark, David Victor, and Jacob Whiton. "How the Geography of Climate Damage Could Make the Politics Less Polarizing." Brookings Institution, January 29, 2019. https://www.brookings.edu/research/how-the-geography-of-climate-damage-could-make-the-politics-less-polarizing/, last accessed October 1, 2019.

Murphy, Edward. "Canadian Hydropower Supplier Says It Has Plenty of Capacity for New England." *Press Herald*, December 6, 2018. https://www.

pressherald.com/2018/12/06/canadian-hydropower-supplier-says-it-has-plenty-of-capacity-for-n-e/, last accessed October 10, 2019.

Muzi, Nico. "Forty Percent of Europeans Say the Next Car They Buy Is Likely to Be Electric—Poll." *Transport & Environment*, October 1, 2018. https://www.transportenvironment.org/press/forty-percent-europeans-say-next-car-they-buy-likely-be-electric-poll, last accessed September 20, 2019.

Nanji, Avaz. "The 10 Industries Most Distrusted by US Consumers." https://www.marketingprofs.com/charts/2017/32764/the-10-industries-most-distrusted-by-us-consumers, last accessed September 30, 2019.

Nareit.com. https://www.reit.com/data-research/reit-indexes/reits-sp-indexes, last accessed October 1, 2019.

Nareit conference presentation, page 8. https://www.invh.com/Cache/1500121118.PDF?O=PDF&T=&Y=&D=&FID=1500121118&iid=4426247, last accessed September 26, 2019.

NASA. "Warmer Earth Greener North." https://climate.nasa.gov/climate_resources/3/graphic-warmer-earth-greener-north/, last accessed October 10, 2019.

NASDAQ. https://www.nasdaq.com/symbol/bep/dividend-history, last accessed October 9, 2019.

NASDAQ. See https://www.nasdaq.com/symbol/duk/earnings-growth and https://www.nasdaq.com/symbol/nee/earnings-growth, last accessed August 30, 2019.

National Centers for Environmental Information, NOAA. Climate at a Glance: Global Time Series, published September 2019. www.ncdc.noaa.gov/cag/, last accessed October 9, 2019.National Climate Assessment. https://nca2014.globalchange.gov/report/our-changing-climate/heavy-downpours-increasing#graphic-16693, last accessed May 29, 2018.

National Oceanic and Atmospheric Administration. https://www.esrl.naa.gov/gmd/ccgg/trends/full.html, last accessed May 21, 2018.

National Oceanic and Atmospheric Administration. https://www.climate.gov/news-features/understanding-climate/climate-change-ocean-heat-content, last accessed May 24, 2018.

National Oceanic and Atmospheric Administration. https://www.pmel.noaa.gov/co2/story/What+is+Ocean+Acidification%3F, last accessed May 30, 2018.

National Renewable Energy Laboratory for the U.S. Department of Energy with data provided by AWS TruePower. https://www.nrel.gov/gis/assets/pdfs/windsmodel4pub1-1-9base200904enh.pdf, last accessed September 26, 2019.

National Renewable Energy Laboratory, see page vi. https://www.nrel.gov/docs/fy17osti/68925.pdf, last accessed October 9, 2019.

National Resources Canada: Energy Fact Book 2018–2019. https://www. nrcan.gc.ca/sites/www.nrcan.gc.ca/files/energy/pdf/energy-factbook-oct2-2018%20(1).pdf, last accessed October 10, 2019.

NextEra 2018 10-K report, page 118. http://otp.investis.com/clients/us/nextera_energy_inc/SEC/sec-show.aspx?FilingId=13234910&Cik=000075330 8&Type=PDF&hasPdf=1, last accessed October 10, 2019.

Northland's 12/17 information matrix. https://northlandpower.com/cmsAssets/ docs/pdfs/Northland_Fact%20Sheet_December_2017_012918_V2.pdf, last accessed September 30, 2019.

Ørsted company presentation November 28, 2018, page 38. https://orsted. com/-/media/WWW/Docs/Corp/COM/Investor/CMD2018/CMD-Presentation-2018.pdf, last accessed October 9, 2019.

Our World in Data. https://ourworldindata.org/co2-and-other-greenhouse-gas-emissions, last accessed September 23, 2019.

Our World in Data, a project of Oxford University. https://ourworldindata.org/ co2-and-other-greenhouse-gas-emissions#future-emission-scenarios, last accessed June 1, 2018.

Penn, Ivan. "The $3 Billion Plan to Turn Hoover Dam into a Giant Battery." *New York Times*, June 24, 2018. https://www.nytimes.com/interactive/2018/07/24/business/energy-environment/hoover-dam-renewable-energy.html, last accessed September 30, 2019.

Penn, Ivan. "Florida's Utilities Keep Homeowners from Making the Most of Solar Power." *New York Times*, July 7, 2019. https://www.nytimes. com/2019/07/07/business/energy-environment/florida-solar-power.html, last accessed September 30, 2019.

PG&E. "Delivering Low-Emission Energy." https://www.pge.com/en_US/ about-pge/environment/what-we-are-doing/clean-energy-solutions/clean-energy-solutions.page, last accessed October 10, 2019.

Popovich, Nadja. "How Does Your State Make Electricity?" *New York Times*, December 24, 2018. https://www.nytimes.com/interactive/2018/12/24/climate/how-electricity-generation-changed-in-your-state.html, last accessed September 29, 2019.

Prairie Climate Centre. "New Maps Highlight Changes Coming to Canada's Climate." http://prairieclimatecentre.ca/2017/10/new-map-series-highlights-changes-coming-to-canadas-climate/, last accessed October 19, 2017.

Raymond, Nate. "China's Sinovel Fined in U.S. Trade Secrets Theft Case." Reuters, July 6, 2018. https://www.reuters.com/article/us-sinovel-wind-grousa-court/chinas-sinovel-fined-in-u-s-trade-secrets-theft-case-idUSKBN-1JW2RI, last accessed October 9, 2019.

Regency Center's 5/2/19 investor presentation, page 6. http://investors.regencycenters.com/static-files/85585786-ec34-4408-986b-e938b8d46d07, last accessed October 1, 2019.

RegisteredNursing.com. https://www.registerednursing.org/healthcare-costs-by-age/, last accessed October 10, 2019.

Renewable Energy Policy Network for the 21st Century. Renewables 2018 Global Status Report. http://www.ren21.net/gsr-2018/chapters/chapter_05/chapter_05/, last accessed October 9, 2019.

Renewables 2018 Global Status Report. http://www.ren21.net/gsr-2018/chapters/chapter_05/chapter_05/, last accessed October 9, 2019.

Robinson, Kim Stanley. *New York 2140*. New York: Orbit, 2017.

Romm, Joe. "Shell Oil CEO Stunner: 'My Next Car Will Be Electric.'" August 3, 2017, https://thinkprogress.org/shell-oil-ceo-says-his-next-car-will-be-electric-fdee683b4e36/, last accessed October 9, 2019.

Samenow, Jason, Ian Livingston, and Jeff Halverson. "How and Why the D.C. Area Was Deluged by a Month's Worth of Rain in an Hour Monday." *Washington Post*, July 8, 2019. https://www.washingtonpost.com/weather/2019/07/08/washington-dc-flash-flood-how-why-area-was-deluged-by-months-worth-rain-an-hour-monday/, last accessed October 1, 2019.

Scott, Michon. "National Climate Assessment Map Shows Uneven Impact of Future Global Warming on U.S. Energy Spending." https://www.climate.gov/news-features/featured-images/national-climate-assessment-map-shows-uneven-impact-future-global, last accessed October 1, 2019.

Shankleman Jess, and Hayley Warren. "Why the Prospect of 'Peak Oil' Is Hotly Debated." *Bloomberg Businessweek*, December 21, 2017. https://www.bloomberg.com/news/articles/2017-12-22/why-the-prospect-of-peak-oil-is-hotly-debated-quicktake-q-a, last accessed September 19, 2019.

Skeptical Science. http://4hiroshimas.com/#Science, last accessed October 9, 2019.

Skeptical Science. https://www.skepticalscience.com/sea-level-rise-predictions-intermediate.htm, last accessed May 29, 2018.

Solar Energy Industries Association (SEIA). https://www.seia.org/solar-industry-research-data, last accessed October 9, 2019.

SolarEdge's 5/6/19 investor presentation, pages 10–11. https://investors.solaredge.com/static-files/2d497b7a-c9c1-4d5e-b49f-48809d20f9aa, last accessed October 9, 2019.

SQM corporate presentation, September 2019, page 6. http://s1.q4cdn.com/793210788/files/doc_presentations/2019/08/New-presentation_august2019_website_final.pdf, last accessed September 15, 2019.

Statistica. "Distribution of Oil Demand in the OECD in 2017 by Sector." https://www.statista.com/statistics/307194/top-oil-consuming-sectors-worldwide/, last accessed September 18, 2019.

Statistica. "Royal Dutch Shell's Oil and Gas Reserves from 2010 to 2018, by Region (in Million Barrels of Oil Equivalent)." https://www.statista.com/

statistics/260332/royal-dutch-shells-oil-and-gas-reserves/, last accessed October 1, 2019.

Statistica. "Real Gross Domestic Product (GPD) of the United States of America from 1990 to 2018 in Billion Chained (2012) U.S. Dollars." July 19, 2019. https://www.statista.com/statistics/188141/annual-real-gdp-of-the-united-states-since-1990-in-chained-us-dollars/, last accessed October 10, 2019.

Statistica. "Revenue of the Worldwide Pharmaceutical Market from 2001 to 2018 (in Billion U.S. Dollars)." June 5, 2019. https://www.statista.com/statistics/263102/pharmaceutical-market-worldwide-revenue-since-2001/, last accessed September 13, 2019.

Statistics Canada. https://www150.statcan.gc.ca/n1/daily-quotidien/170510/cg170510a002-eng.csv, last accessed October 10, 2019.

Stringer, David. "Fastest Electric Car Chargers Are Waiting for Batteries to Catch Up." *Bloomberg*, April 3, 2019. https://www.bloomberg.com/news/articles/2019-04-03/fastest-electric-car-chargers-waiting-for-batteries-to-catch-up, last accessed October 10, 2019.

Suddath, Claire. "Harley-Davidson Needs a New Generation of Riders." *Bloomberg Businessweek*, August 23, 2018. https://www.bloomberg.com/news/features/2018-08-23/harley-davidson-needs-a-new-generation-of-riders, last accessed October 10, 2019.

SunRun 11/18 investor presentation, page 14. http://investors.sunrun.com/static-files/5576bb84-eb9f-4466-b6b0-1bcc406632fc and Vivint 9/18 investor presentation, page 12, https://s2.q4cdn.com/820306591/files/doc_presentations/VSLR-Investor-Presentation_2018_09.pdf, last accessed October 9, 2019.

SunRun. "Repowering Clean." April 5, 2019. https://www.sunrun.com/sites/default/files/repowering-clean-sunrun.pdf, last accessed October 9, 2019.

Tamman, Maurice. "Ocean Shock: Lobster's Great Migration Sets Up Boom and Bust." Reuters, October 30, 2018. https://www.reuters.com/article/us-oceans-tide-lobster-specialreport/ocean-shock-lobsters-great-migration-sets-up-boom-and-bust-idUSKCN1N420I, last accessed October 10, 2019.

Taylor, Jeremy, Nathan Cockrell, Alistair Godrich, and Neil Millar. "The Growing Importance of the 'E' in ESG." Lazard Asset Management. https://www.lazardassetmanagement.com/docs/-m0/67480/TheGrowingImportanceOfTheEInESG_LazardResearch_en.pdf, last accessed October 10, 2019.

Technavio. "Global Wind Power Systems Market 2018–2022." April 2018. Technavio. https://www.technavio.com/report/global-wind-power-systems-market-analysis-share-2018, last accessed October 9, 2019.

Technavio. "Vaccine Market Analysis—Technavio Vaccination Report Portfolio and Segmentation Analysis." https://www.technavio.com/research/vaccine-market-analysis, last accessed September 13, 2019.

Tertzakian, Peter. "Lithium May Be the New Oil, But a Double Whammy Looms for the Battery Market." *Financial Post*, July 25, 2017. https://business.financialpost.com/commodities/energy/lithium-may-be-the-new-oil-but-theres-a-double-whammy-looming-for-the-new-energy-source, last accessed October 10, 2019.

Tihonen, Jari, Pirjo Halonen, Laura Tihonen, Hannu Kautiainen, Markus Storvik, and James Callaway. "The Association of Ambient Temperate and Violent Crime." US National Library of Medicine, National Institutes of Health, July 28, 2017, last accessed October 9, 2019.

TPI Composite's June 2019 investor presentation, pages 16–18. http://s21.q4cdn.com/635504763/files/doc_presentations/2019/06/TPI-Investor-Presentation-June-2019.pdf, last accessed October 9, 2019.

Trading Economics. "Australia—Agricultural Land (% of Land Area)." https://tradingeconomics.com/australia/agricultural-land-percent-of-land-area-wb-data.html, last accessed October 10, 2019.

Trading View. https://www.tradingview.com/symbols/SP-SPN/components/ as of September 30, 2018, last accessed September 29, 2019.

TransDigm's Analyst Day presentation of June 28, 2018. https://www.transdigm.com/investor-relations/presentations/, last accessed October 1, 2019.

Tsao, Jeff, Nate Lewis, and George Crabtree. Solar FAQs, Sandia National Laboratory. Albuquerque, New Mexico, 2006, page 10. http://www.sandia.gov/~jytsao/Solar%20FAQs.pdf, last accessed October 9, 2019.

UC San Diego. http://jacobsschool.ucsd.edu/news/news_releases/release.sfe?id=1094, last accessed October 9, 2019.

Union of Concerned Scientists. https://www.ucsusa.org/global-warming/science-and-impacts/impacts/global-warming-rain-snow-tornadoes.html#.Ww3VsEgvzIU,t, last accessed May 29, 2018.

Union of Concerned Scientists. "What Are Tar Sands?" February 23, 2016. https://www.ucsusa.org/clean-vehicles/all-about-oil/what-are-tar-sands, last accessed September 30, 2019.

US Census Bureau. https://www.census.gov/library/visualizations/2019/comm/num-pop-change-county.html, last accessed October 1, 2019.

US Department of Energy report of September 9, 2016. https://www.energy.gov/eere/articles/computing-america-s-offshore-wind-energy-potential, last accessed October 9, 2019.

US Department of Energy. https://windexchange.energy.gov/maps-data/321, last accessed October 9, 2019.

US Department of Energy. "DOE Releases New Study Highlighting the Untapped Potential of Geothermal Energy in the United States." May 30, 2019. https://www.energy.gov/articles/doe-releases-new-study-highlighting-untapped-potential-geothermal-energy-united-states, last accessed September 17, 2019.

US Department of Health & Human Services MEPS data. "Here's How Much Your Healthcare Costs Will Rise as You Age," last accessed September 13, 2019.

US Energy Information Administration. "Electricity in the United States Is Produced with Diverse Energy Sources and Technologies." https://www.eia.gov/energyexplained/index.php?page=electricity_in_the_united_states, last accessed October 9, 2019.

US Energy Information Administration. "How Much Carbon Dioxide Is Produced When Different Fuels Are Burned?" https://www.eia.gov/tools/faqs/faq.php?id=73&t=11, last accessed October 9, 2019.

US Energy Information Administration. "Today in Energy." January 10, 2019. https://www.eia.gov/todayinenergy/detail.php?id=37952, last accessed October 9, 2019.

US Energy Information Administration. "What Is US Electricity Generation by Energy Source?" https://www.eia.gov/tools/faqs/faq.php?id=427&t=3, last accessed October 9, 2019.

US Energy Information Agency. "Primary Energy Overview." https://www.eia.gov/totalenergy/data/monthly/pdf/sec1_3.pdf , last accessed October 10, 2019.

Vulcan Materials' 2018 annual report, part 1, page 6. https://www.sec.gov/Archives/edgar/data/1396009/000139600919000021/vmc-20181231x10k.htm, last accessed October 1, 2019.

Waki, Yuzo. "China Pays Dearly for Overinvestment." Nikkei Asian Review. https://asia.nikkei.com/Economy/China-pays-dearly-for-overinvestment, last accessed October 9, 2019.

Wall Street Journal. "Barrel Breakdown." April 15, 2016. http://graphics.wsj.com/oil-barrel-breakdown/, last accessed October 1, 2019.

Walton, Rod. "Ten Years After: How Entergy New Orleans Survived Hurricane Katrina." *Electric Light & Power*, August 24, 2015. https://www.elp.com/articles/2015/08/ten-years-after-how-entergy-new-orleans-survived-hurricane-katrina.html, last accessed October 10, 2019.

Wang, T. https://www.statista.com/statistics/183700/us-average-retail-electricity-price-since-1990/, and https://www.statista.com/statistics/201714/growth-in-us-residential-electricity-prices-since-2000/, last accessed October 9, 2019.

We Mean Business. https://www.wemeanbusinesscoalition.org/, last accessed October 9, 2019.

Whitwam, Ryan. "BMW, Porsche Demo Super-Fast Electric Car Charger." *ExtremeTech*, December 17, 2018. https://www.extremetech.com/extreme/282364-bmw-porsche-demo-super-fast-electric-car-charger, last accessed September 30, 2019.

Wike, Richard. "What the World Thinks about Climate Change in 7 Charts." April 18, 2016. http://www.pewresearch.org/fact-tank/2016/04/18/what-the-world-thinks-about-climate-change-in-7-charts/, last accessed October 9, 2019.

Wikipedia. "American Depository Receipt." https://en.wikipedia.org/wiki/American_depositary_receipt, last accessed October 9, 2019.

Wikipedia. "Climate Change Denial." https://en.wikipedia.org/wiki/Climate_change_denial, last accessed May 22, 2018.

Wikipedia entry on Geothermal Power. https://en.wikipedia.org/wiki/Geothermal_power#cite_note-:0-4, last accessed September 17, 2019.

Wikipedia. "Green New Deal." https://en.wikipedia.org/wiki/Green_New_Deal, last accessed October 9, 2019.

Wikipedia. "King Tide." https://en.wikipedia.org/wiki/King_tide, last accessed October 10, 2019.

Wikipedia. "List of Countries Banning Fossil Fuel Vehicles." https://en.wikipedia.org/wiki/List_of_countries_banning_fossil_fuel_vehicles#cite_note-14, last accessed October 9, 2019.

Wikipedia. "List of Largest Cities in Brazil." https://en.wikipedia.org/wiki/List_of_largest_cities_in_Brazil, last accessed September 30, 2019.

Wikipedia. "List of Largest Oil and Gas Companies by Revenue." https://en.wikipedia.org/wiki/List_of_largest_oil_and_gas_companies_by_revenue#frb-inline, last accessed September 15, 2019.

Wikipedia. "Mandatory Renewable Energy Target." https://en.wikipedia.org/wiki/Mandatory_renewable_energy_target#Targets_by_country, last accessed October 1, 2019.

Wikipedia. Map of Temperate Regions of the World. https://en.wikipedia.org/wiki/K%C3%B6ppen_climate_classification, last accessed September 30, 2019.

Wikipedia. "Marcellus Formation." https://en.wikipedia.org/wiki/Marcellus_Formation#/.

Wikipedia. "Northeast Megalopolis." https://en.wikipedia.org/wiki/Northeast_megalopolis, last accessed October 9, 2019.

Wikipedia. Renewables include hydro, wind, solar, geothermal and biomass. https://en.wikipedia.org/wiki/List_of_countries_by_electricity_production_from_renewable_sources, and https://en.wikipedia.org/wiki/Nuclear_power_by_country, last accessed October 1, 2019.

Wikipedia. "Solar Monthly Generation." https://en.wikipedia.org/wiki/Solar_power_in_the_United_States#/media/File:US_Monthly_Solar_Power_Generation.svg, last accessed October 9, 2019.

Wikipedia. "Solar Power in the United States." https://en.wikipedia.org/wiki/Solar_power_in_the_United_States#/media/File:Projected_US_Renewable_Electric_Capacity.jpg, last accessed October 9, 2019.

Wikipedia. "US Monthly Wind Generated Electricity." https://en.wikipedia. org/wiki/Wind_power_in_the_United_States#/media/File:US_Monthly_ Wind_Generated_Electricity.svg, last accessed October 9, 2019.

Wikipedia. "Yield Co." https://en.wikipedia.org/wiki/Yield_co, last accessed October 9, 2019.

Wikipedia 2018 estimates. https://en.wikipedia.org/wiki/List_of_metropoli- tan_statistical_areas, last accessed October 1, 2019.

Wikipedia. https://en.wikipedia.org/wiki/Ulrich_Brechbuhl, last accessed September 27, 2019.

Winck, Ben. "Morgan Stanley: These 7 Pharma Companies Will Be Criti- cal to Fighting Infectious Diseases Brought on by Climate Change." *Markets Insider*, July 25, 2019. https://markets.businessinsider.com/news/ stocks/7-biopharma-companies-most-critical-for-fighting-tropical-diseases- 2019-7-1028384776#glaxosmithkline2, last accessed October 10, 2019.

Wirehn, Lotten. "Nordic Agriculture under Climate Change." Land Use Pol- icy, September 2018. https://www.sciencedirect.com/science/article/abs/pii/ S0264837717308293, last accessed October 10, 2019.

Wood Mackenzie Solar Market Insight of December 2018. https://www.wood- mac.com/research/products/power-and-renewables/us-solar-market-insight/, last accessed October 9, 2019.

The World Bank. https://data.worldbank.org/indicator/EN.ATM.CO2E. KT?view=chart&year_high_desc=true, last accessed May 10, 2018.

The World Bank. https://data.worldbank.org/indicator/EN.ATM.CO2E. KT?view=chart&year_high_desc=true, last accessed May 31, 2018.

The World Bank. https://data.worldbank.org/indicator/EN.ATM.NOXE.KT. CE?end=2012&start=1970&view=chart&year_high_desc=true and https:// data.worldbank.org/indicator/EN.ATM.METH.KT.CE?view=map&year_ high_desc=true, last accessed June 1, 2018.

The World Bank. 2007–2018 National Rankings for Infrastructure and Logisti- cal Competence. https://lpi.worldbank.org/international/global/2018?sort= asc&order=Logistics%20competence#datatable, last accessed October 1, 2019.

World Health Organization. "Climate Change and Health." February 1, 2018. https://www.who.int/en/news-room/fact-sheets/detail/climate-change-and- health, last accessed October 1, 2019.

World Resources Institute. "Infographic: U.S. Businesses Need More Renew- able Energy from the Grid." May 17, 2017. https://www.wri.org/resources/ data-visualizations/infographic-us-businesses-need-more-renewable-en- ergy-grid, last accessed October 10, 2019.

World's Top Exports. http://www.worldstopexports.com/, last accessed Sep- tember 30, 2019.

Xcel Energy. "Our Power Supply." https://www.xcelenergy.com/energy_portfolio/electricity/power_generation, last accessed October 10, 2019.

"Xcel Energy Aims for Zero-Carbon Electricity by 2050." Xcel Energy corporate website, December 4, 2018. https://www.xcelenergy.com/company/media_room/news_releases/xcel_energy_aims_for_zero-carbon_electricity_by_2050, last accessed October 1, 2019.

Xcel Energy's Carbon Report of February 2019. https://www.xcelenergy.com/staticfiles/xe/PDF/Xcel%20Energy%20Carbon%20Report%20-%20Feb%202019.pdf, last accessed October 10, 2019.

Yahoo! Finance. https://finance.yahoo.com, last accessed September 30, 2019.

Index

Publicly traded stocks are followed by their exchange ticker in parenthesis and foreign stocks have their ADR ticker listed if available.

About the Author

James Ellman has more than two decades of experience as a professional investor: first as an equity portfolio manager for Invesco and Merrill Lynch mutual funds, then at hedge funds Seacliff Capital and Ascend Capital. He lives near San Francisco with his wife and sons.